Theory of Constraints
Creative Problem Solving

...I believe that [the] book will be a monument of application of TOC Thinking Processes for creative problem solving. ... [The authors'] perspective of applying TOC Thinking Processes to academia is quite creative and many examples are so vivid that there will be no difficulties in following through the main substance.

...[the] book will be very beneficial to teachers, students, administrators, counselors, and anyone who wants to think clearly for making life meaningful. Personally the Creative Thinker's Toolkit will be a great reference for me to run my class "Thinking Process for Creative Problem Solving."

Wonjoon Choi

Professor of Industrial Engineering, Department of Industrial Engineering, College of Engineering, University of Ulsan, Ulsan, Republic of Korea

Those who practice TOC Thinking Processes appreciate their real value. At first glance it seems to be merely a set of logical diagrams. But, their intrinsic value goes much beyond that. They are designed to achieve breakthrough results in the desired field of operation. Achieving a breakthrough starts with challenging the status quo and overcoming inertia. In order to achieve substantially better results we need to rigorously apply three fundamental powers in our possession: emotion, intuition, and logic. Emotion is critical. Only passionate people have the stamina to march through the tedious road leading to breakthrough results. Moreover, on matters we don't care about, we have zero intuition. Emotions feed the needed intuition to find the right path, to come up with new ideas. Intuition is critical. It fuels logic. Without intuition, applying logic will be, at best, a theoretical exercise with little practical consequence. Logic is critical. Intuition alone can lead us astray. Applying intuition within a logical framework helps us to guide our intuition in the right direction. It helps us to identify missing elements and to devise corrective actions where gaps appear. It helps us to communicate our intuition to other people and to obtain their collaboration. The TOC Thinking Processes support us to achieve this goal. They boost our ability to apply intuition in an area that we greatly care to improve, and when used correctly, to achieve breakthrough results. The authors of this book have applied these tools to the field of higher education. They share their journey on the path to remarkable results in student retention and academic achievement, a core problem of many colleges and society as a whole. But this is just one aspect of their story. Going through the chapters we get an opportunity to learn how the Thinking Processes can be used with students in order to achieve the higher goal of education, which is "to prepare students for life."

Rami Goldratt

CEO, Goldratt Consulting Ltd.
www.goldrattconsulting.com

Theory of Constraints
Creative Problem Solving

Umesh Nagarkatte
Nancy Oley

CRC Press
Taylor & Francis Group
Boca Raton London New York

CRC Press is an imprint of the
Taylor & Francis Group, an **informa** business

A PRODUCTIVITY PRESS BOOK

CRC Press
Taylor & Francis Group
6000 Broken Sound Parkway NW, Suite 300
Boca Raton, FL 33487-2742

Printed on acid-free paper

International Standard Book Number-13: 978-1-138-05605-3 (Hardback)

Library of Congress Cataloging-in-Publication Data

Names: Nagarkatte, Umesh, author. | Oley, Nancy, author.
Title: Theory of Constraints: creative problem solving / Umesh Nagarkatte and Nancy Oley.
Description: Boca Raton, FL : Taylor & Francis, 2018. | Includes bibliographical references.
Identifiers: LCCN 2017011219 | ISBN 9781138056053 (hardback : alk. paper)
Subjects: LCSH: Theory of constraints (Management) | Creative thinking. | Problem solving.
Classification: LCC HD69.T46 N34 2018 | DDC 658.4/0301--dc23
LC record available at https://lccn.loc.gov/2017011219

**Visit the Taylor & Francis Web site at
http://www.taylorandfrancis.com**

**and the CRC Press Web site at
http://www.crcpress.com**

Contents

Foreword

Throughput equals sales minus total variable costs: an appropriate equation if the goal of your organization is to "Make money, now and in the future." But what if your organization's goal is not making money, but money (budget) is a necessary condition of existence? Dr. Eliyahu M. Goldratt's theory of constraints (TOC) spoils its practitioners. They are conditioned to believe that by addressing the system's constraint (steps 1, 2, and 3 of the five focusing steps), the results can only be nothing short of spectacular—anything else would be a "chupchik"—at best, improvements on the margin with a nonconstraint resource.

What if the goal of the system was to enrich its product? How easy is it to define success if the rate of throughput is measured in terms other than dollars? The system is the Mathematics Department at Medgar Evers College (MEC) of the City University of New York. The product is predominantly single, inner city females caught in a struggle to raise their families now or pursue a meaningful career through education in the future. Many of us know of similar situations. The immediacy of the short term overrides the promise of the future in the long term. We know which one wins out in this compromise virtually every time!

I first met with Dr. Umesh Nagarkatte (then professor of mathematics) in the summer of 2001 at the Avraham Y. Goldratt Institute in New Haven, Connecticut. I was the dean of the Avraham Goldratt Institute (AGI) Academy. My role was working with academicians expressing a desire to incorporate TOC into their curriculum. Our experience was that most academicians who become involved with TOC normally do so with the objective of teaching elements of TOC within their existing courses or curriculum, mainly its logistic applications (production drum–buffer–rope, replenishment, Critical Chain Project Management) and to some extent its TOC thinking processes (strategy). After several discussions, this was clearly not the case with Dr. Nagarkatte. His subject matter for applying the TOC thinking process tools was *improving student retention* and, more specifically, female students interested in mathematics. As their efforts were rewarded with success, the focus was later extended to include female students in science and technology. Given the challenges at hand, the current state was woefully short of achieving the desired end state. We needed a strategy of change and the means to manage it.

What do they change, and why? We're all familiar with the adage "To improve one must change. But is every change an improvement?" Given the current state, what would they require in its place, and why is that justified? (construction phase). What was the sequence of tasks that needed to be accomplished? What resources were required, and were they available? (implementation plan phase). From whom did they need to solicit support—who could support and influence the effort, as well as who could derail the effort? (communication phase). Dr. Nagarkatte and Dr. Oley refer to this phase as "TOC also meaning theory of communication" and "theory of empowerment (TOE)." In total, this was the scope of effort behind improving student retention. The strategy went well beyond the Mathematics Department. Direct support of counseling and administration were also critical elements to success. The principal investigators, Dr. Umesh Nagarkatte, Dr. Darius Movasseghi (department chair), and Dr. Joshua Berenbom, professors of Mathematics, focused TOC on a system-level approach across the college, designed with student performance at the core. In nearly all universities and colleges, students flow through the system with the hope of becoming graduates. Professors add value through an accredited curriculum of study leading to the awarding of a degree. *What if the goal of the system was to enrich its product?* That was the theme behind designing the system with student performance at the core. This was a team of professors with the support of the college president and his cabinet, going above and beyond adding TOC content to a course or curriculum.

I was privileged to facilitate the professors' use of TOC to build a better system and enrich the lives of their students. In all my years of TOC (since 1993), and of all the implementations of TOC, this one holds a special place for me, not because the professors were successful in achieving their goal, but because in so doing, they enriched the lives of their students, empowering them to achieve their full potential. What better gift could students receive from their professors? This team of professors provided meaning behind President Jackson's vision of "Creating success, one student at a time."

Of the difference between smart and wise men, Dr. Eliyahu M. Goldratt said, "A smart man learns from his mistakes; a wise man learns from the mistakes of others." Be wise—and learn from works of Drs. Nagarkatte and Oley to enrich your lives and those of your students.

Stephen C. Simpliciano (Steve)
Jonah's Jonah
Guilford, Connecticut

Preface

Thinking is fundamental to being human. The theory of constraints (TOC) has thinking process (TP) tools to help people think systematically. Using them, one can learn how to manage real-life constraints. A constraint is something that stands in the way of achieving a goal. TP tools are based on logic. They are simple enough to be used by kindergarten children for modifying their own behavior and sophisticated enough to be used by chief executive officers to bring their corporations out of bankruptcy. In our experience, TOC becomes theory of empowerment (TOE). It also becomes theory of communication.

This text is intended to help creative thinkers and people who are interested in continually improving knowledge and education, or the Process Of OnGoing Improvement (POOGI). It is especially intended for the higher-education community—students, parents, mentors, educators, advisors, counselors, and administrators. It purposely includes all these audiences since they form components of the *student success system.* TOC needs patience on the part of stakeholders. It is designed to teach TOC and its powerful graphical logic-based TP tools. The tools can be used for creative writing, creative projects, conflict resolution, decision making, and problem solving. The authors feel fortunate in having come across TOC and TP tools and have used them for all their creative work in the school setting and in other activities. They have used the tools for systems approach applications and other related activities described in this book, curriculum development, and preparing reports or presentations. They have used them to write several grant proposals, which have brought in close to four million dollars in external funding for helping students and improving instruction. The first author has used the tools to do research in mathematics; publish three math textbooks, three philosophy books and several articles; and give numerous talks on meditation. The second author has used them in a community setting and to help individuals. Once internalized, most of the time, graphical representations are not necessary. One can see mentally the logical consequences and understand the different sides of an issue, and one can surmise the obstacles and do appropriate project planning without leaving logical gaps. These tools may be applied rigorously to a personal issue, an interpersonal issue, a course content issue, a departmental issue, or an institutional issue. The tools can be used to find win–win solutions for conflicts without compromise or loss for any party. In writing this book, we also hope to encourage open communication between practitioners of TOC around the world.

It is very troubling to see so many young men and women leave school and never fulfill their true potential. We include illustrations in each chapter to show how young men and women, in school or outside in the community, can be empowered to resolve conflicts, make decisions, solve problems, complete school, and succeed. This work is the result of 15 years of research on implementing TOC by two faculty members in an urban undergraduate college who share the common goal (ambitious target) of wanting to stem the tide of student attrition. The authors are aware that this goal cannot be achieved by only one or two people working together, but can be accomplished easily when the entire institution participates in the effort. They feel fortunate that they work in an institution where almost everyone shares this goal. They know that high attrition is due to many factors and is not unique to their college. High attrition is common at many public undergraduate institutions around the country and around the world. It is the authors' belief that their initiative will be replicable in many other institutions that are also struggling to improve retention and graduation rates.

Many educators wonder what to do when their best curriculum developments and well-funded enrichment programs do not greatly improve retention. Their reaction is to give up or to blame the secondary schools for social promotion. They blame distracting TV, the Internet, cell phones, iPhones and iPads, social media, texting, and tweeting. They blame the social structure, or community, or someone else. If their curriculum development programs do succeed, they are local, in the sense that they depend on the personality of the initiator and do not apply globally to the institution. The first thing that we learn in TOC is not to blame anyone, except perhaps *Murphy's law*—what can go wrong, will go wrong—and to provide for it. TOC has a unique way of taking into account not just a student's academic needs, but also his/her personal needs. TOC establishes communication between various stakeholders so that they can work as a unit to address the problem at hand. In that sense, TOC also stands for theory of communication!

TOC asks three basic questions: (1) What to change? (2) What to change to? (3) How to cause the change? TOC considers the issues of all stakeholders—students, faculty, staff, administration, family, and community. Each stakeholder focuses on his/her area of direct control or influence. This means that the president's issues are different from the student's issues. Regardless of who is addressing the problem, TOC has the same logical TP tools. In other words, the same TP tools can be used to solve institutional— academic or nonacademic—as well as personal problems. Since the tools are logical, they transcend the personalities involved. Anyone considering the same issues, having an intuition about them, and following the TOC roadmap will come up with equivalent solutions. TOC teaches one how to think out of the box and how to go beyond one's familiar assumptions by challenging them. Once mastered, TOC becomes a part of the learner's general approach to resolving any conflict with a win–win solution, solving problems systematically, and making decisions that do not lead to negative consequences in the long run. TOC yields insight into a problem situation. Using TOC and their professional expertise, counselors, faculty, or administrators can resolve the problem in a more systematic and coherent manner instead of wasting resources on individual, isolated, or redundant efforts.

TOC empowers a student to lead a successful life without compromising either his/her personal needs or his/her studies. The TP tools help students to be proactive. TOC can be used by a first-year student program to empower students. In order to give freshmen an opportunity to interact with both faculty in his/her chosen major and his/her academic advisors, a TOC course—see the syllabus at the end of Chapter 5—could be taught by a team of academic advisors and academic instructors in different disciplines using examples of TOC in content areas. Hopefully, this will increase students' motivation to continue on in their chosen major. This book is the only textbook available at present at the college level that can be used for a systematic study of TOC and its application to a student's chosen major or discipline.

The textbook has seven chapters. Chapter 1 is the introduction to TOC and its TP tools and explains the importance of studying TOC. Necessity and sufficiency cause-and-effect thinking is explained here with examples. A few sections show how to help develop student's critical thinking. Chapters 2 and 3 answer the question, "What to change?" using the Branch and Evaporating Cloud tools to resolve various types of conflicts. In Chapter 2, the Negative Branch Reservation (NBR) and Current Reality Tree (CRT) are introduced to develop a holistic picture of the person's or institution's current situation. In Chapter 3, we begin with Evaporating Clouds that show students how to resolve daily conflicts. If students resolve one conflict every day, they will quickly learn how to create win–win solutions in their lives. Some clouds help resolve chronic conflicts. Some clouds help empower students. We also show how the cloud tool can be used to develop a persuasive essay. With the Evaporating Cloud and the CRT together, one completely develops an answer to the question: "What to change?" Chapter 4 answers the question "What to change to?" What should the future look like? It teaches cause-and-effect relationships through which students can see the likely consequences of their actions. They are introduced to the Future Reality Tree (FRT) and the Transition Tree (TrT). The FRT and NBR answer the question, "What to change to?" completely and show how to avoid negative consequences of the strategies suggested. Chapter 5 introduces the Prerequisite Tree (PrT) to answer the question, "How to cause the change?" It describes how to uncover the often hidden obstacles that are in the way of achieving goals and shows how to prepare project plans. There are several appendices on everything that one needs to know about achieving academic success, critical chain project management of a course, how to study any course, and why and how to study mathematics. This should help students take responsibility and use the college resources to achieve their goals and not settle for anything less. Chapter 6 can be used for solving institutional problems using the five focusing steps of TOC. One major example of an institutional approach is explicated throughout the six chapters to illustrate the systematic logical link among the TOC concepts discussed in each chapter. Sections on TOC-based program review and strategic planning are very relevant to institutions of higher learning. In Chapter 7, we discuss measurable outcomes of TOC implementation. We discuss the TOC initiative at Medgar Evers College and its overall effects. The answer to the question "How to cause the change?" is not complete unless there are measurable outcomes.

The theory of constraints was developed by Eliyahu (Eli) Goldratt around 1980. TOC has an established track record in industry and the school systems of Singapore, Malaysia, and the Philippines. It is also used in Asia, Europe, Africa, and South America for instruction and community work. In Singapore, TOC is used to produce *paradigm change* in prisoners: TOC changes the way that the prisoners think about themselves so that a high percentage live a productive life in society and do not return to prison. At least 15% of the world's businesses currently use TOC for their operations. TOC is also taught as a required subject in most business schools' M.B.A. programs. But there are several well-known business schools such as Wharton that use TOC or constraint management for all of their operations. The authors' institution, Medgar Evers College (MEC) of the City University of New York, is the first and only liberal arts college where administration, faculty, staff, and students have shown willingness to apply TOC to address the problem of student attrition. It is well on its way to a systemic resolution of the problem. One criticism of TOC is that it has not been applied enough in education as it has been in business and industry. This text tries to show that TOC is as powerful in education as in other fields.

Our experiment with using TOC to address attrition in mathematics courses began in January 2002. Darius Movasseghi, then chair, Joshua Berenbom, and the first author, all faculty in the Department of Mathematics at MEC, participated in formal Jonah training at the Avraham Goldratt Institute (AGI) Academy, New Haven, Connecticut. Tracey Burton-Houle and Steve Simpliciano were the facilitators. The training was funded by an institutional grant for 2001–2004 from the Minority Science Engineering Improvement Program (MSEIP) of the U.S. Department of Education. The attendees used the entire TOC roadmap (described in Chapter 6 of this book) during a two-week intensive workshop to develop a detailed project plan for the Mathematics Department. Their findings were discussed informally by the chair with other faculty in the department, devoting a few minutes of every monthly departmental meeting during the Spring 2002 semester. As the major issues of the department were brought out and discussed in the open, a congenial environment developed that attracted a large number of students to become mathematics majors the following semester. The department developed new curricula and improvements in mathematics tutoring. The faculty developed departmental guidelines that helped all faculty and support personnel work toward student retention. The POOGI of TOC, started in 2002, is so robust that it was still vibrant and expanding at the time of this writing.

TOC analysis addressed the needs of the "whole" student, not just his/her academic needs. The project plan that we developed showed how and where the academic advisors, personal counselors, and the Basic Skills Department could participate with the Department of Mathematics to address the problem of attrition. The facilitator, Steve Simpliciano, made a presentation to the college president, Edison O. Jackson, and his key cabinet members in May 2005, about what the team had learned and offered the *Departmental Guidelines* as a deliverable. President Jackson approved the guidelines and expressed his desire that everyone in the college should learn TOC, starting with the Basic Skills and Freshman Year Program faculty. Two additional institutional federal grants (MSEIP 2004–2007) and Women's Equity in Education Act (WEEA 2005–2007) facilitated the formal Management Skills Workshop (MSW) training at the Avraham Goldratt Institute of key individuals and more faculty. The grants also provided resources to hold various campus workshops for tutors, academic advisors, counselors, and Basic Skills instructors from 2005 to 2007. In the Spring 2008 semester, President Jackson himself, along with his senior administration, reaffirmed his commitment to address institutional issues using TOC. He laid out a logical plan for administrators and middle management designed to reduce attrition during the first year.* The efforts to improve were continued thanks to four more MSEIP grants[†]: institutional and cooperative in 2010–2013, institutional in 2012–2015, and institutional in 2013–2016. In 2011–2013 Victor Nwaokwu, an MEC computer science major student, developed a website http://www.tocforcollege.com as an undergraduate research project supported by the New York City Louis Stokes Alliance for Minority Participation (NYCLSAMP) grants.

Among the faculty attending the formal TOC Management Skills Workshop in December 2005–January 2006, was Nancy Oley, the second author. Actually, as early as 1999, she encouraged the first author to apply TOC to the problem of student attrition. After formal training, she has supported all TOC workshops in the college and made several presentations at conferences. Since 2006 she has applied more TOC tools than anyone else in the college—in faculty development workshops, in her Faculty Senate activities, and in her courses in Psychology. Nancy is a leader in implementing TOC within content areas in an academic discipline. She has helped to develop and edit the TOC for College website: http://www.tocforcollege .com. Dr. Oley received Theory of Constraints International Certification Organization Jonah certification after completing the Constraint Management course (EM 526) taught by James Holt at Washington State University at the end of Spring 2008.

---

* The authors acknowledge the support of colleagues at MEC and Queensborough Community College from the Mathematics Department, Freshman Year Program, Counseling, and SEEK Department.
† Thanks to the reviewers and program officers of US Department of Education.

Acknowledgments

The authors acknowledge the collaboration and support of their colleagues, especially Darius Movasseghi and Joshua Berenbom. Quite a few figures in the textbook are from the joint work of the authors with them at AGI. It was Darius Movasseghi who took the leadership to promote TOC in the department and participated in many international presentations. The authors also received constant encouragement and support from MEC President Edison O. Jackson. They offer their thanks to all at MEC for their support. Many facilitators provided TOC training in a variety of workshops: Howard Meeks of Iowa State University; Kathy Suerken, president of TOC for Education, Inc.; Belinda Small of the Florida School system; Danilo Sirias of Saginaw Valley State University, Michigan; and Janice Cerveny of Florida Atlantic University, Port St. Lucie, Florida. Many advisors, counselors, tutors, and faculty participated in these workshops. We thank them for their support. Alan Barnard of Goldratt Research, South Africa, made an important theoretical presentation at the TOC for Education Inc. 10th International Conference, Florida, in 2007. Some slides from his presentation are included in the book. James Holt from Washington State University, Vancouver, Washington, offered an online Constraint Management course (EM 526) gratis to academics, which triggered a flurry of TOC activity around the college, including presidential retreats to complete the homework of the course. Many slides from the various MEC workshops are included in the textbook with the facilitators' permission. Dr. Holt's critical comments helped us to write Chapter 7—"Epilogue." The authors are indebted to them. Thanks to Eva Chan, director of the Office of Institutional Research, and Janice Cerveny for their help in developing feasible numerical measures for Throughput and Return on Investment in Academia discussed in Chapter 6. These are important logically derived measures, not just the number of graduates. Janice Cerveny also provided some slides related to program review and strategic planning.

Tracey Burton-Houle and Steve Simpliciano were instrumental in covering the TOC roadmap by assigning a lot of homework in the Jonah course in January 2002. Steve Simpliciano introduced TOC free of charge to the first author in 2000 and facilitated the development of a CRT that matched the CRT developed in the Jonah program. Thanks to Tracey and Steve for getting TOC started at MEC. The websites http://www.TOCICO.org and http://www.TOCforEducation.com, international conferences and Tactics newsletter of TOC for Education have been very useful for dissemination and communication of our research worldwide to TOC practitioners in education, in the prison system, and in the wider community. Many educators from the United States and abroad have been encouraging the authors to write a book for professionals in higher education. The authors are grateful to all those and the conference audiences who made these opportunities available. They are especially grateful to Howard Meeks, Philip Ording, and Choi Wonjoon of South Korea, who provided detailed improvements in the text. The contribution of Chuck Gauthier of Vancouver, Washington, toward improving the TP tools discussions was invaluable. We also thank Jordan Pola for suggesting improvements in Chapter 6.

The authors are thankful to Steve Simpliciano for writing the foreword and Rami Goldratt and Wonjoon Choi for writing endorsements for the book. We thank Christine Medansky, Senior Editor, and her excellent editing and the production team at CRC Press, and Michael Tobin for his selection of the cover art. The authors express their gratitude to the late Eli Goldratt for discovering TOC and for encouraging us by saying that we are doing important work for the college. We are sorry that he could not see this book.

Authors

Credit: Bruce Gilbert

Dr. Umesh Nagarkatte received his Ph.D. in algebraic number theory from the Graduate Center of the City University of New York (CUNY) in 1976. He underwent dedicated Jonah training at the Avraham Goldratt Institute with two of his colleagues in 2002. The team became pioneers in higher education to implement the theory of constraints and thinking process tools by using the college as the *system*. He has been certified as a Facilitator by TOC for Education, Inc. (TOCfE).

Dr. Nagarkatte, with the assistance of coauthor Nancy Oley as editor and evaluator, received federal grants in 2001–2004, 2004–2007, 2005–2007, 2010–2013, 2012–2015, and 2013–2016 for using the theory of constraints (TOC)/thinking processes (TP) to address the problem of attrition. He has used TOC/TP with his fellow Jonah, Dr. Joshua Berenbom, to develop three textbooks—*Prealgebra, Elementary Algebra*, and *Intermediate Algebra*—adapting the Singapore Model Method to the college level. Oley and Nagarkatte started working on the current book on TOC/TP in 2010 to empower students, counselors, educators, and other stakeholders to work as a team to ensure student success.

Dr. Nagarkatte taught at the Borough of Manhattan Community College, CUNY, from 1971 to 1976. He recently retired as Professor of Mathematics from Medgar Evers College, CUNY, where he had taught since 1978. His research interests are in algebraic geometry; number theory; applications of mathematics to chemistry and environmental science, philosophy, and meditation; and applying TOC/TP to all areas of interest.

Credit: Tony Gallego

Dr. Nancy Oley received her Ph.D. in experimental psychology from Columbia University and did postdoctoral work in neurophysiology at Florida State University and in neuropsychology at Teachers College, Columbia University. She studied TOC at the Avraham Goldratt Institute and Washington State University, and is currently certified as a Jonah by the Theory of Constraints International Certification Organization (TOCICO) and as a Facilitator by Theory of Constraints for Education, Inc. (TOCfE).

Dr. Oley has pioneered the incorporation of TOC processes and concepts within the content of her psychology courses, helped to develop TOC curricula for incoming college students, created a short TOC course/workshop for remedial math students, and collaborated with coauthor Dr. Umesh Nagarkatte for over 10 years on numerous federally funded TOC-related grants and projects aimed at optimizing the college system to improve curriculum and instruction in mathematics and to reduce attrition.

Dr. Oley has held positions of leadership in university governance as well as in state and national scientific organizations, and has published in the areas of pain/analgesia, memory, nervous system regeneration, olfaction, and the teaching of psychology. She has engaged undergraduate and graduate students at a variety of institutions, among them Augustana College (Illinois), the University of Hartford, Trinity College (Connecticut), Columbia University, and Medgar Evers College, CUNY, from which she recently retired as professor emerita of psychology.

Chapter 1

Introduction

1.1 Organization of the Book

This book is organized into three major sections, dictated by the three basic questions of the theory of constraints (TOC): what to change, what to change to, and how to cause the change. Within each section, there are practical examples followed by discussion of a specific thinking process (TP) tool used to answer the three basic questions, as it applies to understanding and dealing with simple problems. If the knowledge of stand-alone tools is sufficient, the reader-creative thinker or student can study those specific tools and skip some material as directed. In later chapters, the tools are used formally to solve complex system problems within the broader context of TOC. The last chapter is a review of a systems approach using tools discussed in the earlier chapters and the TOC roadmap, and mainly for department heads and administrators who are sincerely interested in the Process Of OnGoing Improvement (POOGI) and are not just interested in a Strength, Weakness, Opportunity, and Threat (SWOT) analysis of their department or institution for a program review or a strategic plan.

1.2 Reasons for Writing This Book

1.2.1 Student Empowerment

An instructor has accepted two students to do research with her during the summer. One student, Cheryl, is very responsible and hardworking. She does her homework regularly while taking care of her three children,

1, 4, and 7 years old, at home. The second student, Mary, did not respond to numerous e-mails that the instructor sent. Before the actual research began, there were several steps that had to be completed such as obtaining Institutional Review Board Certification and attending a workshop. Cheryl completed them in a timely fashion. Mary, on the other hand, came up with different excuses as to why she was unable to get certified. After talking to people in charge of the research, she was granted a 2-week extension to finish the certification. Luckily, Cheryl and Mary showed up on time at the first research meeting. The instructor warned Mary that if she did not complete the certification during the grace period, she would be out of the program. Cheryl helped Mary to register for the certification, and after 10 days, she completed the requirement.

In the meantime, the instructor met with her two students twice a week. Both came on time. However, Mary did not do her assignments most of the time, and whenever she did some work, it was all wrong. She did not follow any of the instructor's directions. She could not concentrate during their meetings, always yawning or showing disinterest in what was going on. Whenever Mary was told that her work was unsatisfactory, she started crying. When asked if she had other issues at home bothering her, she would just nod. However, sometimes, Mary was engaged and came up with unusually good ideas regarding research. This gave the instructor some hope.

During one meeting, she told Mary that she is intelligent but behaves very irresponsibly. Mary whimpered a little. That day when Mary and Cheryl were working together in the next room, she went to see if they had completed the work. There were a couple of papers and a pen lying on the floor. Cheryl said that they belonged to Mary, but that she had been gone for some time. Cheryl mentioned that Mary had expressed disgust with her life in general and had thrown all of her papers and pen on the floor. But after a few minutes, she picked them up. When Mary returned, the instructor asked her what was really bothering her. Mary started sobbing and told her that she was not crying because of anything that the instructor had said to her.

Mary had major problems at home. Her father had passed away when she was young. Her sister was behaving badly, and her mother was seriously ill. Being the only child around her mother and being very shy, she always got blamed for all the difficulties that the family was having. The family was poor. Mary did not have enough money for public transportation to come to school more often. She did not have a computer at home and had to come to school to have access. After hearing her predicament, the instructor advised her to go to a counselor, because she herself was not an expert in handling problems of this nature. Before she left, the instructor assigned Mary homework for the next meeting 4 days later. Mary went to a counselor. Three hours later, she returned to the instructor with a happy face and gave three typed pages of the homework four days in advance of the deadline. She confirmed the instructor's gut feeling that Mary was quite intelligent. Her work was almost perfect; only minor changes had to be made. This was the first time that she had done any satisfactory work. When asked what caused the sudden change in her attitude, Mary said that the counselor gave her some immediate steps to take and told her that anytime that she needed help, the counselor would be there. This reassurance really helped her. The instructor also reassured Mary that if she had any problems in her research, she should feel free to contact her by e-mail. She also advised Mary to spend more time in school studying in order to keep her mind off her situation at home and so she could graduate, get a job, and help her mother. Mary also mentioned how patient Cheryl had been, listening to her problems. Cheryl had also taught her how to use Microsoft Word and Excel.

This day started out to be disastrous, but ended on a very positive note. The instructor was looking at a happy young woman who was ready to handle her numerous problems. The instructor and the counselor had both undergone TOC training and had just implemented it to empower Mary.

In short, **teachers should not give up on a student just because the student is not working up to expectations. The student may have nonacademic issues standing in the way of him/her giving the required time to the academic work. TOC has TP tools which can be used to address both academic and nonacademic issues**. The student should be referred to a counselor, and both the teacher and counselor should work together using TOC tools to empower the student. In this way, TOC becomes a Theory of Empowerment (TOE). This does require training in TOC for both teachers and counselors as well as communication.

1.2.2 Who This Book Is Intended For

■ This book is written for *students at the high school or college levels* who need to have skill in reading comprehension, summarizing, problem solving, and completing projects. Students have dreams. They also have self-doubt. They can conquer their self-doubt by following their dreams. For this, they need to be proactive. **Being proactive means acting appropriately in anticipation of future problems, needs,**

or changes and not being bogged down by the past or blaming someone. These students must know how to resolve conflicts, write persuasive essays, solve problems—academic and nonacademic—know the consequences of any action, make decisions, prepare projects, make presentations, and manage time. They can learn specific TP tools discussed in this book to cover these areas and be proactive. Starting a TOC students' club and repeatedly working on various issues that arise in students' lives would help students to become proactive and help one another to succeed.

In this book, you will see the word *proactive* used quite often, since once the students acquire this quality, the mission of academia is easily fulfilled. These tools are necessary to live a successful life, and the best time to learn them is when one is studying in school or college.

■ This book is written for *creative thinkers* who want to do creative work in any field of research or who are working in the college/university environment and desire to fully understand their environment and to improve it, that is, academics, faculty, counselors, advisors, staff, and administrators. People who have worked with students and who have experienced the issues listed in detail in the next section can also use this book. The sections describing individual tools are also useful for students, parents, community workers, youth counselors, leaders of male/female empowerment initiatives, churches, and even people trying to reform the prison system. One of the most important units of any institution that should learn and implement TOC is administration at the top as well as at the middle level. Since the administrators have power and resources to encourage the units' efforts, they need to work with them and to improve their morale. They must know how to use the power and resources effectively, resolve conflicts, guide, and boost morale of people whom they are serving. If the administrators do not consider consequences of their actions, their institution suffers from litigation and wasted resources.

A preliminary companion website (http://www.tocforcollege.com) has been launched.

■ This book is written for *academics* who are concerned with how to: develop better courses, curricula, or texts; help students resolve their personal conflicts and make good decisions; present material effectively in class; improve processes such as registration; improve morale; and improve the overall functioning of units such as departments and programs. The administration can make or break an institution! "It's ingenuity that will make the difference between a bleak future and a bright one," says Bill Gates.* TOC with its out-of-the-box TP tools can help creative thinking.

■ This book is intended as a *reference* for those seeking to understand and apply TOC and TP in the academic world to activities such as improving thinking skills, time management, project management, presentations, teaching students problem solving, and curriculum development as discussed in Chapter 5. Most TOC texts are designed for management and industrial settings and do not have any direct application to academia. We discuss individual TP tools and show how to apply them in a variety of situations ranging from personal life issues to overcoming departmental and institutional constraints. This is currently the only book based on actual experience written for use of creative thinkers and academia—high school systems and institutions of higher education.

1.2.3 What This Book Is Not Intended For

This book will not be of any use to people who want to make ad hoc decisions and who do not have time to analyze the situation at hand or habitually ignore the consequences of their actions. Studying TOC makes one aware of the consequences of any action. Ad hoc decisions do not necessarily consider consequences, and many result in unintended consequences. This book is useless for people who make systemic decisions to serve their personal interests; these decisions often prove detrimental to the system. If they have no interest in the common good of the system, this book is not intended for them. TOC is ethical and will not harm anyone. If a person is looking for a biased solution, TOC will be useless, since TOC produces win–win, impartial solutions and will not favor one side over the other.

1.2.4 College as a System

A college/university is a complex dynamic system with multiple stakeholders, multiple functional units, and multiple processes focused on a single goal: student success. Each institution is committed to attracting students to its campus, educating the enrolled students, retaining a large number of students in various disciplines so that they progress toward their graduation

---

* Bill and Melinda Gates Foundation Visitor Center, Seattle, Washington.

in a timely fashion, graduating them with good grades, and placing them in careers or graduate/postdoctoral programs in good schools. Every college wants to have employers and graduate/professional schools recruit their graduates. But does every institution reach its goal?

The multiple units of the system encounter many obstacles that stand in the way of achieving their goals. Each individual unit tries to do its best with the resources that it has available. For example, the Faculty Senate of our college, in a sincere effort to stem our student attrition problem, came up with over 30 concerns of students that needed to be addressed. Collectively, the members found that many students have nonacademic as well as academic issues. To address each issue, they proposed a remedial action and the corresponding agency/department in the college that needed to take appropriate action. But who can oversee such a massive effort? Who can tell the department/agency that something needs to be improved? Is there duplication of effort? Are there enough resources to address all the concerns? Who will assess the improvements made?

The academic departments of a college are not equipped to handle students' nonacademic issues. They put all their resources into creating excellent curriculum in terms of the process and content of instruction. They can form articulation agreements with other academic institutions and industries to recruit or place their students appropriately. But it is the dean of students, counselors, and advisors specialized in their own functions who can address students' nonacademic issues, if the students come to see them. The instructor with knowledge of the college resources can direct students to the right person. If the students are themselves aware of these resources, they can on their own approach the appropriate office/person that can help them with their nonacademic or academic concerns. But most instructors, especially adjuncts, do not know what resources the college has to help their students outside of their own department or school. They have an obligation to finish the course syllabus and do not have the interest, time, or expertise to deal with students' nonacademic issues. Some college and university policies do not require students to attend class or to come on time. The instructor therefore does not have to take attendance and may not be aware of students' absences or, if aware, can complain, but cannot do anything about it. The college experiences a dire economic consequence. If each student pays $5000 in tuition per year and due to academic or nonacademic issues, 100 students do not return to the college the following year, the college loses $500,000 by not graduating these students. At many colleges with large attrition, the actual impact would be more severe. Can any college sustain this type of impact? Of course, no college can. Can anything be done about this typical scenario? Yes, of course, use TOC!

The theory of constraints (TOC), properly implemented, establishes the communication necessary among the stakeholders in the system. Each stakeholder becomes a link in the system, doing his/her part by *thinking globally and acting locally*, and not working in a "silo" and disregarding the consequences to other links of the system. There are academic and nonacademic issues, called undesirable effects (UDEs), pronounced "oo dee," in each system. These UDEs are never isolated. These UDEs are the effects of conflicts. A *conflict* is a situation where we do not know exactly which of two opposing actions we should take. Using TOC, we can find the core conflict underlying myriads of UDEs. We can see how the UDEs are logically connected to the core conflict and thus know what needs to be changed. Details on UDEs are given in Section 1.4. TOC/TP tools show what we should change to, and how we can cause the change, all in a very systematic manner. It is amazing that the same TOC tools can be used to address students' personal issues, and to resolve institutional and curricular issues as well.

A typical college system has a hierarchical organizational chart showing the lines of authority as in Figure 1.1. But the college system is better understood as a chain of activities.

In Figure 1.2, the top row shows the sequential links, the responsibility of each link, and the expectations of the system for that link. The actions/entities in the lower two lines (typical actions and desired actions) are in conflict, indicated by a double-ended arrow. Note that, in the first link, working in a

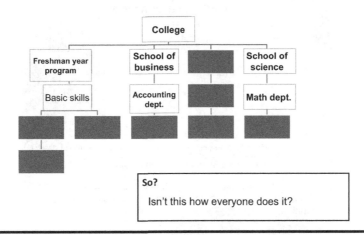

Figure 1.1 Partial organizational chart. (Courtesy of Janice Cerveny, facilitator at several workshops at Medgar Evers College [MEC], New York.)

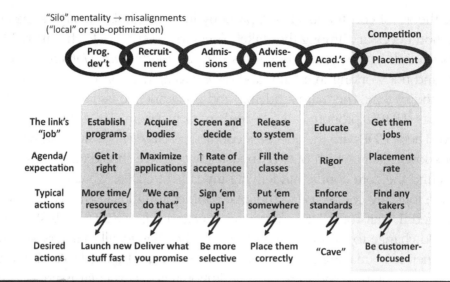

Figure 1.2   Institutional flowchart detailing the functions of each silo.

silo, it takes a considerable amount of time to establish, and many resources to run, a program. But there is also a push from faculty or administrators to launch the program as quickly as possible. Thus, the agendas of the two sets of stakeholders are in conflict. Similarly, actions taken by those working in other silos lead to conflicts. TOC helps to resolve these and other such conflicts by looking at the educational institution as a system.

Figure 1.3 shows a simple linear representation of the university/college system. In this version, the steps in processing students form the system

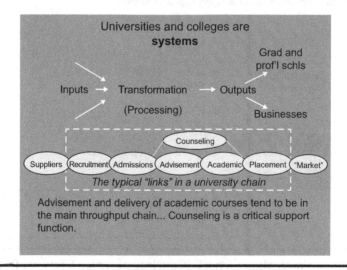

Figure 1.3   Colleges and universities from a system point of view.

chain, and the throughput (output of the system) is usually the number of graduating students. The concept of throughput will be greatly refined to define mathematical measures in Chapter 6.

Members of the community at all levels bemoan the failure of the system to perform at its best. For example, here are some things that stakeholders say:

Students of mathematics, from a survey of students, were found to have the following complaints:
1. I cannot follow the lecture.
2. I feel that I am not capable of doing mathematics.
3. I do not work hard in mathematics.
4. I don't do the homework or prepare for the course.
5. I do poorly on tests.
6. I feel that the exam is too hard.
7. I have difficulty learning the material (in math classes).
8. I have difficulty taking tests.
9. I do not attend my mathematics classes regularly.
10. The instructor moves too fast for students.
11. The instructor cannot teach his/her subject matter.
12. I am not prepared for the course (I do not have prerequisites for the course).
13. I don't have time to do the homework.
14. I don't see the importance/relevance of mathematics.
15. I am unable to attend class on time.
16. I have to take care of my family/personal problems.
17. The instructor does not care about me.
18. There is no help outside of class when I'm free.

Faculty, from a survey in a math department meeting about the performance of students in their classes, have the following complaints:
1. Students do not prepare for class.
2. Students don't attend regularly or on time.
3. Students do poorly on tests.
4. There is insufficient time to cover all the material in the course.
5. Students register late for the semester (they don't start at the beginning of the semester).
6. Students do not have the prerequisite courses for the class.
7. Students aren't learning effectively.
8. I receive very little satisfaction from my work.

9. I feel pressure to pass students who are not adequately prepared for the next course.
10. Students haven't mastered all the prerequisite topics needed for my course.

Staff/counselors/advisors, discussing their issues in a faculty development workshop, have the following complaints:
1. Students coming to see me do not keep my area clean.
2. Administrators do not respect me.
3. The nonacademic challenges of students are often not addressed.
4. The difference between an academic advisor and a counselor is not understood.
5. More and more students have mental health challenges.
6. There are many turf wars.
7. Students do not see connections.
8. The student services department experiences many disruptions.
9. Students come to school hungry (no food, transportation, etc.).
10. College faculty are dismissive of students' personal issues.
11. Students who identify as lesbian, gay, bisexual, or transgender are victimized.
12. Part-time faculty members do not attend to students' needs.
13. Some students fall between the cracks (a first-year student seminar is not required of all students).
14. There is a large dropout rate in science classes.
15. There is inconsistency of outcomes in first-year student classes.
16. Staff morale is low.

Administrators also complain about students' performance:
1. There is a lack of cooperation by some faculty to carry out the departmental agenda.
2. Too many students fail.
3. There is insufficient input by some faculty to address major departmental issues.
4. Some faculty are apathetic.

Each of these complaints or issues is an UDE in the system and will be defined in detail later in the chapter. More concerns can certainly be added, but the reader will get the point: the system of a college/university needs a lot of improvement to perform at its best.

This book has been written to address all these issues in a holistic manner.

1.3 What Is TOC/TP and Why Is It Being Used?

1.3.1 History

The theory of constraints (TOC) was developed by physicist Dr. Eliyahu "Eli" Goldratt (1947–2011) while solving business problems in the early 1980s. In conversation with Eli in 2007, the first author learned that about 15% of the world businesses were using TOC to resolve systemic issues and run their businesses. Among the companies that use TOC are Boeing, Delta Airlines, Ford, General Motors, Proctor & Gamble, Toyota, many others. Specific business applications can be found on the websites http://www.TOCICO.org, http://www.EliGoldratt.com, http://www.goldratt.com, and many more. All TOC books written by Eli are novels. When he was asked why he wrote them as novels, he said that he did not want to leave any logical gaps in his books (E. Goldratt, personal communication, September, 2006).*

1.3.2 Theory of Constraints (TOC) and Thinking Processes (TP)

The theory of constraints teaches how to identify and remove a constraint. A constraint is something that stands in the way of achieving a goal. But it is not just any obstacle! It is a special one, which when addressed, gives us leverage to achieve a goal.

Definition 1.1

A constraint is the most important factor in an organization (or personal life) that needs attention. Giving that attention, dedicating resources to improve that factor, will bring about the greatest change in the organization (or personal life).

For example, a chain is as strong as its weakest link (see Figure 1.4).

At any given time, there is only one *weakest* link. The weakest link is the constraint. By strengthening the weakest link, the performance of the entire chain improves. A system is like a chain. A typical university/college system has been described in Figure 1.3.

---

* From conversation with the authors at the TOC for Education 9th International Conference 9/2006, Leon, Mexico.

Figure 1.4   A chain is as strong as its weakest link (constraint).

In order to move toward improvement in any situation, TOC asks three basic questions:

1. What needs to be changed? (what to change?)
2. What should it be changed to? (what to change to?)
3. How can we change it? (how to cause the change?)

TOC is based on logic, and every logical process is based on assumptions.

The assumptions of TOC are based on Eli Goldratt's observations as follows (Cox III et al., 2012):

1. People are good.
2. Every conflict can be resolved.
3. Every situation, no matter how complex it initially looks, is inherently simple.
4. Every situation can be substantially improved; even the sky is not the limit.
5. Every person can reach a full life.
6. There is always a win–win solution.

Eliyahu Goldratt (1947–2011)
Founder of TOC

These assumptions have been verified by the experience of practitioners who have successfully resolved thousands of problems around the world in all kinds of situations.

In any problematic situation, there are various issues, as seen in Section 1.2. Instead of addressing each issue individually, TOC shows how to find the underlying core conflict. However complex the issues are, or however large the system is, it has been found in practice that there are no isolated issues. In fact, most of the issues can be connected logically to the core conflict. By directing all efforts to resolve the core conflict, resources and time are saved, and all other issues are also resolved very effectively, since they are consequences of the core conflict. In his book *The Choice*

(Goldratt, 2008), Eli Goldratt talks about "inherent simplicity." The following is a summary of a discussion that the first author had with Eli at the 10th TOC for Education, Inc. (TOCfE) International Conference, Ft. Walton Beach, Florida, where his book was first read out loud and feedback requested.

> The more complex a situation is, the more inherent simplicity there is in it.
>
> Finding the cause-and-effect relationships between various components and finding the core constraint, we can discover the inherent simplicity.
>
> By finding the inherent simplicity, we can always find a breakthrough solution to an apparent conflict. (E. Goldratt, personal communication, October 13–14, 2007)

TOC has thinking process (TP) tools. These tools aid in communicating the underlying logic of the situation. Using TP tools, one can find solutions that boost total system performance instead of optimizing individual processes. The *system* in academia consists of students, faculty, services, staff, administration, and their interactions. The system for a person is all the people related to his/her interpersonal and personal issues. *Performance* success is measured in learning, passing rates, graduation rates, being *more* successful in achieving goals, etc. Performance improves due to a *paradigm shift* in how we view the underlying issues and results in changing various policies, measures, and behaviors that are restricting or constraining that improvement.

As quoted in Alan Barnard's presentation (Barnard, 2007),

> Paradigms are frames of references we use to "see" the world and make decisions. Paradigms let through data that match our "expectations" and block data that don't. What may be impossible to do with one paradigm may be easy to do with another. . . . (Barker, 1986)
>
> [Paradigms are] sets of assumptions we believe are valid. We go through "paradigm shift" when we realize one or more of our assumptions are (no longer) valid. . . . (Goldratt, 1986)

There are many thinking processes. If we are dealing with a personal or interpersonal issue, only one or two of the thinking process tools are sufficient. But to resolve a group's, an institution's, or a department's issues, most of the tools are necessary. TOC provides an holistic solution, so whether the issue is personal or of a group nature, we call it a system issue. How this is done will be explained through step-by-step discussions with examples.

The thinking processes were designed to answer three questions, in the following order:

1. <u>What to change?</u> **This step identifies the problem**. Answering this question utilizes data, feelings, and intuition to bring to the surface the root cause or constraint of the current state of the system (or current reality). In TOC, the existence of a constraint inhibits flow through or performance of the system. In this way, TOC tends to view a constraint as positive, since its identification and subsequent treatment result in an order of magnitude improvement in performance. The thinking process (TP) tools that we use here are the **Current Reality Tree (CRT)** (Chapter 2) and **Cloud** (Chapter 3).
2. <u>What to change to?</u> **This step discusses the strategy involved in a TOC solution to the problem**. Once we find the constraint, we apply other TP tools robust enough to develop an indisputable solution that avoids any unintended or undesirable consequences. The tools allow us to visualize what we intend the system to be in the future (future reality) by identifying strategic objectives, the desired effects (DEs). Here, we use the tools called the **Future Reality Tree (FRT)** (Chapter 4) and **Negative Branch Reservations (NBRs)** (Chapters 2 and 4).
3. <u>How to cause the change?</u> **This step discusses the tactics involved in a TOC solution to the problem**. Implementing TOC allows us to determine systematically what obstacles stand between present and desired realities, explain why those obstacles exist, define the steps that will overcome the obstacles, define the order in which those steps should be taken, and recognize when the plan should be altered. We use three TP tools here: the **Prerequisite Tree (PrT)** also called the **Ambitious Target Tree (ATT)** (Chapter 5), the **Project Plan**, and the **Transition Tree (TrT)** (Chapter 5).

1.3.3 TOC for Education, Inc.

TOCfE (http://www.tocforeducation.com) is an organization founded in 1995 that focuses on K-12 education to which Dr. Eli Goldratt has donated his knowledge. The following copyrighted material from the *TACT Workbook* (2003) describing the mission, guiding principles, and ethics of TOCfE has been quoted with permission:

> In spite of all the changes and good intentions of those bringing changes to education, we still have too many problems that prevent us from achieving our "ambitious target" in education: Educators must ensure that all the learning and personal needs of all of their students are addressed. Educators face obstacles such as
>
>   1. Many students do not know how to solve their own problems.
>   2. Many students cannot control their impulsive behavior.
>   3. Many students memorize, rather than understand what they are taught.
>   4. Many students cannot apply what they learn to other situations.
>   5. Many students do not see the relevance of what they learn to their everyday lives.
>   6. Many students do not accept responsibility for the consequences of their behavior.
>   7. Educators are expected to meet the learning and needs of all their students without sufficient resources—time, money and stamina.

In the face of these obstacles, limited resources frequently require teachers to prioritize the learning and other needs of their students. If there is one possible solution: "Develop all students' ability to take responsibility for their own learning and behavior," such a solution would mean that all who lead students would have more time and energy to teach and attain the ambitious target. We need a set of simple yet powerful thinking and communication tools. The answer is TOC thinking tools.*

TOC thinking tools are as follows:

- Simple (they apply to all levels of students and are visually appealing)
- Taught through existing curricula to achieve academic standards and benchmarks to which schools are held accountable
- Applicable to cognitive skills as well as to the behavior and emotional needs of the students

---

* These are also called thinking process (TP) tools, and the authors prefer this term.

1.3.3.1 Mission Statement of TOC for Education

Through the synergy of the TOC tools and visionary educators worldwide, TOC will significantly improve education by enabling learners to think and communicate effectively. Working together toward shared goals, TOC and all who champion students will leave behind a better world (http://www.tocfor education.com/foundation.html).

1.3.3.2 Why Is TOC Important?

Florida teacher Belinda Small, a facilitator at a MEC TOC workshop, gives the following reasons:

- *Students* think of the solutions.
- Students use *their* logic.
- The most important fact is that *students have used it.*

Students make the connection between external academic standards reflected in the Graduate Record Examination (GRE), Medical College Admission Test (MCAT), Graduate Management Admission Test (GMAT), and National Council for Accreditation of Teacher Education (NCATE) and various questions in college course exams.

1.3.3.3 Ethical Code of TOC for Education

The TOC tools were created to find and implement win–win solutions in which no one is harmed through our actions.

1.3.3.4 Users of TOC in Education

Who can use TOC in education? All stakeholders in education including teachers, students, administrators, curriculum developers, policy makers, and parents can use TOC in education. In other words, anyone who is concerned about the quality and the function of education and anyone who wants himself or herself and others to be better in carrying out their various functions in education as well as in their personal lives.

1.3.3.5 How Is TOC Applied?

Within education, the generic TOC thinking tools are applied in three areas:

- Behavior—human relationships
- Administration—systemic improvement
- Curriculum—teaching and learning

Our TOC text, written for high school and college students, counselors, faculty, administrators, and community organizers, to make them proactive in achieving their success, subscribes to the TOC for Education principles and statement of ethics.

1.3.4 Success of TOC in School Settings

The TOC/TP tools are generic and work without regard to age, culture, or political differences. Within only a few years of its founding, the TOC for Education organization has been able to improve student behavior, academic learning, and school functioning for millions of children in 22 countries on five continents. It must be that educators find the TOC for Education methods for improving their educational systems exceptionally practical and powerful!

Educators have used TOC to teach students to resolve conflicts and become better problem solvers. According to repeated studies on international education (National Center for Education Statistics, 2015), over the last 17 years, public school education in Singapore, Malaysia, and the Philippines has been ranked very high internationally. These countries have implemented TOC in their educational systems under the guidance of TOC for Education. They have initiated successful programs for improved curriculum delivery and student conduct.

The TOC for Education website (http://www.tocforeducation.com) has testimonials from all types of stakeholders in education (students, parents, counselors, teachers, principals, superintendents, Ministers of Education) from Brazil, Colombia, the United Kingdom, the United States, Israel, Japan, Malaysia, Mexico, the Philippines, Poland, Russia and the Republic of South Africa, Serbia, Singapore, and Venezuela, among others. In Poland, it is even being taught to Pre-K students. Additionally, the TOC website (http://www.tocforcollege.com) contains several PowerPoint presentations given by educators from these countries at TOCfE international conferences.

1.3.5 TOC in Higher Education

More than 100 universities and schools, including the University of Michigan, Ohio State University, and Wayne State University in the United States and others abroad, use several TOC tools. Many well-known "Ivy League" business schools, such as Wharton, use constraint management to run *all* of their operations. It is a required graduate course in many United States and foreign M.B.A. programs.

1.3.6 Success at MEC

Medgar Evers College of CUNY is the first liberal arts college to use TOC to address the problem of student attrition.

In the following sections we describe various steps of TOC implementation taken by the Department of Mathematics at MEC. Here, we make historical remarks. Some repetition is necessary for the sake of completeness. The grant team considered the goal "to reduce student attrition." To confine it to the faculty's area of responsibility, the team restricted itself to the goal "to reduce student attrition in mathematics courses."

Our experiment with using TOC to address attrition in mathematics courses began in January 2002. Darius Movasseghi, then chair of the department; Joshua Berenbom'; and the first author—all faculty in the Department of Mathematics, MEC—participated in formal Jonah training at the Avraham Goldratt Institute (AGI) Academy, New Haven, Connecticut. Tracey Burton-Houle and Steve Simpliciano were the facilitators. The training was funded by an institutional grant for 2001–2004 from the Minority Science and Engineering Improvement Program (MSEIP) of the US Department of Education. The attendees used the entire TOC roadmap (described in Section 5.10) during a 2-week intensive workshop to develop a detailed project plan for the department. Their findings were discussed informally by the chair with other mathematics faculty, devoting a few minutes of every monthly departmental meeting during the Spring 2002 semester. As the major issues of the department were brought out and discussed in the open manner, a congenial environment developed in the department that attracted a large number of students to become mathematics majors. The department developed new curricula and improvements in mathematics tutoring. They developed departmental guidelines that helped all faculty and support personnel work cohesively toward student retention.

We found that the full TOC analysis addressed the needs of the whole student, not just his/her academic needs. The project plan

showed how and where the academic advisors, personal counselors, and the Basic Skills Department could collaborate with the Department of Mathematics to address the problem of attrition. The facilitator, Steve Simpliciano, made a presentation to the MEC president, Edison O. Jackson and his key cabinet members in May 2005, about what the team had learned, and offered the Departmental Guidelines as a deliverable. President Jackson approved the guidelines and expressed his desire that everyone in the college should learn TOC, starting with the Basic Skills and Freshman Year Program (FYP) faculty. Two additional institutional grants from the U.S. Department of Education—MSEIP (2004–2007) and Women's Equity in Education Act (WEEA) (2005–2007)—facilitated the formal Management Skills Workshop (MSW) training at AGI of key administrators and more faculty. The grants also provided resources to hold various campus workshops for tutors, academic advisors, personal counselors, and Basic Skills instructors from 2005 to 2007. In the spring of 2008, President Jackson, along with his senior administration, reaffirmed his commitment to implement TOC to address institutional issues. He laid out a logical procedure for all administrators and middle management to follow that transcended personalities in order to tackle the problem of attrition as first-year students moved into their academic disciplines. For the college, students, and community, it was unfortunate that President Jackson's retirement caused delay and more obstacles to implementation, as subsequent administrations did not have his patience or vision.*

More details on implementation of TOC and its impact are given in the next section.

1.4 Defining and Solving a Problem

Before beginning to solve a problem, it is necessary to define the problem. Ask yourself, "What is my problem? What is the issue that bothers me?"

Define a problem precisely and you are half way to a solution.

Dr. Eli Goldratt, founder of TOC (Barnard, 2007)
"Bottleneck Is at the Top": 10th International TOCfE Conference,
October 11–14, 2007, Ft. Walton, Florida

---

* These efforts received another boost from three MSEIP grants—Institutional and Cooperative for 2010–2013 and Institutional for 2012–2015 and 2013–16, thanks to the US Department of Education.

Is every issue a problem? No. An issue may be only a symptom of an underlying problem. For example, a fever is symptomatic of an infectious process. By treating symptoms alone, a pill to reduce the fever, you cannot resolve the problem of infection. You must understand what type of infection it is, and treat that infection. Similarly, you must understand the nature and source of the problem if you are to resolve it. Many problems are caused by conflicts. For example, in Figure 1.3, an institution does not function effectively and has low graduation rates or high attrition because of the silo mentality and resultant conflicts. In this case, the underlying problem can be understood in terms of the different conflicts. But addressing every conflict individually will not solve the problem. Using TOC tools, a full analysis of the UDEs of the conflicts itself leads to a clear definition of the core conflict or *the* problem which can then be resolved. In resolving the core conflict, all other conflicts that are logically dependent on it are also resolved.

The sets of concerns (UDEs) stated in Section 1.2.4 are effects or symptoms of problems that need to be addressed. For each concern, there is a conflict which causes the issue and contributes to the problem. But is it necessary to find the conflict underlying every UDE? No. Can the concerns be simply ignored? Some administrators think that by ignoring faculty and staff issues, the issues will go away. Some faculty think that just by doing curriculum development and bringing new gadgets into teaching, all students' problems will disappear. But this is wishful thinking. Issues ignored become threats to the success or even to the existence of an institution.

So, the issues cannot all be ignored. However, all the issues need not be addressed individually. The experience of people who have worked in TOC indicates that **just three important concerns** (UDEs) from diverse areas in the list are enough to find the basic or core conflict or define the real problem. Eli Goldratt, in conversation with the first author, gave credit for this observation to Efrak Goldratt, his daughter, and Dale Houle of AGI, who independently noticed that one comes to the same core conflict regardless of how many concerns that one considers. The second and third chapters are all about how to define the problem or what we need to change ("what to change").

We first review the way that the concerns are formally stated in Section 1.2.2. Each concern is called an UDE.

Definition 1.2

An UDE should be a negative aspect of current reality, be a factual effect, be a description of the state of the system, be a complaint about an ongoing problem that exists, should be a simple complete sentence, not blame someone, not be a speculated cause, [and] not incorporate the solution within the statement.

Theory of Constraints International Certification Organization [TOCICO] dictionary (Cox III et al., 2012)

Each UDE is a simple statement without any connectives such as *or*, *but*, *and*, and *if–then*. It should never blame anyone, explicitly or implicitly! The UDE is often generic. For example, when the first author presented his research at an international TOC for Education conference in Leon, Mexico, in September, 2006, one of the professors from Pueblo, Mexico, said, "I thought you were talking about our students!" The statement of an UDE should not contain a solution to the problem at hand. An UDE is a condition, an effect, and not an action. It does not describe any lack of activity. Each UDE is itself negative or has a serious negative consequence. This and other such definitions come from the TOCICO dictionary (Cox III et al., 2012), whose conventions we follow in the text. When a term is not defined in the dictionary, we follow the usage of experts in TOC.

Which concerns should be tackled first, so that there are quick results? One should start with the area over which one has direct control. This is discussed in the next section.

1.4.1 Span of Control

Any improvement in the system can be made only in the area of one's control and/or in the area of one's responsibility. One must start with the area of control, because rapid progress is possible in areas about which one has intuition and expertise. However, sometimes, individuals are in the unusual position of being involved in issues external to their specific domains, for example, interdepartmental concerns such as recruitment or placement in internships, jobs, or cooperative work with industries or college-wide committees, whose mission is to promote the welfare and interests of people in all areas. In such cases, one should start in the area of responsibility.

A student's area of control is his/her attitude toward education, the number of courses he or she takes, study habits, time management, work, and balancing the time between studying and personal tasks. Any immediate improvement in these areas will be reflected in the student's grade point average. The student's area of responsibility is communication with all the human resources that support his/her studies—family, fellow students, peer tutors, instructors, and staff. Since there are only a few people involved in the student's success system, once the student becomes proactive and takes charge of his or her situation, progress can be very rapid.

1.4.2 Students' Success System

Every student should feel secure, connected to, and protected from all sides. We illustrate in Figure 1.5 the student's safety net. Instructors, tutors, family, and friends are the strongest contacts needed constantly for support. The advisor and chair of the department come next. Counselors and administrators are needed from time to time. The student has to know this safety net is always there to assure him/her success, but the student's own effort is the first resource. Communication between the various stakeholders is essential.

A student TOC club frequented by all stakeholders at various times would certainly help set up this safety net of communication and help students become proactive.

Curriculum development, delivery of instruction, and working with students are under an instructor's control. Working with colleagues in the discipline; referring students to tutors, counselors, and advisors; and meeting

Student success system

All stakeholders connected in student success

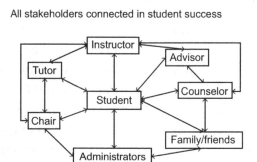

Every student should feel secure and protected from all sides.

Figure 1.5   Students' success system.

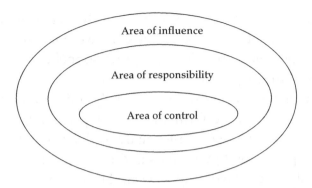

Figure 1.6   Span of control.

various obligations determined by the department and college are areas of responsibility.

Figure 1.6 describes three areas where changes can be made.

1.4.3 Sphere of Influence

In order to make lasting progress in a department or institution, one must have acceptance or "buy-in" from the faculty of the department as well as from senior management. For example, once the chair of the department buys in, the chair can then influence other people involved with the department to bring about the change recommended by instructors. An example follows.

First, the unique features of the college/university system need to be considered. In industry or government, a directive given by superiors is explicitly followed by subordinates. In primary or secondary school, the Board of Education or principal decides on new initiatives and teachers are expected to adopt them. At the college level, no professor will change behavior or adopt new pedagogical strategies, however wonderful, by decree of the department chair or a college administrator. Considering union regulations and academic freedom, senior faculty do not feel obliged to accept any modifications in their normal activities or changes in the curriculum. Any perceived activity extraneous to instruction is usually regarded as an impediment. Thus, faculty acceptance of any new initiative is of paramount importance in a college setting.

We found that after formal TOC training of several key personnel in the MEC Math Department, acceptance by the department faculty, administration, advisors, and counselors was necessary to actively engage all those providing service to the students. The following steps were taken to achieve acceptance or buy-in. They were modified as the personnel changed. Formal steps to buy-in are given in Chapter 6.

Our buy-in steps were as follows: Informally train grant team members who did not participate in the formal training (Spring 2002). Introduce issues (UDEs) and findings (DEs) informally to department faculty (Spring 2002). Prepare departmental guidelines and get departmental consensus (Summer and Fall 2002). Have trainer, Dean Steve Simpliciano of Goldratt Institute, make a presentation to the college president and his cabinet (May 2005). Provide MSW course for other grant personnel and directors of the FYP and Post Secondary Readiness Center (December 2005). Provide a TOC workshop for tutors and counselors (April 2006). Provide a refresher TOC workshop for tutors (March 2007). Provide a TOC workshop for the new FYP director and academic advisors, FY program counselors, and Women's Center counselors (April 2007). Develop a TOC course at the first-year student level: Creative Thinkers Toolkit (2010–2011). Conduct workshops: to train advisors and counselors to teach the course and establish communication with academic faculty (July 2011). Launch the TOC website for college-level audiences (http://www.tocforcollege.com) (July 2011). Present research to the college faculty, staff, and new administration (November 2011, February 2014, February 2015). Arrange for MEC faculty and counselors to attend the TOC for Education conference (February 2012). Hold TOC mentors' workshops for all stakeholders (July 2012, December 2013, January 2015, January 2016). Several first-year student advisors have now received credentials as TOC facilitators to guide students and colleagues.

For the reasons given earlier, in a college, any initiative takes time to get established, and there are many layers of resistance to change. But the people initiating changes should not give up.

We have found that as improvements are made in areas of control, extension of this improvement leads to improvement in areas of responsibility. The area of influence also improves. For example, we wanted to stem student attrition, so we first directed all our efforts toward building a more trusting environment in the Department of Mathematics by openly discussing various concerns about attrition. Then, we collectively made improvements in curriculum content and process, tutorial services, assessment procedures and in the use of technology—whatever the department had direct control over. There was a marked improvement in retention of math students, but the department could not go any further by itself. The enrollment of math majors was 7 in 2000, went up to 29 in Fall 2002, and to 60 math majors and 30 math minors in Fall 2015, with 90% retention for 2012–2015. More than 50 math majors graduated from 2003–2015. The effort of implementing TOC has also brought in a total of eight federal grants worth $3.4 million over 16 years to help support the previously described activities.

With buy-in of the administration in 2005, the area of influence expanded and the department could then reach other departments that dealt with different aspects of student life such as the counselors and advisors. Finally, the college-wide effort to stem overall student attrition was launched: The influence of the initiatives reached a broader constituency, and the narrow area of influence became much wider! The methods of TOC are so robust that the project plan made in 2002 is still viable today and is continually updated as needs change, and the POOGI (discussed in Chapter 6 in detail) continues to be a satisfying experience. Of course, changing administrations play a very important part in slowing down or increasing the rate of improvement.

1.5 Conventions Used

Terms are defined according to the TOCICO dictionary, except as specifically noted. Graphical representations are based on the work of various TOC experts, as noted.

1.6 Logical Foundations of TOC and TP: Necessary and Sufficient Condition Logic

Theory of constraints is based mainly on cause-and-effect logic. We will discuss two types of logic: necessary condition or necessity logic and sufficient condition or sufficiency logic. A cause may be a condition or an action. Given just one simple statement, it is neither a cause nor an effect: For example, suppose we have the following:

I want to graduate from college. I need 120 credits to graduate.
It rains. The street is wet.

None is a cause or effect of the other. When two statements are connected with *if . . . then . . .* or *in order to . . . we must have . . . , because . . .* , we have a conditional statement. We can say, "In order to graduate from a college, a student must earn 120 credits." We can also say, "A student graduates, **only if** the student completes 120 credits." Another way we can say it is, "Because the student needs to graduate, she earns 120 credits." This is a conditional statement using *necessary condition* logic. A need means necessity. That necessity is fulfilled by one or more actions or prerequisites. That is the connection. Graphically, we write a conditional statement with a necessary condition as seen in Figure 1.7.

"If it rains, then the street is wet." This is a conditional statement using *sufficient condition* logic.

We write a conditional statement with a sufficient condition (Figure 1.8).

To describe a necessary condition in terms of an arrow, we use ←, and to describe a sufficient condition, we use →. Necessary and sufficient conditions are discussed in detail below.

Simple statement in a box is called an entity.

Definition 1.3

Entity: A statement, generally in a rectangle or rectangle with rounded corners, that describes a part of the system being studied using a thinking processes diagram. (Cox III et al., 2012)

An entity is always a simple sentence. It has no connectives, such as *or, and, but, if . . . then . . .* , or *in order to . . . , we must have. . . .*

An entity is called a necessary condition if it is required for the effect or result but does not guarantee the result. An entity is called a sufficient condition if it is one of several possible conditions each of which by itself guarantees the effect or result.

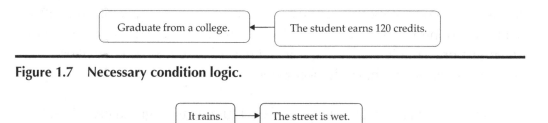

Figure 1.7   Necessary condition logic.

Figure 1.8   Sufficient condition logic.

A *necessary* condition is a requirement that must be fulfilled in order to achieve a result. If the condition is not met, the result is not achieved. For example, in order to graduate from college, a minimum of 120 credits is required. In other words, completing at least 120 credits is a necessary condition. This means that if a student earns 119 credits, the student does not graduate from college. In a necessary condition statement, the effect or result (in the future) is given first. We then find a cause, a state, or a condition, by asking *why* the effect happens. It is possible to have several necessary conditions.

A *sufficient* condition is a condition, which by itself, if met, will *definitely achieve* the result. There may be many such conditions. For example, there are several ways for a street to become wet. For the result "a street is wet," one sufficient condition is "it rains." Another sufficient condition might be "the pipe underneath the street is broken." We say, *"If* it rains, *then* the street is wet" or "If a pipe underneath the street breaks, then the street is wet." The result is the same under both of these two conditions (Figure 1.9).

In a sufficient condition statement, the cause is given first. Then, we derive the result/effect by asking *what will happen* if the condition is met or *what the consequence* of the condition is.

A necessary condition may not be a sufficient condition; that is, the necessary condition may not be enough by itself to attain the result; there might be several more conditions needed for the result to happen. For example, another requirement for graduation is to complete the 120 credits as recommended in a particular discipline (not just a random assortment of credits). Here (Figure 1.10), taking the recommended courses in a discipline is an

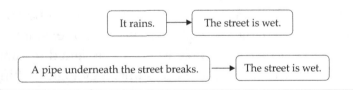

Figure 1.9   Several sufficient conditions for the same effect.

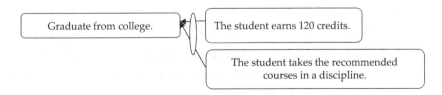

Figure 1.10   Additional cause.

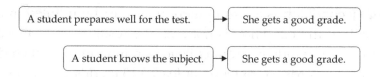

Figure 1.11   Sufficient condition but not a necessary condition.

additional cause or required/necessary condition. The additional cause is indicated by logical *and*, represented graphically by an oval, called a *banana*.

A sufficient condition may not be a necessary condition. There might be several ways to achieve the same result. An example is given earlier. Here is another example (Figure 1.11).

If a student prepares well for the test, then she gets a good grade. Here, the "student prepares well for the test" is a sufficient condition, but not a necessary condition. A student may already know the subject, and thus, she might not prepare for the test to get a good grade.

1.6.1 Applications of Sufficiency and Necessity Logic

For some examples of the application of sufficiency and necessity logic, consider the following statements of a student:

- I don't buy my textbook.
- I want to pass this class.

Each of these is just a statement. Asking the question "what must happen next?" would lead to a *response*, which is the *effect* of the given statement (i.e., the *cause*). The given statement and its response can be connected to make a conditional statement using *if . . . then. . . .* For example, "If I don't buy my textbook, then I won't be able to do the assigned reading." This statement uses is a sufficient condition or sufficiency logic. Asking the same question repeatedly after each response would lead to a chain of cause-and-effect statements (or a "branch") where a cause logically precedes its effect. This chain uses sufficient condition or sufficiency logic and is discussed in detail in the next chapter.

On the other hand, asking such questions as "why?" or "what must you do in order for this to happen?" would lead to finding the cause whose effect is the given statement. The two statements can be connected to make a conditional statement using *in order to . . . I must. . . .* For example, "In order to buy my textbook, I must have financial resources." This is a necessary condition statement or necessity logic. Asking repeatedly the same why question would lead to a chain of cause-and-effect conditions where an "effect" is given first linguistically. This chain uses necessary condition or necessity logic. The technique of making a chain of necessity logic is used in developing a TP tool called the Cloud described in Chapter 3. It is also used in the TP tool called an Ambitious Target Tree (ATT) or a Prerequisite Tree (PrT) and is discussed in Chapter 5. Such a tool can be used in *developing* a project plan. However, *implementing* a project plan would need sufficiency logic.

Definition 1.4

A branch is a sequence of "sufficient condition statements" (connected by *if . . . then . . .*).

For example, if a pipe breaks, the street gets wet. If the street gets wet, it will be slippery. If the street is slippery, there will be more accidents:

Pipe breaks → street is wet → street is slippery → accidents increase

This is a branch.

Here are two examples of student work assigned by Nancy Oley in her Introductory Psychology course.

The example in Figure 1.12 describes the consequences of one's action. Students are asked to buy the textbook, but often don't. To encourage them

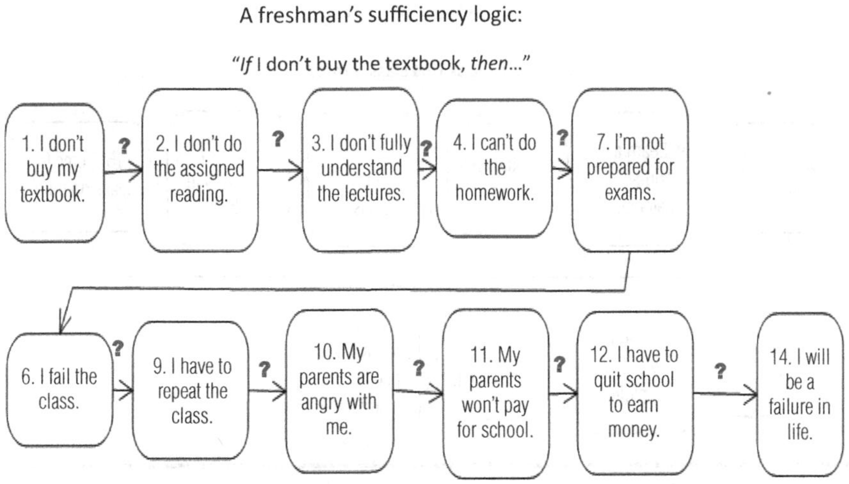

A freshman's sufficiency logic:

"If I don't buy the textbook, *then..."*

1. I don't buy my textbook. **?** → 2. I don't do the assigned reading. **?** → 3. I don't fully understand the lectures. **?** → 4. I can't do the homework. **?** → 7. I'm not prepared for exams.

6. I fail the class. **?** → 9. I have to repeat the class. **?** → 10. My parents are angry with me. **?** → 11. My parents won't pay for school. **?** → 12. I have to quit school to earn money. **?** → 14. I will be a failure in life.

Figure 1.12   Branch developed by a first-year student.

to do so, the professor teaches sufficiency (If . . . then . . .) logic and then gives the student the assignment to create a branch. Each action to the left of the arrow *must* cause the action to the right of the arrow. The question marks are asking "then what must or will happen?" The *completed branch* shows the consequences of not buying the textbook. We have found that students who at least attempt this graded assignment were significantly more likely to get the book and pass the class than those who don't attempt it. The numbers in the Figure 1.12 are statements listed by the student, and then the student arranged some of them logically to fit in the branch.

The example in Figure 1.13 describes how to achieve a goal. Most students begin the class with the idea that they will pass it. However, few have any real plan for doing so. The professor teaches necessity logic (in order to . . . I must) and then gives students the assignment to create a sequence of statements using necessity logic that lays out the necessary actions for passing the class. Each action to the right of the backward arrow is *required* for the action to the left of the arrow to occur. This is an example of an ATT.

Such assignments can be used to make students proactive.

If this seems difficult, take heart. Neuroscientists tell us that we need to practice cause-and-effect logic: ". . . Our brains aren't wired for general logic problems . . ." says neuroscientist David Eagleman (Eagleman, 2011, p. 85). That is the reason we have a difficult time solving puzzles and word problems. The only way to become adept at solving word problems is to solve as many of them as possible. Then, the process becomes automatic.

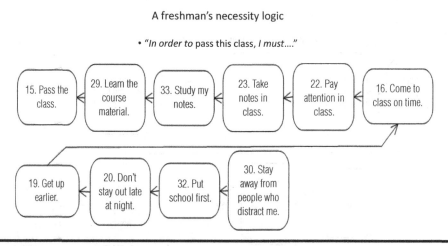

Figure 1.13 **ATT developed by a student using necessity logic. It reveals the logical steps that she must take to pass the course.**

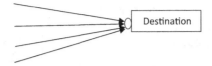

Figure 1.14   Many roads, same destination.

Conflicts sometimes arise because people confuse necessary and sufficient conditions. For instance, assume that John and Mary are travelling in a car and want to reach a destination. John knows at least two roads. Mary insists on using a particular road to reach the destination because she does not know about any other road. A conflict may arise between John and Mary. Here, the road that Mary knows is a necessary condition for her, whereas for John, the road that Mary knows is only a sufficient condition, since there are other roads which he knows will take him to the destination (Figure 1.14).

Another example of a conflict that often arises between a husband and wife is about ways to save money. The goal of saving money can be reached in many ways, but if the husband insists on a way that the wife does not agree with, conflict arises because each person thinks that the only way to save money is the way he/she knows (meaning necessary condition).

Such conflicts also arise in an institution if people in charge are not flexible and open to suggestions from subordinates.

A classic conflict arises when two people decide to take opposite actions to achieve the same goal. This conflict, called a Cloud, is discussed in detail in Chapter 3.

The following example shows how we can use logic to make everyday decisions.

1.6.2 *Everyday Decision Using a Branch*

This example was developed by Ernts Gracia, Math Lab Technician, as the first assignment in the online course on constraint management taught by Dr. James Holt of Washington State University, Vancouver, Washington. The storyline is as follows:

Today it has been snowing. Students and instructors are expecting that classes will be canceled. But classes are in session.

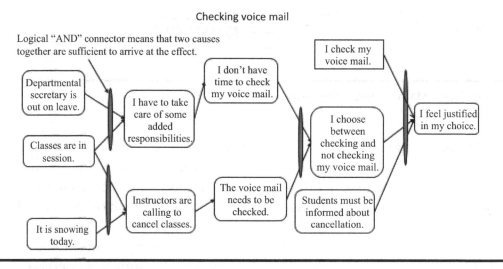

Figure 1.15 Cause-and-effect logic in everyday life.

The secretary is out on leave. There are some added responsibilities I need to take care of. I am not sure whether I should check my voice mail, since this will take time, and I need to take care of other things as well. But, instructors may be calling in to cancel their classes. Students must be informed of canceled classes. So I check my voice mail.

As shown in Figure 1.15, Ernts came to justify his decision to check his voicemail by connecting the related statements using if . . . then logic and explaining his decision via the following branch or "logical twig" called *Checking Voice Mail*. Notice how he wrote each fact or *entity* of the storyline in a rounded box. He arranged the entities and connected the entities with arrows to indicate the cause and effect, and combined several causes together (to make one sufficient cause) with the connective *and* or banana. The rectangular box contains or represents the "injection" or decision.

1.6.3 Application of Cause-and-Effect Logic for Analyzing and Summarizing a Paragraph

We will show how to summarize various points of the following two articles. The main tool we use is cause-and-effect logic. This should give the reader some training in writing summaries.

Example 1.1: To Be Happy Today and Tomorrow

The ultimate goal for a human being is to be happy today and tomorrow. We want to be happy. With our unlimited potential to tap, there should be no need to limit our happiness to any one thing or wait to be happy until some goal is attained or until we have lots of money or fame. Instead, our experience so far in life indicates that when we have "meaningful" time in a day we feel satisfied or happy. On the other hand, when time is wasted in doing something meaningless we feel lousy. We feel our time is meaningful when we accomplish something, even a simple chore completed to our satisfaction. Inner stirrings to do something creative makes us constantly restless to do things. We must know how to channel our energy to finish the big and small activities we undertake. We have to demand the best of ourselves and attain our goals to our satisfaction. Otherwise, we will feel frustrated. Regardless of whether our goal has been attained or not, our constant goal should be that we live a meaningful life—today and tomorrow. It is the yesterday that we cannot do much about except to take appropriate corrective action, instead of brooding over it or blaming someone or ourselves. If our efforts towards achieving a goal have not been sufficient, instead of feeling dissatisfied or unhappy, we should take into account how much we have accomplished and be satisfied with our work so far and continue working. We have to be proactive. (Nagarkatte, 2012)

The preceding paragraph can be summarized as follows (Figure 1.16): In order to be happy today and tomorrow, I must use my time meaningfully. I must take creative actions.

Education brings meaning to our lives. It helps equip us with mental tools to express our innate talents. It gives us choices. It helps us achieve our goals. It helps us widen our horizons. That is the reason we need to study a variety of subjects. We come to college in order to attain our goals. Education can show us to how to be creative and how to use our time meaningfully.

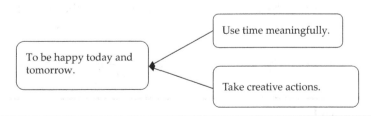

Figure 1.16   Summary of a paragraph.

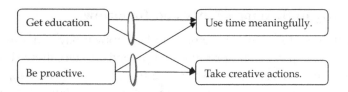

Figure 1.17 Summary of the above two paragraphs.

To summarize the previous two paragraphs: If we have education, we learn how to use our time meaningfully. If we have education, we learn how to take creative actions. But we cannot necessarily attain both, unless we are proactive. This is shown in Figure 1.17.

Example 1.2: A Project

We must discover what obstacles prevent us from achieving our goals. One obstacle is that we have to take care of so many things every day that we first consider the thing that needs our immediate attention. While doing that we are reminded or told of another important thing that needs to be done or another deadline to meet and our attention gets diverted. Now we have to do two things. Thus we constantly keep doing different things without accomplishing our major goals. Everything remains incomplete. That leads to frustration and stress. What we are doing is called multi-tasking. Instead, everything we do that takes some amount of time and effort must be considered a "project." (Nagarkatte, 2012)

At this point, we need to define a project. A *project* is a sequence of logically arranged tasks to achieve some goal. A *task* is a unit of activity. A project is also an example of cause-and-effect logic especially sufficiency logic. If one task ends, then the next begins. For example, a syllabus with a lecture schedule for a course can be considered a project. The tasks cannot be arranged in a random manner. Each task has to be carried out sequentially, one after the other, as in Figure 1.18.

There is a finished product at the end of the project. It is called a *deliverable*. It may be tangible, such as an object or a gadget. Sometimes, it is just acknowledgment by someone (including ourselves) that an intangible goal has been attained. There is some payoff as a consequence of completing the project. It may be a monetary reward. Whatever the project, once

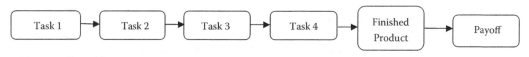

Figure 1.18 A project.

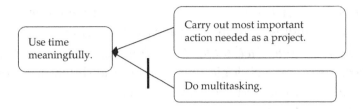

Figure 1.19 No multitasking.

we finish it, there is a kind of satisfaction (happiness), accompanied by an increase in confidence and a sense of accomplishment. That is also our payoff. We can then start another project.

In short, in doing creative actions, we have a choice. We can multitask or we can carry out a single project. Multitasking is a major obstacle. In order to use time meaningfully, we must carry out the most important needed action as a project without multitasking. Note that the line drawn vertically through the arrow negates the relationship (Figure 1.19).

We can summarize the two examples as follows: In order to be happy today and tomorrow, we must use our time meaningfully and perform creative actions. In order to use our time meaningfully and perform creative actions, we must have a good education and we must be proactive. In order to use our time meaningfully, we must also do the most important action of the day (there can be only one at any time) as a project and finish it. We could start another one before finishing the first one, but finishing a project gives satisfaction and other payoffs.

We need both necessity- and sufficiency-based logic to justify our actions, and we must know the difference between the two.

1.6.4 Application of Cause-and-Effect Logic to Solve Word Problems in Mathematics

Mathematics is all logic. We come across necessary conditions (in order to . . . we must or ". . . only if . . ."), sufficient conditions (if . . . then . . .), and necessary and sufficient conditions, in pure mathematics. Solving word problems is an essential skill in any subject where mathematics is applied. Other applications are commonly found in the natural and social sciences. Knowing the two types of logic helps studying mathematics and its applications.

In order to solve word problems, we can use sufficient condition logic. We discuss two examples. The first of the two following examples is taken from *The Singapore Model Method for Learning Mathematics* (Hong, 2009) but solved here using explicit logic. We connect the different statements using if . . . then . . . logic and develop a branch connecting the givens with the required answer. In Chapter 4, we will show how a word problem can be solved using necessary condition logic. Some algebra problems require necessary condition logic.

Example 1.3

The ratio of the number of boys to the number of girls is 5:6. It is given that 30% of the boys wear glasses, and there is an equal number of boys and girls who wear glasses. What percentage of the girls wear glasses? (Hong, 2009, p. 130, Example 18).

SOLUTION

(Note that if a ratio is given, the actual fraction is obtained by multiplying a variable x by the numerator and denominator of the ratio. You must also know how to convert a percentage into a decimal.) We analyze each sentence in the word problem as a conditional statement.

1. If the ratio of boys to girls is 5:6, then the number of boys is $5x$ and the number of girls is $6x$.
2. If 30% of boys wear glasses, then $0.3(5x) = 1.5x$ boys wear glasses.
3. If an equal number of boys and girls wear glasses, then the number of girls who wear glasses is $1.5x$.
4. If the fraction of girls wearing glasses is $1.5x/6x = 1.5/6 = 1/4$, then 25% of the girls are wearing glasses.

Thus, the answer is that 25% of the girls are wearing glasses.

Most problems using arithmetic are solved similarly using sufficient condition logic.

Example 1.4

A woman had $10,000 that she invested in two funds, a fund that earned 9% and one that earned 7%. If she earned $880 in interest from the two funds, how much was invested in each fund?

Table 1.1   Investments, Interest, and Total Interest

	Rate 9%	*Rate 7%*	*Total*
Investment	x	10,000 − x	10,000
Interest	0.09x	0.07(10,000 − x)	880

SOLUTION

The first step is to examine the givens and the unknown. Givens
(assumptions)—The woman invested $10,000, some of which earned 9%
interest and the rest, 7%. The total interest is $880. The unknown is the
investment in each.

There are four things that we deal with: the two investments, the total
investment, the interest from each investment, and the total interest. We can
arrange them in a table (see **Table 1.1**) or just analyze them without a table.
The second row gives the equation, which can be solved.

WITHOUT A TABLE

Investment: If x is the amount invested at 9%, then the rest of the amount is
10,000 − x at 7%, because both investments must add up to 10,000 or (x +
(10,000 − x) = 10,000).

The *interest* on each investment is given by 0.09x and 0.07(10,000 − x).
The total interest in algebraic terms is 0.09x + 0.07(10,000 − x), and the total
actual interest is $880. We equate them:

$$0.09x + 0.07(10,000 - x) = 880$$

After this step, we need only to know how to solve an equation in one
variable.

To solve this equation, we get rid of decimals by multiplying every term
by 100 to get

$$9x + 7(10,000 - x) = 88,000$$
$$9x + 70,000 - 7x = 88,000 \quad \text{(removing parentheses)}$$
$$2x = 18,000 \quad \text{(simplifying)}$$
$$x = 9000$$

The woman invested $9000 at 9% and $1000 at 7%.
Both are examples of the branch.

1.6.5 Improving the Quality of the Educational Team and Environment with TOC

Teachers are specialists in their own areas. They like their subject because they have found it very interesting. They have found the inherent simplicity in it. They have found connections. Teachers need to bring out that simplicity for their students. In general, instructors should teach their students to find the inherent simplicity in whatever they do. Regardless of their discipline, teachers can learn TOC and its TPs and teach it to their students to make them proactive, that is, help them anticipate events and take control over their academic and personal lives.

Table 1.2 shows a TOC/TP tool for each specific task that an instructor has to perform.

TOC can also be used more broadly to develop an environment conducive to learning. The starting point is mutual love and respect, to encourage and celebrate the unique talents of each colleague. A department, a school, a college or a university can save much energy wasted in fighting interpersonal conflicts and channel it into more productive uses such as helping students succeed. If any issues arise, people should be able to discuss and resolve them objectively without fear or compromise. An *Evaporating Cloud*, as discussed in Chapter 3, helps bring to the surface hidden assumptions that are involved in the actions that cause conflicts. By challenging some of the assumptions, we can arrive at a break-through solution to a conflict. A *branch* can link various issues and give us insight into apparently isolated issues. It can also make us see the consequences of an action and help us to write a summary, as shown in Chapters 2 and 4. An Ambitious Target

Table 1.2   Tasks of an Instructor and Relevant TP Tool

Task	Tool
1. To resolve conflicts	1. Cloud (Chapter 3)
2. To make students proactive. Students understand consequences of their actions	2. Branch (Chapter 2)
3. To engage students by making the lecture/ discussion challenging, interactive, and interesting	3. TrT (Chapter 5)
4. To teach problem solving—uncover the logical connections between givens and the unknown	4. TrT, sometimes ATT (Chapter 5)

Tree can help point out obstacles and actions to overcome them. The action plans can be developed into well-designed projects, as given in Chapter 5. A Transition Tree can help develop presentations, as discussed in Chapter 5. A chairperson or administrator can work effectively to develop harmony in his or her area following the pointers given in Chapter 6. **The skills needed to be a leader—the ability to resolve conflicts, solve problems, and make decisions—are illustrated by example throughout the book**.

1.7 Assumptions and Injections in Thinking Processes

The word *assumption* comes from the verb *to assume*.

Definition 1.5

Assumption: A statement, condition, or belief about why a logical relationship exists between entities. (Cox III et al., 2012)

In the theory of constraints, assumptions are surfaced (brought to the surface) using thinking processes, and if they are causing conflicts, they then can be challenged. This often changes our thinking and leads to conflict resolution. One TOC/TP tool, the Evaporating Cloud, teaches us how to think "outside the box" and to challenge false assumptions.

Example of assumptions and challenging them: Suppose a student says, "I cannot do mathematics because it is difficult and I could never do it in school."

It is a common assumption that mathematics is difficult. We can question this assumption—have the student spend some time with peers or mentors who are good in mathematics, study some of its ubiquitous applications in any modern field, and spend some time on a regular basis with it—then the student's assumption may prove to be invalid. The second assumption of the student is that because his/her previous experience with mathematics has been mathematics is difficult and he/she has no ability to do mathematics. Since mathematics is logical, if he or she had some logical gaps in her/his learning in her school, then he or she might find it difficult. But we make the student recognize that he or she is not the same person now as she/he was in school. He or she is mature and has a better understanding of the world and the importance of mathematics in the world. Now, he or she can relearn math faster because of motivation and leave no logical gaps. Thus, we can challenge her/his two assumptions.

1.8 Checking the Validity of Logic: Categories of Legitimate Reservation

1.8.1 Validity of a Conditional Statement

Keep in mind that the truth of a conditional statement can always be challenged. Consider the statement: "If you smoke, then you will get lung cancer." Here, we are saying that smoking is a sufficient cause of cancer. This means that smoking is enough, by itself, to cause cancer. Smoking produces lung cancer. This is represented in Figure 1.20.

In order to check the validity (correctness, or truth) of the statement, you will have to do an experiment on yourself that might be quite risky, or observe data from others who have cancer, and draw a conclusion. Indeed, there might be several other causes of lung cancer, such as prolonged exposure to radon. Smoking may not actually be necessary or sufficient to get cancer. However, the data comparing the number of smoking and nonsmoking people who get cancer strongly suggest that the previous conditional statement is true.

Breakthrough solutions in TOC are obtained by challenging the assumptions that underlie various confining conditional statements.

1.8.2 Categories of Legitimate Reservations

This section is for constant reference as we study TOC and develop logically rigorous solutions. Before we deal with a *branch* in detail in the next chapter, we must check that there are legitimate statements or cause-and-effect pairs. The following discussion provides a guide as to how to check the validity of the logic. A challenge to the validity of an implication, or the logic of an if . . . then . . . statement, is called a legitimate reservation. We must "raise the categories of legitimate reservation" in the most respectful and unemotional way possible.

This is group work. As the branches (or "trees" made of branches) connected with if . . . then . . . are presented, the reviewers in the audience should scrutinize the logic. There are *three levels* consisting of seven steps of categories of legitimate reservation.

Figure 1.20   Sufficient cause.

In the following discussion, you will come across the word *entity*. As stated earlier, an entity is usually a rounded box that contains a simple statement, whether it is a cause, an effect, or a fact of life (FOL).

1.8.2.1 Level I: Clarity Reservation

Level I seeks *clarity* and *understanding* of the tree builder's intentions (TOCICO dictionary).

Sometimes, people make statements which need clarification to be understood.

1. The student says, "If I see a word problem, then I freeze." A clarity reservation such as "I don't understand what you mean" makes the student restate, without emotion: "I have difficulty in doing word problems." (clarity in entity).

   Sometimes, the cause–effect relationship is not clear. Asking questions such as, "What does this mean?," "Is that really so?," or "Does this really cause that?" can make clear the cause-and-effect relationships. Here are some examples:

2. The student says, "Mathematics is not for girls." Or, as implied in that statement, "If you are a girl, then you can't do mathematics." The reviewer asks, "Why is that so?" or "Is that really so?" If you say that "mathematics is not for girls," then that is based on your assumption about girls. This assumption can be challenged. Since some of the well-known mathematicians are women, perhaps you should reconsider your assumption.

3. "If I did not do well in science in high school, then I will not do well in science in college." This logic is represented in Figure 1.21.

   "Does your past experience really lead to your future experience? Does it really cause that? What about your effort in the present? Can't you do something different now?"

Figure 1.21   Sufficient cause for not doing well in science in college.

Figure 1.22 Causality existence reservation.

1.8.2.2 Level II: Causality Existence and Entity Existence Reservations

Level II examines the validity of an entity: does the entity really exist and does the causal relationship between specified entities really exist? (Cox III et al., 2012).

1. *Entity existence reservation:* "Does it exist?" "How is it possible?"
   A first-year student says, "I will not take mathematics."
   The scrutinizer asks, "How is it possible?" Most colleges of the university require at least one course in mathematics. If the student's statement comes from an assumption that mathematics is difficult for him or her, let the student restate the condition, for example, "I find mathematics difficult."
2. *Causality existence reservation:* Sometimes, the effect is not a direct effect of the cause. We need to add further explanations to make the effect logically flow from the cause. In fact, we might have to add a whole series of cause–effect entities.

In the following example (Figure 1.22), the effect is not an immediate logical consequence of the cause. Such an arrow is called a *long arrow*.

It needs several more steps called *intermediate* cause–effect entities such as "I do not know the subject." This cause–effect relationship is discussed in detail in Chapter 2.

1.8.2.3 Level III: Cause Insufficiency, Additional Cause, Predicted Effect Existence, and Cause–Effect Reversal (Tautology) Reservations

To use level III's *four* reservations, the scrutinizer must actively assist the presenter by proposing a change such as adding or changing some words and/or suggesting a missing condition or an entity that appears to be omitted (Cox III et al., 2012).

1. *Cause insufficiency reservation:* Sometimes, insufficiency in logic can be challenged. Here, *insufficiency* means that the cause is not sufficient for the effect. The first example that we discussed was "Earning just 120 credits does not guarantee that you will graduate." The added condition or cause was "earning the credits in a recommended coursework in a discipline."

   As illustrated in Figure 1.23, a student says, "If I have to attend to my personal responsibilities, then I cannot get good grades." We challenge this only in a friendly helpful manner.

   The mentor says, "Why can't you get good grades?" "How does the effect follow from the cause?" "The logic does not flow. Is it because you do not get time to study?"

   The student then says, "If I have to attend to my personal responsibilities *and* I do not get time to study, then I cannot get good grades." This is summarized in Figure 1.24.

2. *Additional cause reservation:* An if . . . then . . . statement may not fully account for the effect unless an additional cause is supplied. There might be several sufficient conditions to produce this effect.

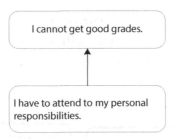

Figure 1.23 Insufficient cause.

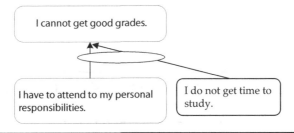

Figure 1.24 Sufficient cause.

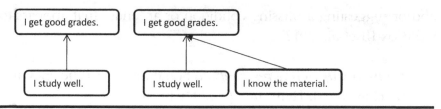

Figure 1.25 Additional cause.

By removing one of the conditions, the effect is still attained. Here, in Figure 1.25, the additional cause is *or* (not connected with a banana).

If you know the material, then you do not need to study and can still get good grades.

3. *Predicted effect reservation:* Sometimes, the cause-and-effect statement cannot be checked directly. But another effect for the same cause can be checked. If the second effect does not happen, then the cause entity probably does not exist.

Here, it would be disastrous to wait to see the first effect of getting cancer! Instead, it is easier if samples of the air can be checked for toxins by analyzing them using chromatography and principal component analysis. In other words, the second effect (Figure 1.26) is easier to check.

4. *Cause–effect reversal reservation:* Sometimes people confuse the cause with the effect. Sometimes, the cause-and-effect are reversed as shown in Figure 1.27.

We cannot conclude that the car is being burglarized. If the car is being burglarized, then the alarm will, of course, sound, but it is possible that someone bumped into the car and the alarm is activated and there was no burglar.

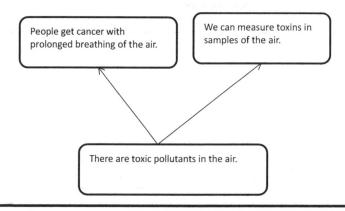

Figure 1.26 Predicted effect.

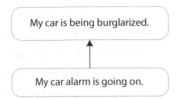

Figure 1.27   Cause–effect reversal.

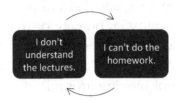

Figure 1.28   Infinite loop.

Sometimes, two statements in a proposed cause–effect statement are really just two different ways of saying the same thing, and one is not really the "cause" of the other.

For example, we could say, "If I have 6 oranges, then I have half a dozen oranges." We could just as correctly have said, "If I have half a dozen oranges, then I have 6 oranges." They mean the same thing.

Sometimes, a cause-and-effect relationship may be in "an infinite loop" as shown in Figure 1.28, such that the cause of one entity is the effect of the other and vice versa.

These loops may be neutral, positive or negative. It is important to recognize when a loop exists (see Chapter 2).

To summarize,

- Level I seeks clarity and understanding of the tree builder's intentions, that is, finding out what the words and phrases in the logic diagrams' entities really mean and how they are being used.
- Level II examines the validity of an entity: does the entity really exist and/or does the causal relationship between specified entities really exist?
- In each of level III's four reservations, the scrutinizer must actively assist the presenter by proposing a change such as adding or changing some words and/or suggesting a missing condition or an entity that appears to be omitted. Scrutinizers should proceed from level I to level

II to level III reservations until they have satisfied their concerns. That is, they should first seek clarity, next assure appropriate causality, and finally propose improvements in a logic diagram. Note that the tree builder is free to accept or reject any reservation at any level (Cox III et al., 2012). This concludes the discussion of categories of legitimate reservation of if . . . then . . . pairs.

Practical note: Discussing a logical chain of if . . . then . . . or cause-and-effect statements (i.e., a logical twig, branch, or tree) with others requires making many changes, insertions, and deletions. Having a large poster board on an easel or a smooth wall and a set of "Post-it" notes (or notes with a sticky back for ease of moving around) of different colors on hand is very helpful.

Exercises

1. Complete the statement *I am.* . . . Study the example in Figure 1.12, in Section 1.6.1. Build a branch–chain of *If . . . then . . .* statements, starting with *If I am . . . then. . . .*
2. Describe the meaning and give examples of necessity-based and sufficiency-based conditional statements.
3. Select a case study on the branch from http://www.TOCforEducation .com, and write it in your own words.
4. Select a paragraph from a newspaper. Make a list of conditional statements in the paragraph that involve (a) necessary conditions and (b) sufficient conditions.
5. Make a list of obstacles that prevent you from achieving a goal. Rewrite them as an ATT. A detailed explanation will be given in Chapter 5.
6. Develop a storyline for a decision that you had to make in your life recently. Use PowerPoint to illustrate the story using a branch as in the example, Checking Voice Mail.
7. Solve a word problem in mathematics, using the *If . . . then . . .* logic and connecting explicitly the givens and the unknown.
8. Describe popular assumptions in five *If . . . then . . .* conditional statements which are wrong or detrimental (misconceptions). Show how you will challenge them.
9. What is a "paradigm"? Research this using the Internet, and write a paragraph in your own words explaining what paradigm change means.

References

Barker, J. (1986). Discovering the future: The business of paradigms (video). Retrieved from http://www.joelbarker.com.

Barnard, A. (2007, October 11–14). *How to SEE and UNLOCK inherent potential within each of ourselves and others*. Paper presented at the 10th Theory of Constraints in Education International Conference, Fort Walton Beach, FL.

Cox III, J.F., Boyd, L.H., Sullivan, T.T., Reid, R.A. & Cartier, B. (2012). *The Theory of Constraints International Certification Organization Dictionary*. 2nd ed. NY: McGraw Hill.

Eagleman, D. (2011). *Incognito: The Secret Lives of the Brain*. New York: Pantheon.

Goldratt, E.M. (1986). *The Goal*. Great Barrington, MA: North River Press.

Goldratt, E.M. (2008). *The Choice*. Great Barrington, MA: North River Press.

Hong, K.M. (2009). *The Singapore Model Method for Learning Mathematics*. New York: Houghton Mifflin Harcourt.

Nagarkatte, U. (2012). Motivational guide. January 22, 2017. Retrieved from http://www.TOCforCollege.com: http://www.tocforcollege.com/motivational-guide.html.

National Center for Education Statistics (2015). *Trends in International Mathematics and Science Study (TIMSS)*. Retrieved from http://nces.ed.gov/timss.

Suerken, K., Goldratt, R., Goldratt-Ashlagratt, E. (2003). *TACT Workbook*. Niceville, Fl: TOC for Education, Inc.

Chapter 2

What to Change? Part 1: Branch, Current Reality Tree, and Future Reality Tree

2.1 Example: Conflict Resolution

Nancy Oley's story: I had an interesting experience shortly after learning about TOC. The psychology laboratory (which I directed) had been moving toward collapse on a number of levels for some time, and things finally reached a crisis. The two lab techs were not cooperating, and they were unable to solve some serious technical problems that, if unresolved, would render the lab useless. I called a meeting of the parties involved. Everyone was upset. But instead of the usual, I decided to try TOC approach of developing, collectively, a Current Reality Tree (CRT).

First, we agreed upon a common goal: to have the lab running smoothly and effectively. We put Post-its on the whiteboard, one for each undesirable effect (UDE) standing in the way of that goal. UDEs are discussed in Section 1.4, and in detail in Section 2.3. We agreed that there would not be criticism of any idea, and we continued until we ran out of ideas. Then, we arranged the UDEs in *if–then* order. This revealed four clusters of problems, each cluster emerging from a more generic UDE. This took 3 hours and took into account everything from resentment over being paid too little and late, to not knowing enough to solve the problem. We were able to work as a team without rancor, and many ideas for solutions popped out right away (interventions to cut the negative branches). Both lab techs

49

started working together and discovered a workaround for the technical problem in less than a day. I recognized that I had to take care of some issues at my end as well. We didn't get to the *core* conflict formally, but the progress was amazing! I needed to put it down on paper and present it to the administrators with the power to solve some of the problems. ... That wasn't as easy.

This chapter is about building branches from a list of issues that can be logically linked to produce a solution.

2.2 Overview

TOC asks three questions: What to change? What to change to? How to cause the change?

Chapters 2 and 3 develop TOC thinking processes needed to answer the first question: What to change. We divide the material into two chapters because of the large number of pages and for logistical reasons. It is easier to discuss the cause-and-effect or sufficient condition logic alone, which we discuss in this chapter. But for the complete answer, both chapters need to be studied.

Many institutions take up strategic planning without addressing the first question. The changes that an institution makes as a result of strategic planning may not address some of the key institutional issues at all or may involve duplication! For example, curriculum development without regard to the actual concerns of a department either is short lived or does not lead to any significant changes in how the department functions.

We need to solve a problem whose symptoms we have enumerated. As seen in Chapter 1, we need to address the *constraint* of the system. In Chapters 2 and 3, we learn how to turn a set of systemic issues into a core conflict in order to identify the constraint or main problem in the system.

In Section 2.3, we see how to describe the issues in a simple nonemotional, nonconfrontational manner. When you ask some people what needs to change, they get emotionally charged and start blaming people and circumstances, policies, and laws or say that we don't have this or that and that it ought to be this way or that way and suggest ways to improve. Instead, TOC practitioner goes coolly about making improvements in a logical and systematic manner and suggests win–win solutions that last. We review how an issue must be defined as an UDE. We also define a desired effect (DE).

In Section 2.4, we observe that the issues (UDEs) of a system—personal or organizational—are never isolated, that some or all are logically connected, and that we can start a cascade of improvements by dealing with the *one* issue from which the network of issues originates. Example 2.1 shows that it is possible for the issues to form a chain or a loop. We can then break the loop with an injection (or intervention) in one or more places. We call the branch consisting of "if … then …" statements a Current Reality Tree (CRT). The tree might also consist of disconnected branches related to several basic dissimilar issues. The CRT can be used as a stand-alone tool. But without considering another tool, the Cloud, discussed in Chapter 3, the CRT does not give us a complete understanding of the key systemic problem from which all the issues arise. We will use it to deal with whole systems in Chapter 3.

In Section 2.5, we introduce the idea of a Negative Branch Reservation (NBR) and a positive branch. A negative branch helps us to visualize the negative and/or unintended consequences of an UDE or an action that we want to take. A negative branch is an easy way to practice "if … then …" or sufficiency-based logic. A negative branch can be trimmed by interventions, called "injections." Similarly, a positive branch with injections helps us to visualize the positive effects of the corresponding DE. Both negative and positive branches have to be used for an effective change to take place. In Example 2.6, we discuss a system-wide solution for a typical student's issue.

2.3 UDEs and DEs

What are the problems in our system that need fixing? What keeps the system from performing at its best? What are the current issues? As seen in Chapter 1, a system may be viewed as a chain or a network leading to an outcome, and not every link needs to be strengthened to improve the system's performance. We can get the quickest and most significant improvement by concentrating on the weakest link, the constraint of the system. Thus, the most negative condition is the first to be addressed. First, we prepare an environment in which people feel comfortable stating the issues as UDEs. We review the definition of an UDE and then list the issues as UDEs in a nonthreatening way.

Step 1: This is the most important step. Basic respect and human dignity are essential throughout the process. If there is a conflict with another person on some issue, make sure you remember that clear thinking can happen only when there is no "heat" generated in the argument. Therefore, instead of "fueling the heated situation" or keeping the argument going, or thinking about who is winning, put the issue on pause. If the conflict is within you, don't get frustrated or angry with yourself. Take a break. If you feel like it, discuss the issue with a friend, a mentor, a guide, an elder calm person, or a counselor whom you trust, even if the person does not know TOC. If the issue is too personal to discuss with anyone, then just write the various issues down clearly as UDEs.

Step 2: Write your issue as an UDE.

Definition 2.1

An UDE should be serious, be a condition not a lack of an activity, not blame anyone, happen frequently, have a serious negative outcome, and not incorporate the solution within the statement. (Cox III et al., 2012)

State what bothers you in a simple, clear, complete sentence, not a compound sentence using *but, and,* or *because.* An UDE is not a negative effect in itself or a symptom of the problem. It should be a "benign" statement; that is, it should not hurt anyone. It should have no emotion. An issue or UDE creates a want or an action or a condition as the result of a want or an action. The UDE should focus on a current fact or condition.

Examples of UDEs are as follows:

1. Tommy takes too much time to get ready in the morning—unacceptable UDE. This is how a counselor feels about her son. It includes a judgment—too much.
2. I am disturbed by students talking in my class.—UDE of an instructor.
3. I have no prerequisites for this class—student's UDE.
4. I don't have time to do the homework—student's UDE.
5. I have difficulties in my math course—student's UDE.
6. There is no communication between instructors and tutors—instructor's UDE.
7. I am unhappy because of your unnecessary activity—unacceptable UDE of a married couple. It is not a simple statement. It also blames another person.
8. I do not attend my classes on time—student's UDE.
9. I am not authorized to hire a tutor—a tutorial coordinator's UDE.
10. I am not up to taking mathematics as my major—a student's UDE.

Definition 2.2

A DE is the logical opposite of an UDE.

For example, if the UDE is, "I do not attend my classes on time," then the DE is, "I attend (or do attend) my classes on time."

A DE plays an important role in creating a "positive branch." We discuss a positive branch in Section 2.5. It is also useful in answering the second basic question, what to change to? We will discuss this aspect in detail in Chapter 4.

2.4 Branch

Definition 2.3

A branch is a sequence of *sufficient condition* statements (connected by if … then …).

We have several examples of branches in Chapter 1. In everyday life, we make decisions using a logical sequence of thoughts, connecting them with if … then logic.

In this section, we will study an elaborate branch called the Current Reality Tree (CRT) that consists of a logically connected set of UDEs.

In Section 2.5, we will study how to build a branch that brings out the consequences of an action. If the consequences of the action are negative, that branch is called a "negative branch," which needs to be scrutinized using a process called the Negative Branch Reservation (NBR). The negative branch can then be "trimmed" by one or more interventions called injections. To convince ourselves that the consequence of an initiative or measure to be taken will be positive, we need to develop a positive branch.

2.4.1 The Current Reality Tree (CRT) as a Stand-Alone Tool

Once we have a list of UDE's, we try to link them using sufficient condition (if … then …) logic, providing additional causes as needed to make the logic solid. This gives rise to a CRT. The CRT may not necessarily be one single tree, but a bunch of branches (see Figure 2.2). The CRT shows that the UDEs are not isolated.

2.4.1.1 Example of a CRT

Example 2.1

Consider a few student UDEs from Section 1.2.4, Chapter 1.

1. I cannot follow the lecture.
2. I perceive that I am not capable of doing mathematics.
3. I do not work hard in mathematics.
4. I don't do the homework or prepare for the course.
5. I do poorly on tests.
6. I feel that the exam is too hard.
7. I have difficulty learning the material (in math classes).
8. I have difficulty taking tests.

Definition 2.4

An injection is a state or condition used as an intervention that breaks cause and effect relationships in a CRT. In typical usage it may be an action, but it is usually expressed as a system condition. (Cox et al., 2012)

When we link these UDEs with sufficiency logic as in Figure 2.1, we get a loop. This is the student's CRT. The numbering of the entities comes from the original list of UDEs. We read this loop as follows, starting at no. 4: "If I don't do the homework or prepare for the course, then I have difficulty learning the material (in math classes). If I have difficulty learning the material (in math classes), then I have difficulty taking (math) tests. If I have difficulty taking (math) tests, then I

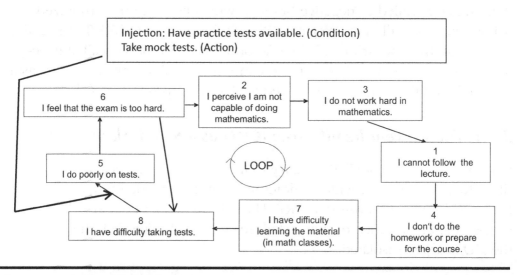

Figure 2.1 CRT with an injection.

do poorly on tests, etc.," This is a negative feedback loop: The less homework I do, the less homework I will keep doing. If not remedied, this loop becomes a downward spiral for the student. However, this negative feedback loop can be broken by an injection at any one of several places. For example, we can introduce an injection between UDE 5 and UDE 8: Have practice tests available and make sure that the student takes them as mock tests.

For any set of UDEs, a CRT can be constructed easily as shown previously. Note that not every CRT forms a loop and that not every loop has to be a negative one.

Example 2.2: Case Study: Issues of Students Taking Basic Skills Courses

In order to study attrition in basic skills courses in mathematics and English, we considered the following UDEs collected by basic skills instructors.

1. More than 20% of the students attend the class irregularly.
2. The students who are absent have the most difficulty understanding the lessons.
3. The majority of students do not study at all at home.
4. Most of the students do not review/practice the exercises and examples of the concepts that were presented in class.
5. Students do their homework in a hasty manner.
6. Most of the time, students copy from other students who took their time to complete the homework at home.
7. Many students do not have the class textbooks.
8. Many students cannot afford the high cost of the textbooks.
9. A few of the evening students come to class very tired from work.
10. Some evening, students fall asleep during class lectures.
11. A few students, especially the younger ones in the math classes, seem not to have interest in the course.
12. Many students, especially those in the math classes, develop fear and anxiety of the course.

The CRT of these UDEs is given in Figure 2.2. The entities which have three-digit numbers are additional clauses to make the logic robust. FOL stands for a "fact of life" which we must accept. The tree consists of four different branches indicating the four basic types of student behaviors that we accommodate.

The CRT does not have a "root" tying all or most of the UDEs together. Making a single CRT with a unifying root out of disconnected sets of UDEs needs additional work and knowledge of an additional tool called a Cloud (described in Section 3.2).

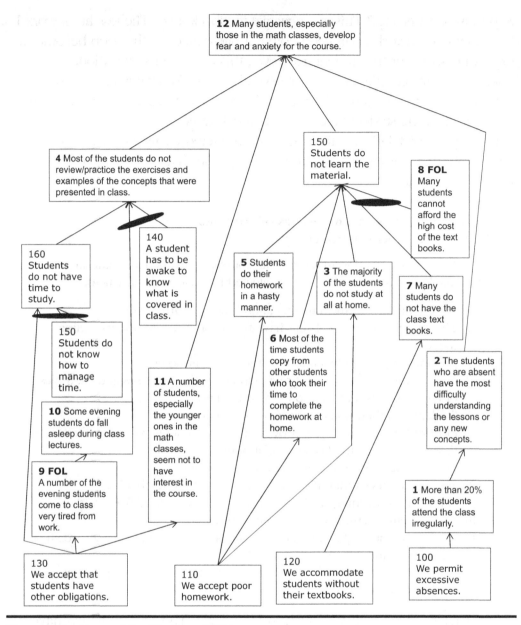

Figure 2.2 Current Reality Tree (CRT).

2.4.2 Use of CRT

A CRT can be used as a stand-alone TP tool. It is simple enough for kindergarten children and sophisticated enough for corporate/institutional use. With practice, you will be able to see connections after looking at a set of issues—UDEs—without drawing the CRT. In addition, by looking at a possible future action, you will be able to determine the consequences of that action without verbalizing them or drawing a logical short branch or "twig."

A CRT by itself does not give insight into the whole system. We only learn that the UDEs are logically connected; we do not know how to fix them within the system or how to resolve conflicts so that these UDEs do not arise. A CRT partially answers the question: What to change? This is not good enough. You need the next chapter to arrive at a complete answer. It shows not only how to resolve conflicts, but also how to create a positive alternate reality in the future involving DEs, the opposites of UDEs.

2.5 Negative and Positive Branches

2.5.1 Negative Branch Reservation: NBR

For any action, policy, statement, or behavior, there might be negative outcomes. If detailed consequences are thought out, written out, read aloud, or discussed with someone, we can envision the possible negative UDEs before actually taking action. This is called a Negative Branch Reservation or an NBR. We can then take a corrective action or use an injection to prevent the negative outcome. Implementing the injection is called "trimming" the branch.

NBRs are used to evaluate and address the deficiencies of "half-baked ideas" that are being proposed.

> **Definition 2.5**
>
> A half-baked idea is an idea which is not well thought out. A measure, proposal, action, or behavior suggested to overcome one negative effect may cause other negative effects that were not intended.

A half-baked idea is one proposed to overcome a negative situation while not thinking about other negative consequences that may arise if the idea is implemented. Many ad hoc policies laid down by administrators are half-baked ideas. For example, when designing a course, syllabus, and related activities, the departmental faculty set the number of credits and contact hours for the course based on students' background, so that most students would be able to complete the course. Without consulting the faculty, the university board or administrators decided to lower the credits or hours on their own because they cost too much money in terms of faculty salaries. Such decisions are half-baked ideas. Some possible negative consequences are that students are poorly prepared to handle the next class and/or there will be a higher failure rate in these courses.

Often, when a presenter puts forth a half-baked idea, the audience says, "yes, but" or just keeps quiet. The presenter may feel that any criticism is unfair and is not prepared to answer the criticism or says, "Let me think about it …" or "I will clarify it tomorrow." Sometimes, the presenter is obstinate, and instead of confronting the presenter, the audience keeps quiet and communication breaks down. The half-baked ideas are hard for others to accept.

In a personal setting, a negative branch may arise from an action or behavior that resulted from a half-baked idea or a sudden decision. In an institutional setting, negative branches resulting from policy decisions need to be carefully scrutinized.

Definition 2.6

An injection is a state or condition that is proposed to overcome, or 'trim,' a negative branch reservation. (Cox et al., 2012)

Definition 2.7

An injection is a state or a condition that is proposed as a means for converting undesirable effects into desirable effects through a chain of cause and effect entities in a positive branch or future reality tree (FRT). (Cox et al., 2012)

Example 2.3

The head of a student advisement department at a college enunciated a policy that all students must have a realistic schedule to prevent them from taking too many credits or taking only difficult courses in one semester. The reason for this was to avoid student academic failures. However, she did not think through the consequences of this policy. This is a half-baked idea. The negative consequences are given in Figure 2.3. We also show the injections used to trim the negative branches. This figure was generated while developing a Future Reality Tree for the department as part of a Jonah course at AGI in January 2002.

The entities next to the entity 180 (all students must have a realistic schedule) are justifications or additional *causes*. They are put in to make the overall logic more sound (see Figures 2.5 and 2.7 for examples for justifying a negative branch). Other justifications needed to explain why the effect is inevitable are

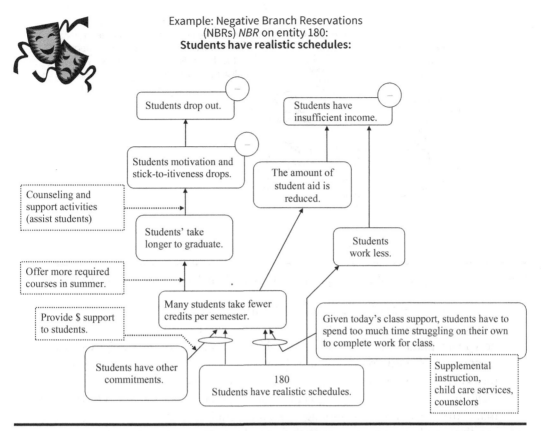

Example: Negative Branch Reservations
(NBRs) *NBR* on entity 180:
Students have realistic schedules:

Figure 2.3   NBR on "Students have realistic schedules."

not given here. The negative outcomes are that students drop out or students have insufficient income. The injections are given in rectangular boxes.

Many UDEs result from policies or measurements by an organization. In TOC, policies, measurements, and behaviors play a role in answering the question, what to change? Once we have a policy or rule, we need to take some measurement to ensure that the policy is being followed. When people know they are being measured, they behave according to how they are measured. This is illustrated in Figure 2.4.

The following examples clarify this point.

Example 2.4: How the UDEs Arise from Implemented Policies That Are Half-Baked Ideas

This example is from industry and may be skipped.

On an assembly line of an industry, various parts made in different departments are put together to make a product. In order to make a complete product, all parts have to be available at different stages on the assembly line.

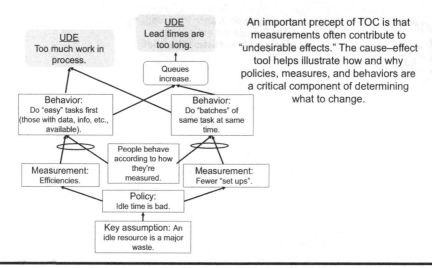

Figure 2.4   Company policy—a half-baked idea. (Courtesy of Janice Cerveny.)

A company makes a policy that no department should remain idle. The natural measurements are (a) the efficiency of each department in terms of how many parts that they produce and (b) how many times the machines have stopped and started. In other words, how many *setups* have been made. Each measurement results in a corresponding behavior of the employees. And several UDEs result. Too many critical components might be made. If fewer setups are made, then there might be shortages of other required parts to make the product, thus resulting in a longer time to finish (lead time of) the product.

Example 2.5: How Policies in a University Create UDEs: PATHWAYS–A Half-Baked Idea

A university has a number of autonomous colleges. A top administrator feels that a student wanting to transfer from one college to another should be able to do so without having to repeat the basic general education already taken. The question came down to how many credits and which courses constitute *general education*. The university committee consisting of some administrators and faculty from various colleges selected to answer the questions decided that 30 credits is an ideal minimum number of general education credits required and came up with courses in different areas. The administrator forced the colleges to abide by the policy promising reprisals if the policy was not followed. We call this policy PATHWAYS.

Various UDEs arose as a result.

1. The uniqueness of a member college's general education program was lost.
2. Some important college disciplines that had required more than 30 general education credits could no longer offer their courses.

We will see some consequences of this policy in terms of measurement and behavior in Figure 2.5.

Example 2.6 Why Are There So Many Incomplete Grades?

Gary is a typical student who is overwhelmed by homework, take-home projects, and an upcoming exam. He is frustrated and says, "I give up. I cannot keep up with my coursework."

You are concerned and Gary trusts you. You want to help him. You ask him, "If you can't keep with the coursework, then what will happen?" He says, "I have to ask instructors to give me makeups or INC (incomplete) or ABS (absent) grades." This is represented in Figure 2.6.

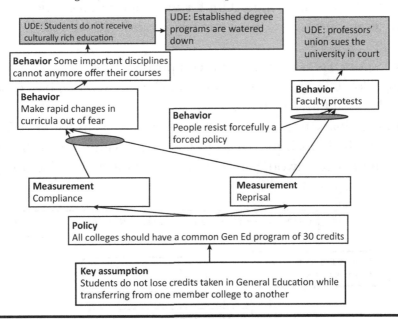

Figure 2.5   PATHWAYS—university policy—a half-baked idea.

Figure 2.6   Gary's negative branch (start).

There is a logical gap here. The effect does not directly follow from the cause. Ask, "What is the direct result of not keeping up with the coursework?" With each answer, keep asking, "then what will happen?" You will have the following consequences from Gary's point of view. They are numbered consecutively for convenience.

Note that these are all potential or predicted UDEs that will happen in the future. We can do something in the present to prevent them from happening.

1. I start preparing at the last minute for tests or projects.
2. I do not perform well on my assignments and tests.
3. I have to request makeup exams.
4. I have to drop courses important for my major or take longer to finish.
5. I have to ask instructors to give makeups and INCs or ABSs.

In order to discuss Gary's situation completely, we need to consider an Evaporating Cloud. Evaporating Clouds and Gary's example, based on these UDEs, are discussed in Chapter 3.

First, a preliminary negative branch is developed as in Figure 2.7.

We develop the branch further as in Figure 2.7 with the root "I cannot keep up with the coursework." In this case, the branch is called a negative

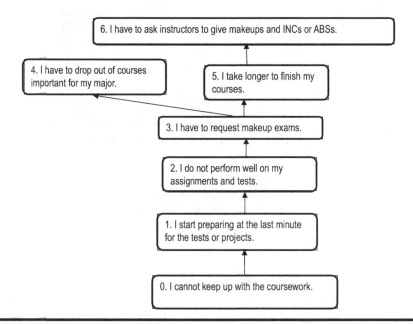

Figure 2.7 Gary's negative branch.

branch because by raising concerns (reservations) or asking questions, these consequences were surfaced and represent negative effects. The logic, shown in Figure 2.8, is made robust with additional statements of justifications or supporting statements, labeled a, b, c, d, and e. For convenience, we used round boxes for each of the previous sentences, also called entities, and square boxes for justifications. After scrutinizing the negative branch, we prevent the outcomes by using an injection to "trim" the branch.

Read this branch as follows: If I cannot keep up with the coursework, then I start preparing at the last minute for the exams or projects because my grade depends on the exams and projects in the course. ... If I start preparing at the last minute for the exams or projects, then I do not perform well on my assignments and tests because there is not much time to understand the topics on tests and projects ... (read the entire branch aloud to make sure that there are no logical gaps).

This negative branch can also be read as follows: "If I cannot keep up with the coursework and if my grade depends on the exams and projects in the course, then I start preparing at the last minute for the tests or projects (this means that I cannot escape taking the test or doing the project). If I start preparing at the last minute for the tests or projects and if there is not

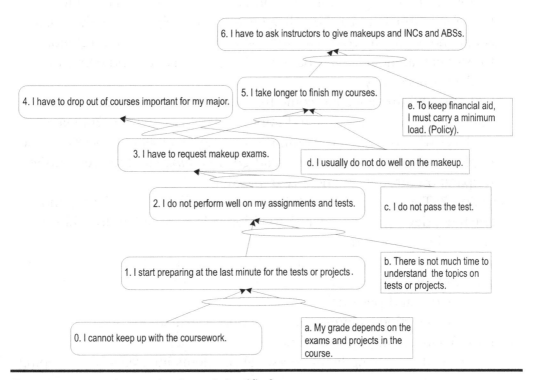

Figure 2.8   Gary's negative branch justified.

much time to understand the topics on tests, then I do not perform well on my assignments or tests. ..."

In order to trim Gary's negative branch, it is a good idea for him to work with a counselor, a role model, or a guide at the college; he cannot do it alone.

2.5.2 Positive Branch

Developing and trimming a negative branch may not be enough. It is also necessary to construct a positive branch.

Let us now construct an institutional solution to the dilemma faced by all students who are like Gary. We will develop a positive branch that reinforces Gary for keeping up with the coursework. See Figure 2.6.

Can you think of an injection in this situation that will negate or invalidate Gary's assumptions? This injection (or injections) would help resolve these issues for Gary, and Gary can, of course, propose some injections himself. But the following is a college-wide solution to help all students like Gary.

Gary's college has the motto: "Success, one student at a time." It has mechanisms in place to support the injections. The college's injections are as follows:

Injection 1: The college administration/faculty have a mechanism to
(a) inform students that the college is ready to help address their personal and academic concerns and follow up with them and (2) monitor student attendance and daily/weekly performance and contact the student if necessary.

Where did this injection come from? The college has made a commitment to reduce attrition and improve passing rates and graduate students who will be successful, responsible members of society. Before implementing that injection, the *college must make* all the prerequisite preparation through the next two injections.

Injection 2: The college, through its curricular offerings, guidance, and teaching, develops its students' confidence in their ability to achieve success in school and in life.

Injection 3: Through TOC and its TP tools, students get training and guidance in time management and conflict resolution to help them balance coursework and personal responsibilities.

These injections address the assumptions that students such as Gary have regarding their personal needs:

– Correctly resolving family/personal problems interferes with keeping up with coursework.

– Personal responsibilities don't get fulfilled on their own.
– I have to take time from schoolwork to do those things.
– There is no one else to fulfill my other obligations.
– My other obligations can't/won't go away.
– I can't postpone my other obligations.

Where do these assumptions come from? This will be discussed in Chapter 3 where we develop Gary's Evaporating Cloud.

Injection 4: College faculty understand that the contributions they make to helping students solve or get insight into their difficulties are recognized as meaningful by the administration.

This injection is essential for the faculty, who would spend more time helping students and therefore less time doing research and publishing in refereed journals. If the college does not recognize their time and work with students, they will feel that their time is wasted and that they had better turn to doing research. But again, there is another injection which can get rid of this fear. That injection is as follows:

Injection 5: Faculty can work with students on publishable research that can be brought to the students' level. This injection has rewards for both students and faculty.

Injection 6: Faculty and advisors help students get the academic skills to keep up with the coursework.

Where does this injection come from? This injection comes from an assumption in Gary's Evaporating Cloud in Chapter 3: "The only way to achieve As and Bs is to keep up with the coursework."

This injection trims the negative branch in Figure 2.2 at the first box 0.

The UDE "I cannot keep up with the homework" also requires Gary to see the positive branch. This doubly assures that if students such as Gary focus on their coursework without neglecting their personal problems and obligations, this will bring them and the college to a win–win solution. This positive branch comes from the injections in place at the college.

Definition 2.8

A DE is a statement which is the logical opposite of an UDE.

Let us now develop DEs using sufficiency logic for Gary's UDEs. The college may state the DE more generally to cover all students like Gary. Hence,

Table 2.1   UDEs and Generalized DEs

UDEs	(Generalized) DEs
1. I start preparing at the last minute for the tests or projects.	1. Students are good at keeping up with all aspects of the course.
2. I do not perform well on my assignments and tests.	2. Students perform well on regular tests.
3. I have to request makeup exams.	3. Students do not need to take makeup exams.
4. I have to drop courses important for my major or take longer to finish.	4. Students graduate in greater numbers, and the college has a low attrition rate.
5. I have to ask instructors to give makeups and INC and ABS grades.	5. Students get good grades.
6. I cannot attend my classes on time (typical student).	6. Students attend their classes on time.
7. I must attend to my family responsibilities. There is no one to help me.	7. Students keep in touch with faculty and counselors as they progress (this addresses the second UDE in 7).

these DEs are stated in general terms, not just as logical opposites of the UDEs (see Table 2.1).

A positive branch consists of DEs linked with cause-and-effect logic and with the injections.

2.5.2.1 Conventions

There is no rule regarding using rounded or rectangular boxes. We usually use rounded boxes for entities and rectangular boxes for injections. Different-colored Post-its can substitute for drawings. We usually write injections on a colored (shaded) background and in rectangular boxes, the DEs using a different color (shade) background in boxes with rounded corners, and the intermediate effects (to complete the logic) on a white background in boxes (entities) with rounded corners. We can rearrange the arbitrary numbers of DEs in the process to be more convenient (see Figure 2.9).

In Figure 2.9, we start with the college's intervention procedures and resources in place to help the students. These lead us finally to the DEs.

In the Figure 2.9, DE 5 summarizes DE 2, DE 3, and DE 5 from Table 2.1.

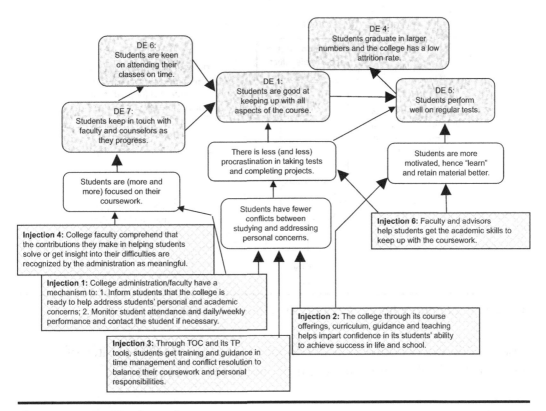

Figure 2.9   Positive branch.

Consideration of the negative and positive branches completes the discussion of Gary's and a typical student's conflict. Both the branches need to be developed and discussed for a lasting solution.

2.5.3 Summary of a Negative Branch Reservation and a Positive Branch

Figure 2.10 gives a general setup for a negative branch. A positive branch depends upon the injections and has **no** *and* or banana in the diagram.

1. Write the entity that is leading to the NBR at the bottom of the page.
2. Write the potential UDE at the top of the page.
3. Read "If [entity], then [UDE] because …," and write all statements that come after the word *because*.
4. Insert the statements in the negative branch using cause-and-effect logic.
5. Check the logic by reading the negative branch aloud.

The negative branch reservation (NBR)

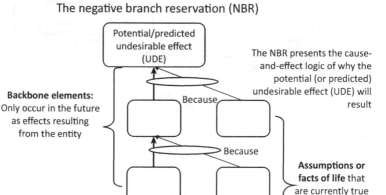

Potential/predicted undesirable effect (UDE)

The NBR presents the cause-and-effect logic of why the potential (or predicted) undesirable effect (UDE) will result

Backbone elements: Only occur in the future as effects resulting from the entity

Because

Because

Because

Assumptions or facts of life that are currently true (needed for logical sufficiency or clarity).

Entity

Figure 2.10 Template for NBR. (Courtesy of Janice Cerveny.)

A positive branch is developed by creating DEs as logical opposites of potential UDEs along with injections to make them happen.

Exercises

1. Select a case study on the negative branch from http://www.tocforedu cation.com, and write it in your own words.
2. List the issues that you have that stand in the way of doing your course-work. Develop a CRT and suggest injection/s.
3. A student says, "I have family responsibilities, so I cannot do well in school." Develop a negative branch starting from "I have family responsibilities" and ending with "I cannot do well in school." Then, develop a positive branch.
4. "I found science hard in school, so I will not do well in science in the college." Develop a negative branch and a positive branch based on that statement.
5. A student is thinking of leaving her family home. Develop logical branches showing the positive and negative consequences. Use injection/s to trim the negative branch and reinforce positive branches. Then, comparing the two branches, decide whether it is worth it for her to leave home.
6. Suppose that you are going to make a presentation in class today. Write down the steps that you need to take in order to prepare in a logical

order giving justifications for each step. Check if there are any half-baked ideas in any step. If so, write down the consequences and trim any branch that has negative consequences.

7. The administration decides that a student can take credit-bearing courses while doing basic skills zero-credit courses in mathematics. This is a half-baked idea. Develop a negative branch and suggest injection/s to trim the negative branch.

Read a chapter from a textbook. Develop a branch from the beginning to the end of the chapter. If there are any formulas, describe in your own words how they are developed in the book.

Reference

Cox III, J.F., Boyd, L.H., Sullivan, T.T., Reid, R.A., & Cartier, B. (2012). *The Theory of Constraints International Certification Organization Dictionary.* 2nd ed. NY: McGraw Hill.

Chapter 3

Chapter 3

What to Change? Part 2: Evaporating Clouds

3.1 Overview

TOC asks three questions: What to change? What to change to? How to cause the change? This chapter develops the TOC thinking processes (TPs) needed to answer the first question: what to change. In the second part of the discussion, we develop and implement the concept of Evaporating Cloud (EC) (or simply, Cloud). We need to solve a problem whose symptoms we have enumerated. As seen in Chapter 1, we need to address the *constraint* of the system. Here, we learn to identify the constraint or problem in the form of a core conflict.

In Chapter 2, we saw how to describe the issues in a simple nonemotional, nonconfrontational manner. Each issue should be stated as a simple sentence with no connectives such as *because, or, but, and*, etc. The TOC practitioner goes coolly about making system improvements in a logical and systematic manner and suggests win–win solutions that last. We saw how an issue must be defined as an UDE. We also defined a DE.

We observed that the issues (UDEs) are never isolated, that some or all are logically connected to each other, and that we can start a cascade of improvements by dealing with the one issue from which the network of issues originates. We learned what a Current Reality Tree (CRT) is. The tree might also consist of disconnected branches as seen in Figure 2.2, and can be used as a stand-alone tool. We also used a negative branch to visualize the negative and/or unintended consequences of the UDE, and the positive branch with injections to visualize the positive effects of the corresponding DE. The CRT and negative and positive branches use "if . . . then . . ." or sufficiency-based logic. We will see that these tools are useful in resolving "chronic conflicts."

In Section 3.2, we study a TP tool called the *Cloud* or *Evaporating Cloud* based on necessary condition logic. We develop the Cloud for specific issues. We show how it is a great tool to describe the conflict underlying an UDE in a logical way. We "surface" (bring to the surface) and analyze various assumptions. We challenge these assumptions. If we can show them to be invalid, we can move to a resolution of the conflict and "evaporate" the Cloud.

In Sections 3.3 and 3.4, we study five different types of Clouds. A practitioner of TOC will find that such a detailed discussion is not readily available in the TOC literature.

The Cloud is a stand-alone tool, but it can also be used to resolve complex systemic issues.

In Section 3.5, we select three important diverse or representative UDEs from among all the UDEs identified in our system, and develop a Cloud for each of them. From these Clouds, we develop a generic or Core Cloud. We check, if necessary, whether a similar Core Cloud results when a different set of three representative UDEs is selected. We thus assure ourselves that the Core Cloud is in fact the systemic Cloud that represents all of the UDEs. We surface the assumptions underlying the various necessary condition statements contained in the Core Cloud. We then provide the Core Cloud as a visual and logical base of the CRT. We see that all of the UDEs are connected within the CRT. We call this the Conflict/Communication Current Reality Tree (CCRT). The CCRT provides the deepest insight into the core problem or the constraint of the system and includes all of the UDEs. It is used to communicate with stakeholders. The CCRT has important regions which give additional visual insight into negative feedback loops that are maintaining the negative current reality. This is explained with a simple example in Section 3.5.4.

Section 3.6 discusses "evaporating" or resolving the Core (conflict) Cloud of the system. By examining the assumptions surfaced in the Core Cloud, we can come up with an idea called the *Bright Idea* to resolve the core conflict. Once we have found the Bright Idea, we are on our way to proposing ways to implement it. Pursuing the Bright Idea is the subject of Chapter 4: what to change to?

We discuss a case study—Writing a persuasive essay in Section 3.7. Section 3.8 summarizes the concept of the Cloud. The steps to answer "what to change?" are summarized in Section 3.9.

3.2 The Cloud as a *Stand-Alone* Tool

3.2.1 TOC Has a TP Tool Called "an EC" or "Cloud"

The Cloud is a communication tool to clearly describe a conflict. The Cloud uses necessary condition logic.

To recall how such a statement is formed, consider the following: An instructor says, "In order that my students have a quality education, I can (must) not communicate with tutors." or "Because my students must have a quality education, I cannot communicate with tutors." We replace the set of words "In order to . . . I can (must) . . ." by a backward arrow. No questions are asked about the rationale for this statement. Figure 3.1 graphically represents the above sets of words: "In order that . . . I must . . ." or "Because . . ., . . .".

Example 3.1: Instructor's Communication Problem

To create a conflict Cloud, we start with an UDE. Consider an instructor's UDE: "There is no communication between instructors and tutors." This is a condition. What is the conflict here?

A storyline explains why this is a conflict. Developing a storyline usually helps us create a Cloud from an UDE.

Storyline: An instructor wants to do all the instruction herself, does not feel the need for additional help, and hence does not want to use tutoring or any other supplemental help that would be beneficial to students. The instructor also feels that tutors or supplementary instruction might confuse her/his students. Thus, she does not communicate with tutors. At the same time, the department insists that it is important for all faculty to use the available resources including tutoring. Therein lies the conflict. The common objective for the instructor and his/her department is, of course: "Be a responsible instructor."

Department's UDE: There is no communication between instructors and tutors. There are two sides to the UDE, the instructor's and the department's. The instructor does not communicate with tutors although the department requires that she should. Each party acts this way because of certain needs.

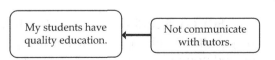

Figure 3.1 Instructor's reasoning.

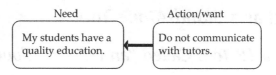

Figure 3.2   Instructor's need and action/want.

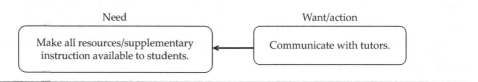

Figure 3.3   Department's need and action/want.

The instructor's side as stated earlier (Figure 3.1) can be seen in terms of the instructor's need as described in Figure 3.2.

Here, "My students have a quality education" is the instructor's need. In the instructor's words, "In order to fulfill my need/requirement that my students should have a quality education, I do (must) not communicate with tutors." Just by looking at this conditional statement, one does not see how to make any sense out of it. But there are assumption/s or perception/s of the instructor that underlie the arrow in this necessity-based logic statement that we will discuss later in this section.

The department's need as a necessary condition statement is shown in Figure 3.3.

The department policy says, "Instructors should communicate with tutors (a resource) in order to make all resources/supplementary instruction available to students." or "Because we need to make all resources/supplementary instruction available to students, instructors must communicate with tutors." (note that we can state a necessary condition this way also).

Each of these needs statements is itself a necessary condition to achieve the common goal: "Be a responsible instructor." This discussion can be put together in a Cloud, described in the following.

3.2.2 Cloud: Definition and Structure

Definition 3.1

An Evaporating Cloud (EC), Conflict Cloud, or Cloud is a TOC thinking process tool that analyzes the details of a conflict, meaningful action and a decision in a concise and non-provocative way (Cox III et al., 2012).

The Cloud helps to define and analyze a conflict. As in Example 3.1, we start by converting the UDE into a conflict. We do this by considering the UDE from two different viewpoints. This enables us to see the outcome of two logically opposed actions. A conflict is well defined when two opposing actions (wants) are shown to lead to the achievement of a common goal. Such a goal should be broad, overarching, and general. Both actions are logically linked to the common goal by two different needs. Again, the Cloud uses necessary condition logic.

The Cloud analyzes the details of the conflict *in terms of wants* by studying the five aspects of a conflict: If there are two parties, X and Y, with opposite wants and a common goal, we consider the following:

X's want (action)
Y's want (action)
X's need
Y's need
The common objective (goal)

The conflict may be internal to an individual. For instance, the conflict, "I must attend to my family responsibilities or I must study," is internal. The Cloud may be between two parties, for instance, between an instructor and her/his department, as discussed in Section 3.2: "The instructor must communicate with tutors on a regular basis and the instructor feels s/he cannot do so."

The Cloud's structure is built of five entities (boxes) connected by logical arrows. The arrows indicate the four *necessary condition* statements: two on X's side and two on Y's side with the common goal or objective. Each box addresses one of the five aspects to help describe the conflict. Figure 3.4 shows the structure of a Cloud.

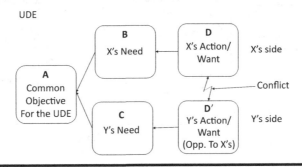

Figure 3.4   Structure of a Cloud/EC.

Here, the entities D and D′ are logically opposite wants or actions, while A is an objective, B and C are requirements or critical needs, and A, B, and C are thus states or conditions to be fulfilled or satisfied. The needs B and C should never conflict. A conflict arises when there are two opposite actions or wants. We read the Cloud from left to right: first the top side and then the bottom side: "In order to have or obtain objective A, we must first fulfill or satisfy need B, and in order to fulfill or satisfy need B, we must have or do D. At the same time, in order to obtain objective A, we must have need C. In order to have C, we must have or do D′. D and D′ are logically opposite and are in conflict (or, this is a conflict)."

Using the five-entity structure, we can formulate the example in 3.1 as a Cloud in Figure 3.5.

Example 3.1: Instructor's Communication Problem (Continued)

We read the Cloud: "In order to be a responsible instructor, I must ensure that my students have a quality education, and in order that my students have a quality education, I must not communicate with tutors. At the same time, in order to be a responsible instructor, I must have all supplementary instruction available, and in order to have all supplementary instruction available, I must communicate with tutors." The actions "not communicate with tutors" and "communicate with tutors" are in conflict.

Evaporating Cloud

UDE: "I have no communication with tutors." *(Instructor's UDE)*

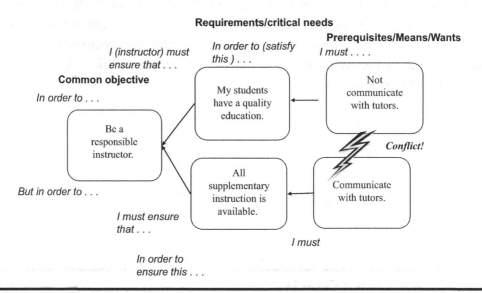

Figure 3.5   Instructor's EC.

To review, an UDE is caused by a specific action/want. At the same time, there is a more desirable action/want that is opposing it. A conflict arises within a person internally, between two persons, between a person and a group, or within an institution, when a decision has to be made as to whether or how to perform the desirable action instead of the undesirable one. Regardless, there is always a common goal or objective for an issue/UDE. The goal is attained when the *need* on each side is satisfied. These nonconflicting needs are generated because each side looks at the issue with certain, often differing assumptions. Each side wants to fulfill those needs in a particular way. In a conflict, the two wants are specific actions and are opposites of each other.

Needs are conditions and they never oppose each other. But the satisfaction of need B is jeopardized by carrying out or having D', and the satisfaction of need C is jeopardized by carrying out or having D. We say, "need B is 'jeopardized' by D'" and "need C is 'jeopardized' by D" as a shorthand.

Before we can resolve the conflict, we must ask *why* each action fulfills the corresponding need. This questioning surfaces the assumptions and this questioning process gives rise to a fully developed Cloud, as shown schematically in Figure 3.6 and applied to our current example in Figure 3.7.

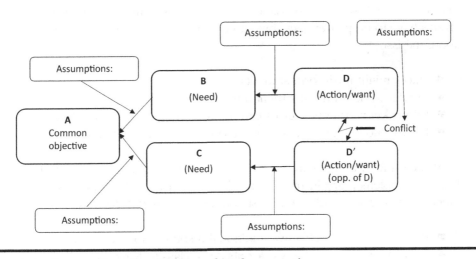

Figure 3.6 Evaporating Cloud with surfaced assumptions.

Evaporating Cloud – Surfacing Assumptions

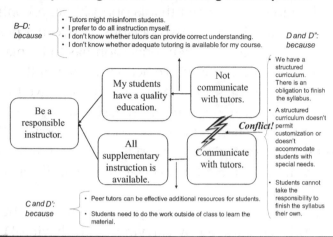

Figure 3.7 Figure 3.5 modified.

Example 3.1: Instructor's Communication Problem (Continued)

Exercise

Surface the reasons/assumptions for the following two necessary condition statements (for guidance see the assumptions written after {s} in Figure 3.7):

A ← B   and   A ← C.

We should not be critical of any assumptions raised at this point. That will come later. We read the Cloud: "In order to be a responsible instructor, I must ensure that my students get a quality education. In order to ensure that my students get a quality education, I must not communicate with tutors, *because* (list all the possible reasons you can think of; they don't always have to be proven facts but can also reflect your feelings/opinions about the issue).

- Tutors might misinform students.
- I prefer to do all the instruction myself.
- I don't know whether tutors can improve student understanding.
- I don't know whether adequate tutoring is available for my course.

At the same time (But), in order to be a responsible instructor, I must have all supplementary instruction available. In order to have all supplementary instruction available, I must communicate with tutors, because

- Peer tutors can be effective additional resources for students.
- Students need to do the work outside of class to learn the material.

An instructor cannot both communicate with tutors and not communicate with tutors because of the following:

- The statements are contradictory to each other.
- We have a structured curriculum (to finish the syllabus topics by certain dates).
- The deadlines don't permit customization or don't accommodate students with special needs.
- Students cannot take the responsibility to finish the syllabus on their own.

3.2.2.1 Finding Win–Win Solutions: Resolution of Instructor's Conflict in Example 3.1

Now that most assumptions are surfaced for the instructor, we are ready to find an injection so that the instructor's conflict is resolved.

Since needs never oppose each other in *any* conflict, if we consider the needs of both sides and fulfill them by *one want or action*—injection—*agreeable to both sides*, then the conflict evaporates! Or, to put it another way, if even one assumption is shown to be invalid and an appropriate injection for it is accepted, then the conflict is resolved. No compromise is necessary. A win–win solution arises.

Definition 3.2

An injection is a state or condition that invalidates one or more assumptions underlying the relationships between the objective and requirements, or between requirements and prerequisites or between the two prerequisites of an evaporating cloud (Cox III et al., 2012).

Note the use of the word *injection* in different contexts used here and in Chapter 2. The intention of an injection is the same, to remedy the current negative effect/conflict or make something positive happen.

A win–win solution is a solution that fulfills both sides' needs. The problem is that in order to satisfy its needs, each side usually insists on getting its conflicting wants. The UDE, a Cloud to communicate the conflict, and uncovering assumptions without blaming anyone, are the keys to conflict resolution.

Thinking within a win–win framework requires us to shift the focus from getting what we want to obtaining what we need.

Example 3.1: Instructor's Communication Problem (Continued)

In satisfying the instructor's needs, the assumption that "Students cannot take the responsibility to finish the syllabus on their own" was considered, and a *student-centered* syllabus with detailed day-to-day course outlines including exam dates, resources available, grading, and attendance policies was prepared. The instructor's assumptions regarding tutors were considered by making effective well-trained tutors available and advertising about tutoring. A booklet entitled *Departmental Guidelines* was developed and presented in a meeting to explain to all stakeholders the roles of the students, instructors, and tutors (supplemental instruction). This made it clear that students need to be proactive in their success. Thus, a win–win solution was obtained for the instructor and department. At this point the instructor had a paradigm shift, and the conflict was resolved by her accepting D′.

3.2.3 Developing a Cloud Step by Step from an UDE

We will now discuss how to *develop* the Cloud in terms of actions. We use the following steps to examine a conflict using a Cloud with another person. An injection, a proposed action to make the issue disappear, may be added at an appropriate time. Never lose focus on resolving the conflict and achieving the objective!

With practice, you will not need to draw a Cloud every time you encounter a potential conflict; you will be able to discern the issues and assumptions on both sides mentally and to find a win–win solution, so that no one has to compromise. Thus, you are in a position to avoid an actual conflict.

Step 1: State the UDE. An UDE relates to two opposite wants. Wants are actions to be taken.

Step 2: Start with D, the specific action *that caused* the UDE.

Step 3: Write its opposite action in D′. D′ prevents the UDE.

An action D fulfills a need and D′ fulfills a different need.

Step 4: To fill in B, write the general need for the want D. Do not rehash D, the want. D is specific. B is general or generic. B is also the need that D′ prevents us from fulfilling (according to the assumption of B–D).

Step 5: Fill in C. Again, C should be something general; it is not the opposite of need B. D′ is specific. C is the need that D prevents us from fulfilling (according to the assumption of C and D′).

Step 6: Fill in A, the common goal or objective that will be achieved if the needs of B and C are both satisfied. This can be summarized by the Cloud in Figure 3.8.

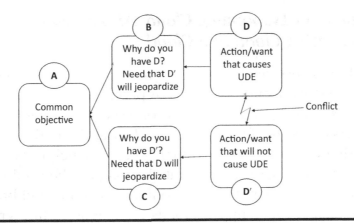

Figure 3.8   Checking the logic.

This will be explained further through specific examples.

The word *common objective* in A is the goal that both sides strive to achieve. This section describes how a Cloud can be used to resolve five different types of conflicts.

3.2.3.1 Presenting a Cloud to Another Person

The order in which we develop and analyze a Cloud is not always the most effective way to communicate the Cloud to another person. The other person probably has more interest in resolving the conflict on his/her side of the Cloud than on yours.

Step 1: So, start by reaffirming your collective common goal of objective (A). It might take some discussion to reach a consensus on this.

Step 2: Then, state the other person's side, A, B and B–D. This shows that you have thought carefully about his/her needs and wants. If you have stated his incorrectly, get clarification and restate it.

Step 3: Then, present your side, A and C, C–D′. This shows the other person why the conflict exists.

Step 4: Let the other side come up with injections or erroneous assumptions if he/she can.

Step 5: Continue to surface assumptions, and identify the one(s) that you think that you can invalidate.

Step 6: Invalidate as many assumptions as you can with the other person's help using appropriate injections. Voila! The conflict is resolved.

3.2.4 Examples of Evaporating Cloud, Also Known As a Conflict Cloud or a Cloud

We start with two very simple examples from personal experience that will give the reader the "feel" of how the process works. We also consider several examples pertaining to major issues of concern in a college/university setting, for example, student attrition, that can also be addressed using Clouds. The Cloud tool is easy enough to be used by kindergarten children but is sophisticated enough to be used by corporations and educational institutions for conflict resolution and breakthrough solutions. In Poland, for example, Clouds are taught to third graders (Hetmanczyk-Bajer, n.d.).

3.2.4.1 Resolving Day-to-Day Problems

The following is an example of a day-to-day conflict. It was presented by a college counselor about a conflict between a mother, Maryann, and her 8-year-old son, Tommy.

> **Example 3.2: A Mother's Problem**
>
> Storyline: Maryann wants Tommy to get ready faster in the morning so that both can leave the house on time. The result is that Maryann yells at Tommy to hurry up and Tommy complains.

In order to resolve the conflict, we examine the two sides of the issue. "Breaking the Cloud" leads to a win–win situation. The following steps can be followed to analyze any day-to-day conflict. In each step, just look at the relevant parts of Figure 3.9 and not the entire figure.

Step 1: We correct any poorly stated UDEs, for example:

Maryann yells at Tommy in the morning.
Tommy complains in the morning.

These are *symptomatic UDEs*, meaning reactions or secondary actions rather than the originating action. They also express emotions. We must remove the emotion. We remove the emotion and rewrite the UDE in terms of a *systemic UDE*, meaning the actual condition.

UDE: Tommy does not get ready on time in the morning.

Step 2: We write complete simple sentences clearly describing the two conflicting behaviors/opinions/situations/procedures in the two boxes, D and D′, with the *unwanted action in D and the conflicting action in D′*. Start with D. Then, write its logical opposite, D′.

D: Take more (my) time.
D': (Tommy) Take less time.

These are in direct conflict with each other. These boxes describe the two opposing wants.

Step 3: Now, in order to see the needs that require the actions in D (Tommy's, son's) and D' (Maryann's, mother's), we write the two needs in boxes labeled B and C as shown. Remember that a need is something you must fulfill, and in your/their view, D or D', a particular action, does so. The logic arrows are right to left. You are writing the necessary action that fulfills your need. Start with B.

As a general rule, after finishing every step, we read it aloud: "In order to fulfill the need B, I must perform or have D." We must see that the logic makes sense. Otherwise, reword the statements so that each statement is logically sound.

(Tommy's side) "*In order to* finish all my different morning chores, *I must* have help from Mommy." B ← D

Then, fill in the box C. "In order to fulfill the need C, I must perform or have D'."

(Maryann's side) "*In order that* each of us does our respective chores, I do not help Tommy." C ← D.

Step 4: There is a common objective in box A: "Get ready on time." The two logic arrows are placed right to left from B and C, respectively, to A.

We read aloud: "In order to attain the objective A, *Tommy must* have or satisfy B. On the other hand (or at the same time) in order to attain the objective A, *Maryann must* have or satisfy C."

More specifically,

(Tommy's side) "In order to get ready on time, I must finish all my different morning chores. At the same time (Maryann's side), in order to get ready on time, we must each do our respective chores." (We can adjust the language as needed to flow more smoothly.)

After developing the Cloud (Figure 3.6), Maryann brought to the surface the assumptions on both sides. She had heard Tommy's usual complaints (assumptions B–D). It was important not to criticize or argue with Tommy's assumptions, so long as they were clear and understandable. Then, she also verbalized her own assumptions C and D'; she had explained assumptions 1 and 2 that morning to Tommy. These assumptions are read as follows:

Tommy: "In order to finish all my different chores, I must have help from Mommy.

. . . because I need more sleep.

. . . because Mommy can help me more.

. . . because I can't give myself enough time to do everything I need to."

Similarly, the complete sentences C and D′ and Maryann's assumptions must be read aloud before we proceed to resolve the conflict.

Maryann developed a solution to the problem on her own by challenging two of her own assumptions and also considering Tommy's assumptions, that is,

> Everything usually done by Tommy has to be done by him (it doesn't).
>
> Tommy has to do everything that very morning (he doesn't).
>
> Tommy wants Mommy to help him more (and Mommy can do that).

With all the assumptions surfaced, we now have the complete resolution as in Figure 3.9.

A, B, and C are conditions (states). D clearly jeopardizes C. D′ jeopardizes B, because Tommy does not finish all his morning chores if Mommy does not help. B and C sound similar, but the important thing is that B and C should not oppose each other.

The injection is that Tommy does not have to do everything that morning. This idea comes from looking at the surfaced assumptions on both Tommy's and Maryann's sides. Read the resolution in Figure 3.9. In the proposed solution, Tommy has fewer things to do by himself every morning. He would naturally take less time to do his things to prepare. Maryann has found a "win–win" solution. Read the Cloud and the resolution again to see that there is no compromise made by either Tommy or Maryann. At this

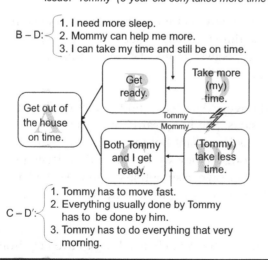

Issue: *"Tommy (8-year-old son) takes more time to get ready in the morning"*

B – D:
1. I need more sleep.
2. Mommy can help me more.
3. I can take my time and still be on time.

Get ready.

Take more (my) time.

Get out of the house on time.

Tommy
Mommy

Both Tommy and I get ready.

(Tommy) take less time.

C – D′:
1. Tommy has to move fast.
2. Everything usually done by Tommy has to be done by him.
3. Tommy has to do everything that very morning.

Resolution: Tommy does not have to do everything that morning. He can be told to pepare the previous night the clothes that he is going to wear the next day. I must help him more to get ready in the morning. I must make Tommy breakfast so that he will have fewer things to do by himself in the morning. This will enable him to be ready at the required time.

Figure 3.9 Tommy's Cloud.

point, there is a paradigm shift that occurred as a result of challenging the assumptions on both sides. The paradigm shift resolved the conflict.

Example 3.3: Instructor's Cloud: "Talk, No Talk" Problem

An instructor developed the Cloud and resolution as given in Figure 3.10.

UDE: Students' talking in my class is disruptive.

The first step is to write a brief explanation of the UDE. Questioning offers another technique to develop the Cloud. In order to verbalize the needs, she asked herself and answered the following questions:

- What important need are you having trouble achieving because the issue or UDE exists? This is B.
  I have the need to cover the syllabus.
  It is necessary for students to hear the lesson without noise distractions.
- What do you often end up *doing* to deal with this problem? This is D.
  I keep asking my students to stop talking.
  I talk to the disruptive students out of class.
- Why do you have to deal with the problem? (Or, what sometimes happens when you *do* try to deal with the problem?) This is an assumption for B–D.
  Students who are talking disrupt my thinking. I won't be able to cover the material.
  Students who want to learn also get annoyed. They don't hear the lesson.
- What action do you sometimes (often?) *prefer* to be taken (D')?
  I talk to the disruptive students outside class without embarrassing them in the classroom.

The D' box is the logical opposite of D. She filled out the box C and assumptions for C–D', the needs and assumptions for her students, from her observations, and having spoken with the students outside of class. A is the common goal for the students and the instructor. This discussion leads to the Cloud in Figure 3.10.

Observe that B and C are general and D and D' are logical opposites. D' jeopardizes B, and D jeopardizes C. The resolution came from considering the assumptions underlying the needs of both the instructor and her students. The conflict was resolved here by sometimes accepting D and sometimes D'.

Did the instructor or her students have to compromise? Students talked in their groups and when answering the instructor's questions. This satisfied their need to have a favorable learning environment by interacting with one another. The instructor held students' focus on the lesson by engaging them. They stopped talking to one another disruptively, and the conflict was resolved.

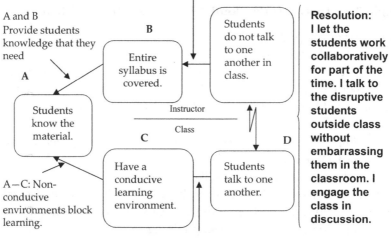

B–D
I will have to stop teaching if they keep talking.
Other students won't hear the lesson while there is talking in class.

A and B
Provide students knowledge that they need

A–C: Non-conducive environments block learning.

C and D′
1. Students learn to participate in the class by interacting.
2. Students lose focus in a long lesson.
3. Sometimes they do not understand what I have said and they want to ask their neighbor.
4. Students do not realize that they are disruptive.

Figure 3.10 Instructor's Cloud—"Talk, No Talk" problem.

3.2.5 Directions for Developing Clouds to Resolve Day-to-Day Conflicts

This subsection summarizes the steps to develop Clouds for resolving day-to-day conflicts and is based on the presentation of Janice Cerveny, the facilitator of the MSEIP July 2011 TOC Mentors' workshop for counselors, advisors, and faculty.

Step 0: Select an appropriate conflict.

_____

_____

Write a brief explanation (story) describing it.

_____
_____
_____
_____

Steps 1–6 (Figure 3.11)

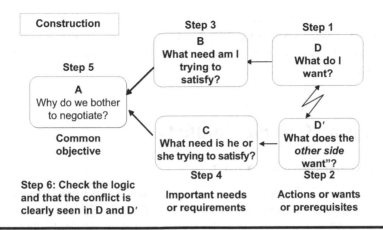

Figure 3.11   Day-to-day personal conflicts.

As shown in Figure 3.11, need B can be found by asking why I want what I want in D. Need C can be found by asking why I want what I want in D′.

3.2.5.1 Surfacing Assumptions and Finding a Solution

Surface at least three of the assumptions on your side only: B–D.

Read aloud B ← D and say "because of assumption 1." Read aloud B ← D and say "because of assumption 2" and so on. Read again emphasizing different keywords. Perform the *logic check*, "Does this make sense?"

When surfacing assumptions, stay on your side. Do not over justify the want D, but do emphasize the need B.

Similarly, surface the assumptions for C and D′.

While communicating the Cloud, start in the reverse order. Start with the other's side C and D′. Invite the other side to modify the need C to make it fit their need better. Surface assumptions on your side B–D. Wait for the other side to surface assumptions C and D′. If the other side cannot come up with any assumptions, leave the Cloud. The other side may come up with the assumptions later. Do not damage the relationship by pressing this point.

Exercises

1. Develop a Cloud to resolve some day-to-day conflict on your own. Use the template provided at the end of the chapter. Use the previous reasoning to form the Cloud.

2. Prepare one Cloud a day for a different conflict that you face. Surface the assumptions and suggest a resolution to the conflict. Scrutinize the Clouds of fellow classmates or friends if you are studying TOC in a class.

3.3 Addressing Chronic Conflicts

Definition 3.3: Chronic Conflict

A conflict for an individual is a chronic conflict if the person feels trapped, does not see any other choice and feels powerless to remove the conflict. The individual submits to the reality unwillingly. The issue is long term, highly emotional, with little effort being given to addressing the issue. The issue may be personal or interpersonal.

Avraham Goldratt Institute, Management Skills Workshop Course (MSW), booklet 3.

Any conflict not addressed directly has a tendency to become a chronic conflict, unless, because of time or change in the situation or maturity, the issue no longer exists. Chronic conflicts, for example, between a boss and worker or a husband and wife, can be solved using the TOC technique.

Remember that a Cloud has box A as the common goal, boxes B and C as general needs, and boxes D and D' as specific, logically opposite wants. D and D' cause the conflict, while A, B, and C do not. For example, for the student who has the chronic problem and wants to resolve it, *the Cloud must be broken on his/her side, the B–D side. He/she doesn't want D to happen. D is the cause of the UDE for the student.* However, he or she has to accept the other person's side, the C and D' side, without neglecting his/her own need B. This Cloud requires the use of the negative branch (already discussed in Chapter 2) to improve the solution. This also requires help and support from people representing the other side. To complete a solution, the positive branch (already discussed in Chapter 2) is also necessary. How to present the Cloud to the other party is discussed at the end of this section.

To address chronic conflicts, the goal is to help individuals identify and evaluate possible solutions until they find one that they feel comfortable pursuing. This technique is also an *initiating skills* tool.

3.3.1 Example of Chronic Conflicts

Example 3.4: A Student's Dilemma

UDE: "I cannot attend my classes on time."

This is an example that requires the college to take some action to help the student and to address student attrition.

Storyline: Gary is a student with family and personal responsibilities and cannot attend his math classes on time. Sometimes, he has to be absent, and many times, he is late for his class. But he and his course instructor (or college) want him to attend classes on time. This creates a conflict in the student's mind. Gary works with the instructor or a counselor on this Cloud (see Figure 3.12).

The numbers in Figure 3.12 indicate the order of the steps that we take to create a Cloud.

Remember that after finishing every step, we read it aloud to make sure that the logic makes sense; otherwise, we reword the statements so that each statement is logically sound. Each statement is *simple* and grammatically *complete*.

Observe that D and D′ are logical opposites of each other.

Then, the entire Cloud is read aloud by Gary. "In order to have success in personal life," I must "be responsive to take care of family/personal problems." And in order to "be responsive to take care of family/personal problems," I must "remain absent or be late to my classes." At the same time, in order to have "success in personal life," I must "know the course material."

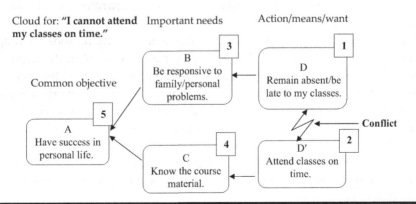

Figure 3.12 Student's dilemma.

And in order to know the course material, I must "attend classes on time." D and D′ are in direct conflict. "I don't know what to do," Gary opined.

Once we have created the Cloud, we must find the assumptions underlying the logic arrows:

B ← D, C ← D′, and the conflict, D ↔ D′. Surfacing these assumptions takes time and might seem tedious, but it is essential. Challenging these assumptions leads to breaking the Cloud and resolving the conflict.

There are two scenarios: institutional and personal. If there are many students in the college like Gary, it is necessary for the college to make certain changes. However, that takes time, since there are many individuals and departments involved. But an individual student can make appropriate changes more rapidly.

Example 3.4: A Student's Dilemma (Continued)

Gary feels that there is no one else to fulfill his obligations at a certain time. This is included in the analysis as: In order to attend to family responsibilities or personal problems, I must remain absent or be late to my classes because there is no one else to fulfill my obligations at a certain time.

A detailed discussion of Gary's case among the mathematics faculty and some students revealed the following *assumptions* underlying logic arrows: A ← B, A ← C, B ← D, C ← D′, and D ↔ D′ (see Figure 3.13).

Here, we are using the idea of surfacing assumptions between D and D′, that is, why there is a conflict in the first place. Surfacing these assumptions reveals some institutional policies, written or unwritten, which can be addressed by the institution.

On the institutional side, two bolded statements in the reasons (assumptions) for D and D′ led to a viable strategy for improvement in the department: The department offers programs tailored to the needs of the students. Classes can be easily switched without penalty if a student's work schedule changes. Support services will be offered if needed. Intervention occurs when a student remains absent or is not performing, via the faculty member contacting the counselor or talking to the student. This way, the student could be move to a win–win situation. In the Mathematics Department, this approach has led to synchronization of course sections and enhancement of support services.

The student himself could break the Cloud if he saw the importance of both sides and arranged his situation or classes with the help of his family

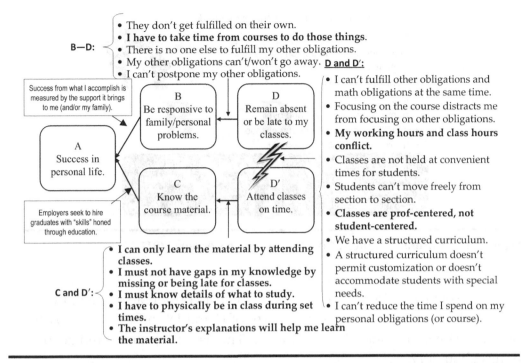

Figure 3.13   Student's dilemma—surfacing assumptions.

members, if necessary, to both study and take care of his personal responsibilities using different options. He does not have to sacrifice one for the other. A college education offers the student the means to improve his financial situation, to have a broader perspective and to help his family. This observation is derived from the assumptions for the logic arrow A ← C and A ← B.

Fleshing out the different assumptions in Figure 3.13 is the hard part. They could only be revealed through group discussion, in the case of the department, and discussion with the family members or a counselor in the case of the student.

We have discussed the negative branch and the positive branch in Chapter 2. To complete the discussion on Gary, this is a good time to go back and reread those sections.

3.3.2 Importance of the Chronic Cloud

What is a chronic conflict? Figure 3.14 contributed by Janice Cerveny summarizes the situation.

Identification: Indicators that this tool is required

- Same fight
- Many fights—same person
- High emotion
- Total acquiescence
- Feel trapped
- Same complaints over and over
- Inability to even talk about the issue
- "Here we go again"—the script...

Effect on the organization?	Effect on individuals?
Mistrust, poor morale, absenteeism, turnover, cynicism, inertia . . .	Demoralized, absenteeism, turnover, "revolving door," cynicism, inertia . . .

Figure 3.14   Chronic conflicts. *Courtesy of Janice Cerveny, 2011.*

The resolution of chronic conflicts requires a considerable amount of work by both parties involved. The party of C and D′ must help the party of B and D with the injections and work. The list of injections and actions brings about a *paradigm shift*.

A chronic conflict is always between two individuals, or one individual (upper side) and the other (lower) side, where the other side is an institution or department. A conflict full of emotion between two family members can also be resolved in this manner. A typical shared goal for a family is to be happy. Conflicts will not arise between two members of the family if the person who is a student of TOC keeps in mind the needs of both family members and fulfills them. In addition, while fulfilling his/her own needs, the other family member should provide support to the other. The following steps resolve a chronic conflict. *Note that the strategy involved in presenting the Cloud and its resolution to the other party is different from the one that you used to analyze the conflict.*

1. Let's assume that you are a student of TOC and wish to resolve a chronic conflict. In this case, the arrow B ← D (your side) has to be broken. The entities or boxes B and A should not be neglected.
2. The other side's want or action, D′, has to be accepted, meaning that D′ is or will be the desirable or changed or new behavior after discussion.
3. Write the assumptions for B ← D.
4. Think of an injection to break B ← D.

5. Construct a negative branch arising from the injection that you have thought of.

6. Communicate the chronic conflict in a meeting with the other party as follows:

    a. Say: "I would like to make a fresh start." Present the A–C–D' as you see it. Ask if this adequately represents the other side's viewpoint. If not, adjust the entities as needed.

    b. Find out the other party's issues (UDEs) that your want (D) has caused. The other party may be suspicious of opening up, but your genuineness will keep the communication channel open.

    c. Present your side A–B–D and the assumptions for B–D: "In order to fulfill my need (B), I have D, because I feel . . . (see assumptions B–D)."

    d. Present the injection that you are willing to make.

    e. Present the negative branch that you have constructed. Ask the other side to help you figure out how to avoid the negative consequences of your injection.

    f. Your solo work is over at this point. Now both parties must exert an effort to move forward. Be patient and allow the other party to think about an injection to trim the negative branch, unless the party has already thought of an injection.

    g. Maintain communication with the other party and observe the relationship. If there have been arguments, mentally go over the mistakes that you may have made in anger or without considering the other side's assumptions.

7. Trim the negative branch at different arrows. It is better to trim the arrows at lower levels with injection/s with the help of the other side. If the other side doesn't come up with injections, focus on the common objective and remain sensitive to the other party's need. Stay open and do not force the solution. Never go back to want D. *A conflict does not exist if there are no opposing wants.* Even though at present, there is no solution to your liking, stay focused on a win–win situation with the common objective. Your positive efforts will never be wasted.

Exercise

Do you have a chronic conflict that you are afraid to work with? Work through a Cloud and discuss it with your academic or personal counselor.

3.4 Empowerment Clouds

The conflicts that we have seen so far illustrate how, when a conflict is resolved, each of the people involved in the conflict is empowered. That is what *winning* does to a person. It generates a feeling of confidence and a feeling of empowerment. Since no one loses, it is empowerment for both parties. Here are other examples for empowerment:

In the following example, a student wants to select mathematics as a major but is hesitant. The argument can be similarly developed for any other major.

Example 3.5: Empowering a Student to Select a Major

Storyline: Shanaya wants to major in mathematics, but given her past experience in mathematics, she feels that she is not up to it. She does not have confidence that she can do it. She wants to get As and Bs, and she feels that she can do this easily in other majors. However, she wants to go into a technical career. She goes to a mentor who develops a Cloud and discovers her reasons or assumptions for not being a math major by asking her questions. The numbers in Figure 3.15 indicate the order in which the mentor *develops* the Cloud for Shanaya. She checks the logic to make sure that satisfaction of the need in box B is jeopardized by D′, Shanaya's proposed choice; that is, if she does not become a math major, she cannot do well in a technical curriculum.

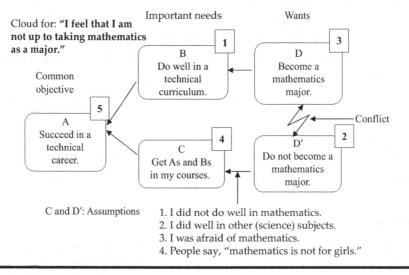

Figure 3.15 Shanaya's empowerment Cloud.

The mentor knows that the department has taken the following measures to overcome students' fear of learning mathematics, but she does not immediately share this information with Shanaya.

INJECTIONS

1. The Department of Mathematics, through course offerings, curriculum, guidance and teaching, imparts confidence in all its students in their ability to achieve success in school and in life.
2. Through TOC and its TP tools, students get training and guidance in time management, problem solving, and conflict resolution to address negative experiences and deficiencies.
3. By remaining in the department and working constantly with teachers and students who love mathematics, Shanaya will also love mathematics.
4. The department believes that anyone can excel in mathematics, provided that there is a favorable learning environment. The department has already created such an environment.

ACTIONS THAT SHANAYA MUST TAKE

Shanaya's goal is a long-term goal. She needs to apply consistent effort. She should create an Ambitious Target Tree (ATT) as discussed in Chapter 4. To do this, she would list her obstacles and the intermediate objectives needed to overcome the obstacles and then perform the actions required to attain the intermediate objectives. In order to work with faculty, Shanaya, with an open mind, should ask other students and have interactions with all faculty before selecting a mentor. Not all department faculty like to work with, guide, and do undergraduate research with students. She should find a faculty member with a compatible personality to plan her coursework and undergraduate research. Being consistently in the company of lovers of mathematics will help her to focus on the goal. She can learn how to study mathematics and get good grades. She should take on each course as a *"project"* and make a project plan for the entire semester even before she has a mentor. See how to work on a course as a project, how to study any subject, and how to study mathematics in the *Motivational Guide* (Nagarkatte, 2012). There is also an appendix to Chapter 5 where the project plan is discussed in detail.

PRESENTING THE CLOUD

Once the Cloud is constructed, **in order to *discuss* the Cloud with Shanaya, the mentor starts in a different order.** She starts at the goal A and reads the Cloud, "In order to succeed in a technical career (A), you must do well in a technical curriculum (B). And in order to do well in a technical curriculum, you must become a mathematics major (D) because

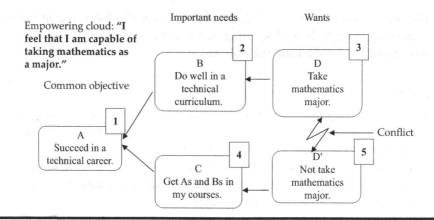

Figure 3.16 Explaining the Cloud to Shanaya.

mathematics provides tools, concepts, and skills to succeed in a technical curriculum (assumption B–D not written). On the other hand, in order to succeed in a technical career, you must get As and Bs. And in order to get As and Bs, you must not become a mathematics major (i.e., opt for some other major), because you did not do well in mathematics in the past, etc. Becoming a mathematics major, and not becoming a math major is a conflict. In order to break the conflict, you must break the link between C and D′; that is, you must be able to get As and Bs in mathematics courses also. That is the reason that the plan of action suggested earlier is necessary."

The numbers in Figure 3.16 indicate the order in which the mentor discussed the Cloud with Shanaya. Compare this with Figure 3.15.

USING THE CLOUD TO TAKE ACTION

The order in which Shanaya should interpret the Cloud from the point of view of action is given in Figure 3.17 and is different from the way it was developed or discussed with Shanaya.

To resolve the conflict, Shanaya should break the connection between C and D′ with injections from the following list.

1. Through TOC and its TP tools, I can get training and guidance in time management, problem solving, and conflict resolution to address negative experiences and deficiencies.
2. By remaining in the department and working constantly with teachers and students who love mathematics, I will also love mathematics.
3. I feel comfortable in this learning environment because the department believes in me; I can excel in mathematics.

Once she has done that, it becomes clear that if she becomes a math major, Shanaya can fulfill both needs: get As and Bs in her courses and do

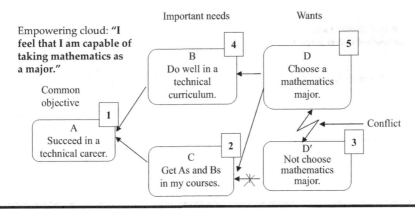

Figure 3.17   Shanaya's interpretation of the empowering Cloud.

well in a technical curriculum. This result is represented by the arrow C←D. Note that D′ was Shanaya's original choice and that D would be her decision after working through the Cloud.

The previous Cloud was written for a student who wanted to be a mathematics major. Similar empowerment Clouds can be developed for any other subject.

Conflicts sometimes arise when a person feels inadequate in a job because of certain official or unofficial rules. We want to develop a conflict resolution paradigm that empowers a person in such cases.

Example 3.6: Empowering a Person at Work (or the Lieutenant's Cloud)

Storyline: Charles is a senior who has been appointed as a tutorial coordinator by Dr. Kelly, chairperson of the Department of Biology in an urban college. Dr. Macy is in charge of tutorial services for biology. Charles is talented, trustworthy, responsible, and well versed in computers and does research with Dr. Kelly. He is well liked by all students. However, Dr. Macy has made a rule that all tutors must be approved by him. He has been sick for 2 days and the midterm test week is coming close. Students are coming to the department for tutorial help. There is a great need for a tutor and a tutor is available. But because of Dr. Macy's rule, Charles cannot by himself hire a tutor. He comes to Dr. Kelly for help.

Dr. Kelly tries to contact Dr. Macy several times, but he is unreachable. Dr. Kelly guides Charles to come to a decision using what is called the *Firefighting* or *Lieutenant's Cloud*. It is an empowerment Cloud. Figure 3.18 shows the initial Cloud constructed by Dr. Kelly.

After constructing the Cloud, Dr. Kelly first brought out the assumptions, which allowed him to come up with injections, as shown in Figure 3.19:

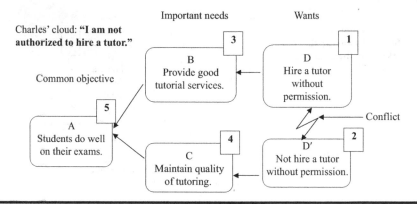

Figure 3.18   Lieutenant's Cloud/Firefighting Cloud.

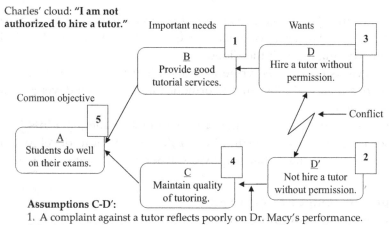

Assumptions C-D':
1. A complaint against a tutor reflects poorly on Dr. Macy's performance.
2. Dr. Macy is the only person who is experienced in judging quality of tutoring.
3. Dr. Macy doesn't like his authority undercut.

Figure 3.19   Dr. Kelly reads the Cloud to himself, 1 through 5, and surfaces assumptions.

INJECTIONS

1. Only hire a tutor with a good academic record and interpersonal skills.
2. The chair will explain to the faculty supervisor for tutoring the overarching goal of the department, and monitor objectively the quality of the tutor's work and his/her students' performance (along with other tutors' work) documented by the tutorial database.
3. A *bad* tutor does not reflect poorly on the supervisor's performance but on the department.
4. The chair recognizes the faculty supervisor's efforts and concerns about maintaining quality and assures him that the same standard will be followed by the department even in Dr. Macy's absence.

Injection 1 prevents complaints about tutors to Dr. Macy, the tutorial supervisor. Injections 2 and 3 elevate tutoring responsibilities from the supervisor to the department. Injection 4 is to make sure that the chair does not insult the supervisor.

The win–win effort helps the department to maintain harmony among the faculty.

The order of the boxes in Figure 3.18 was used to develop the Cloud, by first making sure that the proposed need B is jeopardized by the policy in D′. Dr. Kelly explained it to Charles in the order shown in Figure 3.20 which is the same as in Figure 3.18.

The actions that Charles must take are shown in Figure 3.21 in the form of a combined injection which breaks the link between C and D′. Read the

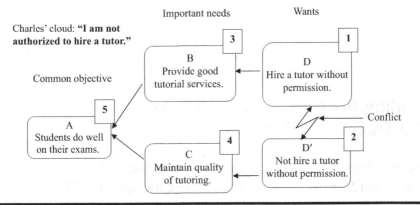

Figure 3.20   Reading the Cloud to Charles—start from need D and then surface assumptions C-D′ of Figure 3.19.

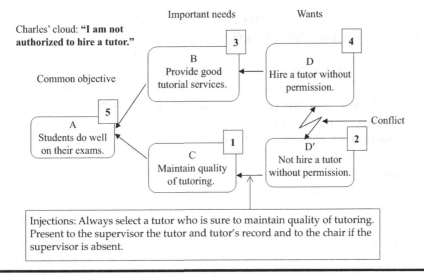

Figure 3.21   Final step in empowerment Cloud with injection.

Cloud in the marked order of the entities to understand why the rule D′ was made in the first place. This conflict is resolved by meeting the needs 1 and 3 to achieve the objective 5.

Note that D′ no longer causes a conflict, since it is now not an absolute policy. Here the resolution comes from keeping D′ but using permission from the chair, thus extending the permitting authority.

If this satisfies your need, skip to Section 3.7 and then to Chapter 4, to learn the PrT/ATT.

If you are working with children, skip to Section 3.8 and then go to Section 6.8 of TOCfE.

However, if your situation is more complex, keep reading.

Exercise

Work with your instructor to help empower you to graduate in your major and develop a project plan (studying Chapter 5 for this purpose will help).

3.5 Finding the Core Conflict Using the Three-Cloud Process

TOC also provides a rigorous way of identifying and fully understanding a deep or core conflict underlying all or most of the system's UDEs using Clouds.

Example 3.7: Institutional Problem Solving: Department of Mathematics, Medgar Evers College

Here, we relist some of the UDEs from Section 1.3.*
Students complain about the following:

1. The instructor moves too fast for students.
2. The instructor (knows his subject matter but) cannot teach.
3. **I feel that I am not capable of doing mathematics.**
4. I am not prepared for the course (prerequisites for class).
5. **I don't have time to do the homework.**
6. I don't see the importance/relevance of mathematics.
7. I am unable to attend class regularly and/or on time.
8. The exams are too hard.
9. I have to take care of my family/personal problems.

* This work was done by the first author and colleagues Joshua Berenbom and Darius Movasseghi (chair until 2009) at the Avraham Y. Goldratt Institute, New Haven, Connecticut, in January 2002, with facilitators Tracy Burton-Houle and Steve Simpliciano and with the support of an MSEIP grant (2001–2004) from the US Department of Education.

10. I (some students) go blank on exams (poor test taker).
11. The instructor does not care about me.
12. **There isn't help outside of class when I'm free.**

Faculty complain about the following:

1. Students do not prepare for class.
2. Students don't attend regularly or on time.
3. Students do poorly on tests.
4. There is insufficient time to cover all the material in the course.
5. Students register late and don't start classes at the beginning of the semester.
6. Students do not have the prerequisites for class.
7. (No matter how well I teach,) Students aren't learning effectively.
8. I receive very little satisfaction from my work.
9. We feel pressure to pass students who are not adequately prepared for the next course.
10. Students haven't mastered all the prerequisite topics needed for my course.

Administrators complain about the following:

1. There is a lack of cooperation by some faculty to carry out the departmental agenda.
2. Too many students fail.
3. There is insufficient input by some faculty to address major departmental issues.
4. Some faculty are apathetic.

3.5.1 Developing Clouds for Three Representative UDEs

We selected three representative UDEs of students, since faculty and department UDEs depend on students' UDEs. The highlighted UDEs are 5, 7, and 12. For each UDE, we developed an EC (see Figures 3.22 through 3.24).

We read each Cloud aloud and worked on the wording until each necessary condition sounded logically and grammatically correct.

3.5.2 Developing the Core Cloud from Three Clouds

We developed the Core or Generic Cloud from the three Clouds as follows:

From the goals A1, A2, and A3 of the three Clouds, we formed A. We developed a goal statement sufficiently broad to encompass the goals of the three Clouds. From the entities B1, B2, and B3 of the three Clouds, we formed B. From the entities C1, C2, and C3 of the three Clouds, we formed C. From

Evaporating cloud no. 1

Issue no. 5: "I don't have time to do the homework."

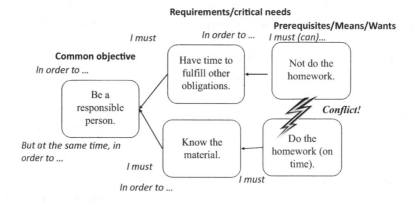

Figure 3.22   Cloud for issue no. 5.

Evaporating cloud no. 2

Issue no. 7: "I am unable to attend regularly and/or on time."

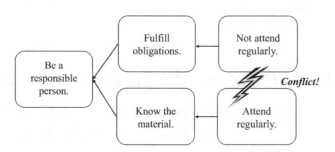

Figure 3.23   Cloud for issue no. 7.

the entities D1, D2, and D3 of the three Clouds, we formed D. From the entities D′1, D′2, and D′3 of the three Clouds, we formed D′. The resulting Cloud shown in Figure 3.25 is called the Root Cause, Core Cloud, or Generic Cloud. Note that sometimes, it will be necessary to switch B with C, or D with D′ in one or more of the three Clouds for the Core Cloud to make sense.

Evaporating cloud no. 3

Issue no. 12 : *"There isn't help outside of class when I'm free."*

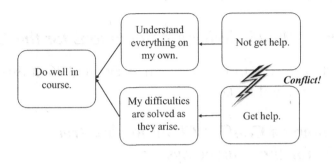

Figure 3.24   Cloud for issue no. 12.

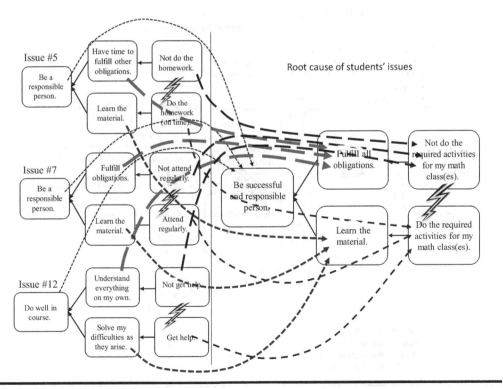

Figure 3.25   Constructing the Core Cloud.

We also studied Clouds created from another set of three UDEs and found that the Core Cloud was the same. This confirmed what research has shown: Only three representative Clouds are needed to develop the Core Cloud. That work is not presented here.

3.5.3 Surfacing the Underlying Assumptions for the Core Cloud

The fully developed Core Cloud is shown in Figure 3.26. It lists the assumptions for B–D, C–D′, and D–D′.

3.5.4 Developing a Conflict Cloud Reality Tree (CCRT) for the College System

This tree is designed to help the TOC facilitator to communicate the system's current reality to the stakeholders. We developed a Conflict Current Reality Tree (CCRT) for our college using the Core Cloud as the base of the tree of UDEs. This tree is huge and to present it requires two sheets. Only one part of the tree is shown in Figure 3.27. The other part of this tree is in Figure 3.28.

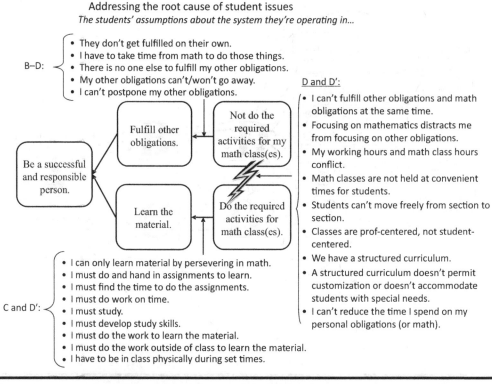

Figure 3.26   Surfacing the assumptions of the Core Cloud.

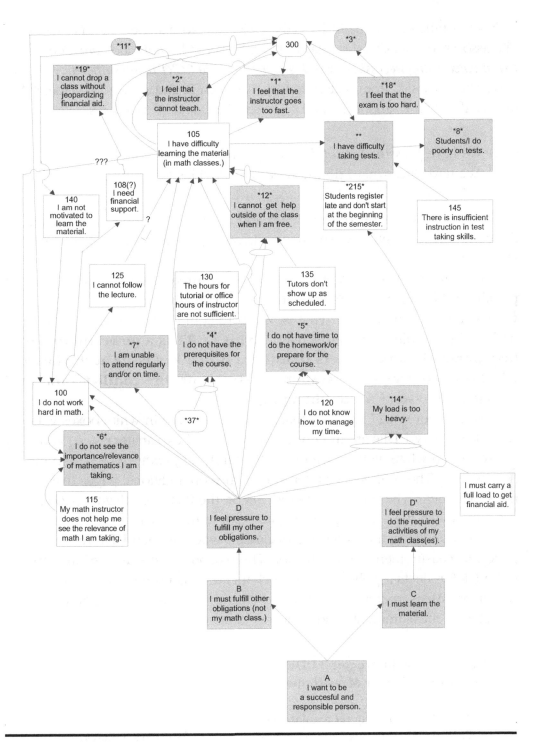

Figure 3.27   CCRT (page 1).

Note that the root of the CCRT is the entity A, placed at the bottom of the tree. The associated Core Cloud is rotated 90° to be vertical. *Unlike the Core Cloud that was created using necessity-based logic, we read the CCRT using sufficiency-based logic.* The arrows go from bottom to top: "If A then B, and at the same time, if A then C. If B then D, and if C then D′. We rewrite D and D′ as follows:

D: We have *pressure* to *not* do the required activities for math classes.
D′: We have *pressure* to do the required activities for math classes."

For the CCRT, the needs, entities B and C, are now effects of the cause, the common goal entity A. The needs drive or pressure the actions or wants D and D′.

If we have developed the Core Cloud using three systemic UDEs, most, if not all, of the original UDEs are likely to be logically connected with D, to yield a single, unified CCRT. That is, the core conflict gives rise to all of the undesirable conditions in our situation. **This CCRT is a powerful tool to help persuade stakeholders that there is one key issue at the heart of all the problems—the system constraint or core conflict—and that the current system needs changing.**

Note in Figures 3.27 and 3.28 that student UDEs are in white boxes with asterisks; faculty UDEs are in gray. Some additional explanatory steps and clauses are in white without asterisks. "P" stands for *policy*, discussed in the next section. The oval entities refer to branches on additional pages that are not shown here. The entity numbered 105 on the first page (Figure 3.27) is connected with the second page (Figure 3.28) of the CCRT.

After developing the CCRT, we discussed whether each UDE relates to a policy, a measurement, or a behavior. The reason for this discussion is that if the UDE reflects a policy, it can be changed. Policies give rise to measurements. Measurements give rise to behavior. A change in policy will be reflected in measurements and hence in behaviors.

Example 3.8: Instructors' UDEs Describing Behavior, Policy or Measurement

1. Students don't attend regularly or on time (behavior).
2. Students do poorly on tests (measurement—of students' behavior).
3. There is insufficient time to cover all material in the course (policy—of department, that all material should be covered. Students' preparation prevents this).

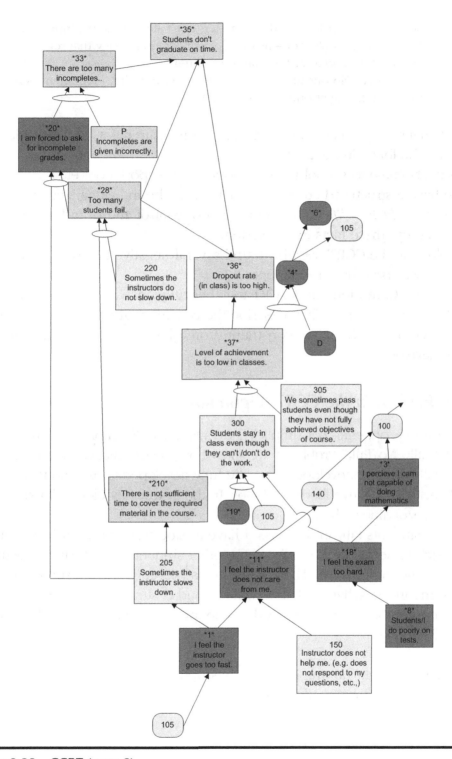

Figure 3.28 CCRT (page 2).

4. Students register late for the semester (don't start at the beginning of the semester) (behavior—result of administration policy that registration is continued after the stated deadline).
5. There isn't help outside of class when I'm free (policy—of department to offer tutoring at only certain times).

Not all UDEs can be classified as a policy, a measurement, or a behavior. Consider the following example:

Students come to school hungry (no food, transportation, etc.)

We have a structured curriculum that cannot be individualized.

These are *facts of life* (FOL) in our area of control and/or influence. We have to accept these facts in our system.

Looking at the CCRT, we also found several negative feedback loops, one of which was presented in Example 2.1.

Thus, the Core Cloud and CCRT together fully answer the first basic question, "What to change?" They describe the constraint and the current reality. The base of the CCRT is the constraint (Core Cloud) from which the current reality develops.

3.5.5 Regions in the CCRT (Optional)

This section is optional. For simplicity, we again take Example 3.3—Instructor's Cloud: "Talk, No Talk" Problem.* We show how the Conflict Current Reality Tree (CCRT) can be developed from the fully developed Cloud and that the CCRT includes negative feedback loops. In the instructor's Cloud: "Talk? Don't Talk?" the storyline is the following:

When students talk in my class, I have to stop teaching until I can get my class back under control. If I don't, the other students can't hear the lecture and miss the information. These disruptions prevent me from presenting everything in the syllabus. This conflict Cloud is summarized in Figure 3.29 and, ignoring the assumptions at this step, presented vertically to develop the CCRT in Figure 3.30.

■ UDE: Students' talking in class is disruptive.
■ D: Students do not talk in class.

---

* This section was developed during a TOC workshop in Riverhead, New York, January 2011, with Chuck Gauthier, facilitator.

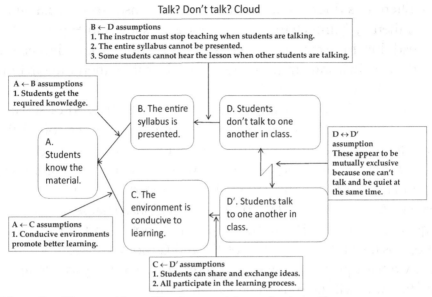

• D jeopardizes C because without talking they cannot share and exchange ideas.
• D′ jeopardizes B because disruptions prevent the instructor from covering the entire syllabus.

Figure 3.29   Talk, Don't Talk Cloud.

Turn the cloud around. Change the arrows.

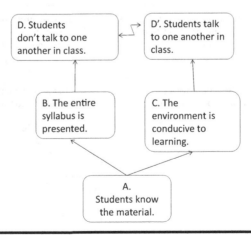

Figure 3.30   Developing the CCRT.

As written, this does not immediately make sense, so we change the logic to "if . . . then . . ." and change a few words as shown in Figure 3.31.

We read this, for example: "If we want students to know the material, and if a conducive environment promotes better learning, then the environment must be conducive to learning."

We now consider the assumptions in Figure 3.29. Instead of separating them from their places, we prefer to look at them with their connections for inserting them into CCRT. We start with the top layer of Figure 3.31.

We add more assumptions and if . . . then . . . pairs (see Figure 3.32), we see in Figure 3.33 that the original conflict leads to UDEs that are the opposite of A, B, C, D, and D′, arranged in regions. That is, the logical consequences of D and D′ are their opposites (not D and not D′), as well as the opposites of A (not A), B (not B), and C (not C). If we don't see these regions, we have probably missed something in our analysis. Organizing the regions this way will help us to create the CCRT.

We see in Figure 3.34 that regions tend to create feedback loops, positive or negative, that work to maintain an undesirable situation. Identifying these is helpful in explaining the situation to others using the CCRT.

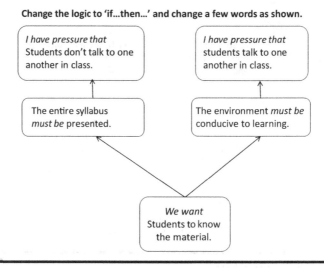

Figure 3.31   **Developing the CCRT (contd.).**

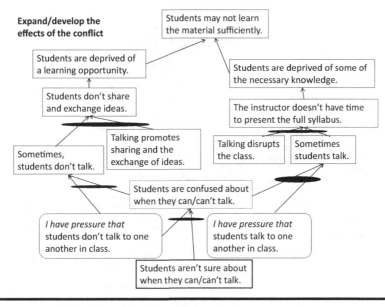

Figure 3.32 Expand/develop the effects of conflict.

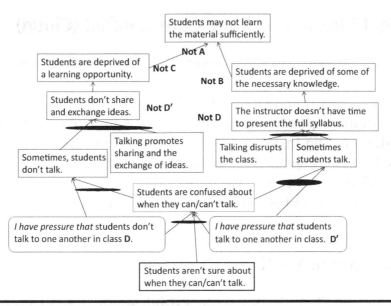

Figure 3.33 Identifying regions of the CCRT.

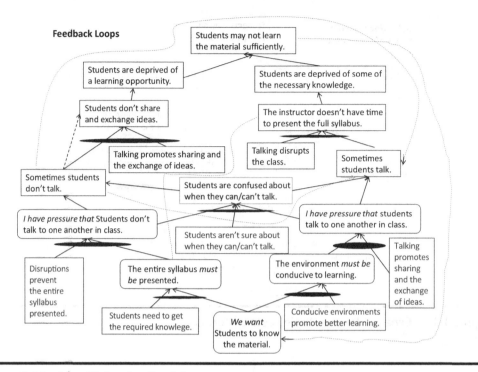

Figure 3.34   Identifying feedback loops.

3.6 Bright Idea to Break the Core Conflict (Cloud)

We now return to our earlier discussion of the Core Conflict. Consider Figure 3.35.

The assumptions D and D′ in Figure 3.25 and repeated in Figure 3.35 indicated that the department could obtain a systemic solution by proposing a Bright Idea* or main injection: "The department offers programs tailored to the needs of its students." This is the start of answering the second basic question, "What to change to?" We started working on the second question from our areas of control and influence, discussed in Chapter 1.

3.7 Application: Writing a Persuasive Essay

The Evaporating Cloud is an excellent thinking process tool for developing a persuasive essay or preparing for a formal (or informal) debate.

---

* The credit for proposing the Bright Idea goes to Darius Movasseghi.

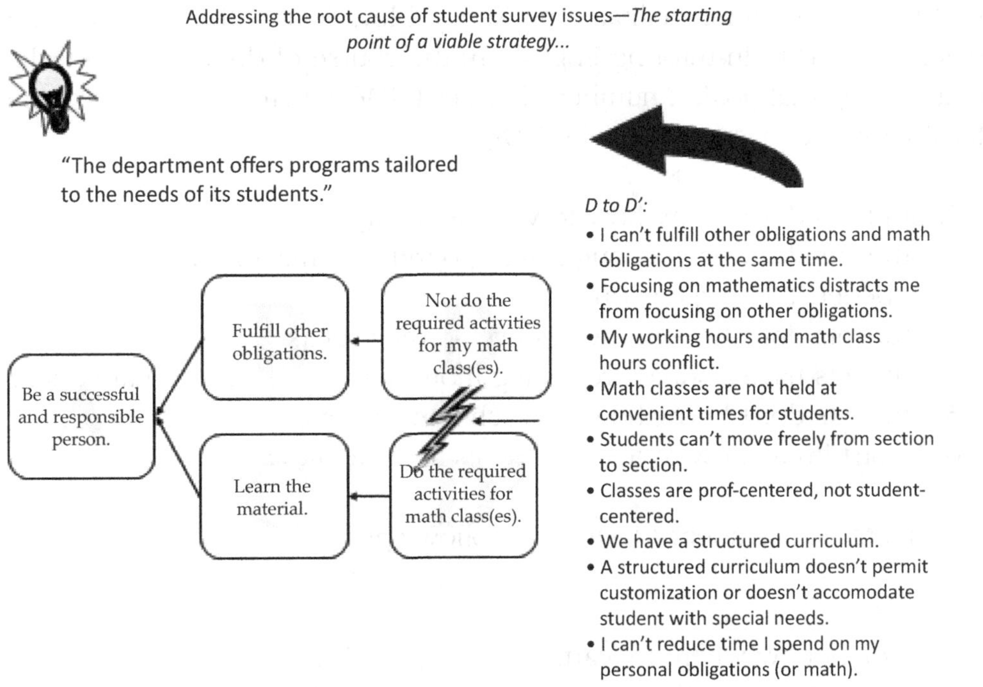

Addressing the root cause of student survey issues—*The starting point of a viable strategy...*

"The department offers programs tailored to the needs of its students."

D to D′:
- I can't fulfill other obligations and math obligations at the same time.
- Focusing on mathematics distracts me from focusing on other obligations.
- My working hours and math class hours conflict.
- Math classes are not held at convenient times for students.
- Students can't move freely from section to section.
- Classes are prof-centered, not student-centered.
- We have a structured curriculum.
- A structured curriculum doesn't permit customization or doesn't accomodate student with special needs.
- I can't reduce time I spend on my personal obligations (or math).

Be a successful and responsible person.

Fulfill other obligations.

Learn the material.

Not do the required activities for my math class(es).

Do the required activities for math class(es).

Figure 3.35   Bright Idea to break the Core Cloud.

It teaches students how to think about both sides of an issue in a structured, methodical, nonemotional way. In the process of working through the Cloud, students come to think clearly and unemotionally about (and therefore state more clearly) the underlying conflict, and are led to propose at least one well-reasoned solution to the problem being discussed. The need to think about both sides of a controversial issue—even if only one side is eventually argued—is certainly not new to college writers/speakers; it is a key to good persuasive writing in all disciplines. However, in contrast to traditional methods of instruction, the TOC approach directly addresses both the intellectual and motivational obstacles articulated by instructors and their students (mentioned in the following) who are faced with the daunting task of having to develop ideas and actually write. The Cloud structure also reduces the stress associated with the inevitable critique from peers and faculty, by focusing on the ideas, not the person presenting them. How to use this technique is illustrated in the following example:

3.7.1 Using TOC to Write a Persuasive Essay

The idea for this application came from an all-day MSEIP grant workshop for Math and English tutors at MEC in March 2012. One of the breakout sessions for the English tutors, facilitated by Nancy Oley, dealt with how to use various tools of TOC in tutoring English. In the course of discussing obstacles to achieving that goal, a number of issues (UDEs) were raised, for example, faculty say the following (faculty UDEs):

1. Students don't know how to write an essay.
2. Students don't have enough background information/facts or personal experience to write about.
3. Students don't know how to develop their ideas.
4. Students have trouble presenting more than one side of an argument.
5. Students don't know how to reach conclusions.
6. I don't know how to teach students to write an essay.

Students say (students' UDEs) the following:

7. I have no ideas.
8. I don't know where to start.
9. I am afraid of writing.
10. I don't like/want to accept criticism.

Leaving aside the outcome of this particular workshop for the moment, let us focus more generally on how TOC can be used to help both students and their instructors overcome their writing UDEs. The persuasive essay is a good place to start. What are the elements of a persuasive essay? According to "Study guides and strategies: persuasive or argumentative essays" (2012), this task involves "establishing facts, clarifying relevant values, prioritizing, sequencing, forming and stating conclusions, logical arguments, and persuading the reader that your conclusions are based on the agreed-upon facts and shared values." TOC provides tools to help students identify values and think logically, and formal structures to assist faculty in teaching those tools. In the following, we outline the steps taken to help students develop a persuasive essay using a Cloud and the negative branch.

Step 1: Generate a topic.

Although students often struggle to find things to write about, they are quick to identify things in their lives—personal, school, work, community, national, and international—that they don't like, the UDEs of their lives. For example, after reading about the life of a young person in prison, a student identified the following UDE about which he felt strongly: "Too many young people are being imprisoned for possession of small amounts of marijuana." This is an issue that has been a topic of current political discourse as well as a familiar event in the communities of many of our students (there were, of course, many other UDEs not discussed here). Having identified an UDE to work with, the student might have to do some research to more precisely define the UDE, for example, What is a small amount of marijuana? What is meant by "possession"?

Step 2: Define the conflict underlying the UDE.

The important next step is to decide what fundamental issue or conflict underlies the UDE. For example, is it the imprisonment? Or is it really the current policy that leads to imprisonment—criminalization of marijuana use? Assuming the latter, and using the Cloud structure, the student is helped to formulate the underlying conflict in terms of D and D′, where D is the want or action advocated by, for example, "the authorities," that caused the UDE, and D′ represents the want or action that the student supports. D and D′ must be logical opposites. That is,

D: "Criminalize small amounts of marijuana."
D′: "Don't criminalize small amounts of marijuana."

We fill in D and D′ in the Cloud structure with these opposite wants as shown in Figure 3.36.

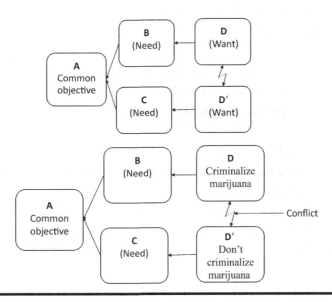

Figure 3.36 Developing the Cloud.

Students might question why both D and D′ must be considered. Whether writers wish to present only one side of the issue or both sides*, they still have to understand and anticipate the arguments of the other side in order to persuade the reader. The nonemotional method of representing issues and examining assumptions using a visually-based Cloud analysis makes this task easier.

Step 3: Identify the common goal and needs.

Part of the persuasive process involves finding common ground, a common goal (A) to which both sides can subscribe and from which the writer can argue his/her position. The student must also develop a good understanding of the needs of both sides (B, C) so as to anticipate and develop the arguments to be made. This can be quite challenging for a student who is strongly committed to one side of the issue and has not thought much about the other side's perspective.

The instructor helps the student to think about what need of the authorities (B) is satisfied by criminalizing marijuana (D). This is done in a nonemotional, analytical way. If the student is unfamiliar with this side, she might have to do some background research on the history of the relevant law in order to develop a reasonable (B). The student will usually have less difficulty identifying what need (C) is satisfied by decriminalizing marijuana (D′), since this is her basic position. For example,

B: "Get marijuana users off the street."
C: "Maximize personal freedom."

Then, the instructor helps the student to think about what common, overarching goal both she and the authorities could possibly share. For example, one such goal might be the following:

A: "Have a harmonious society."

The implications of this shared value might be quite different for the student and the authorities.

The conflict is presented in the more fully developed Cloud in Figure 3.37.

Step 4: Uncover the explicit and implicit assumptions of each side that underlie the conflict.

---

* Research suggests that a "balanced" two-sided argument is more persuasive among more highly educated people than a one-sided one.

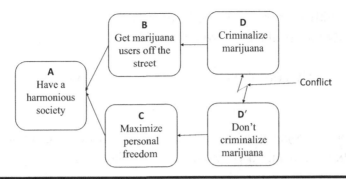

Figure 3.37   Developed Cloud.

To persuade the reader to accept her viewpoint, the student must convince the reader that her own reasoning is correct, but that of the authorities is flawed. In order to do this, the writer must carefully examine all the assumptions underlying her own arguments and try to imagine all the assumptions made by the adversary. The instructor encourages the student to express feelings and thoughts without criticism and helps the student to determine whether or not the assumptions are valid. Many of these assumptions come from just thinking about the situation, but in some instances, the student would need to do some outside research. The research could be online, in the library, and/or interviews with peers or experts. A couple of online sources are in the footnotes of this chapter. It is often helpful if the assumptions are phrased in an exaggerated way—"always," "never," etc. Not all of the assumptions have to be used in the final essay or in the same form. Some possible assumptions of the student and the "authorities" are the following:

A and B: "In order to have a harmonious society, we must get marijuana users off the street because" of the following:

1. People who use small amounts of marijuana are drug users.
2. Drug users always commit crimes.**
3. Drug use always leads to violence.**
4. Drug users never contribute positively to society.**
5. Drug users always disrupt communities.**

A–C: "In order to have a harmonious society, we must maximize personal freedom because" of the following:

1. Societies without personal freedom are never harmonious ones.
2. Governmental regulations are always intrusive and make people unhappy.**
3. People can only contribute positively to society when given their freedom.**

B–D: "In order to get marijuana users off the street, we must criminalize small amounts of marijuana because" of the following:

1. Marijuana use is always a danger to society.**
2. Marijuana users will always go on to use "heavy" drugs.**
3. If there are no users, there will never be dealers.**
4. There is no other way to get users off the street.**
5. By criminalizing marijuana use, there will be many people who can easily be sent to upstate prisons; there are economic incentives to "feed" the "prison–industrial "complex" (Schlosser, 1998).

C and D′: "In order to maximize people's personal freedom, we must not criminalize small amounts of marijuana because" of the following:

1. Small amounts of marijuana are only for personal use.
2. People should always be allowed to ingest any substance that they want to.**
3. People always make good decisions about what is best for them.**
4. The government should never intrude on an individual's behavior that does not hurt others.
5. Marijuana use is never a threat to society.
6. Marijuana is only a recreational drug, like alcohol.
7. Marijuana is not always a gateway drug.

D and D′: "We cannot simultaneously criminalize and decriminalize the use of small amounts of marijuana because" of the following:

1. A law is never ambiguous or logically inconsistent.
2. The Federal and State laws must always be consistent.**

Step 5: Find the flaws in the arguments.

Now, the student must check each assumption to see if it is supported by facts, logic, or common sense. Again, some research may be required.

Suppose, for example, that the assumptions with double asterisk (**)
above are judged by the student to be invalid or at least questionable.
If the invalid assumptions are on the student's side, these are potential
weaknesses in her argument that must be strengthened or avoided in the
essay. If the invalid assumptions are on the adversary's side, these can be
pointed out in the essay to weaken the adversary's position. It is possible
that, having thought through the arguments on the two sides, the student
will decide that the adversary's position is the better one, and adopt that
one.

In the course of examining the assumptions, the student is likely to come
up with some good ideas (Bright Ideas) that will, in essence, resolve the
conflict. For example, take the assumption B–D: "There is no other way to
get users off the street." The student might reason that rather than sending
small-time marijuana users to jail to get them off the street, one could send
them for treatment and educational programs instead. This may be enough
for the student to actually write the essay. However, an even more thorough
analysis can be achieved by thinking through the implications of the conflict. This is discussed in Step 6.

Step 6: Identify and remove the negative consequences of criminalization.

This step involves the negative branch. Once the student has become
engaged in the issue, it will not be difficult for her to think of many negative
things (UDEs) that occur as a result of criminalization of small amounts of
marijuana, the D in the Cloud. Some of these are below:

1. Young people are sent to prison for long terms.
2. Young people's education is disrupted.
3. Families are torn apart.
4. Whole communities are disrupted.
5. Young people have a criminal record.
6. People can't get jobs when they are released.
7. Convicted persons can't vote.
8. Young people are negatively influenced by hardened criminals.
9. Upstate prisons are overcrowded.
10. The economic benefits are moved outside of the communities to the
    prison towns.

Using sufficiency, if–then, logic, the student connects these UDEs to D
to create a negative branch. These UDEs and their logical relationship can
be mentioned in the essay. By "injecting" the Bright Idea—decriminalize

small amounts of marijuana and get drug users off the street by putting them into treatment, the student can "trim" this negative branch to create a better *future reality*. In summary, by following these steps, the student develops some basic arguments for the essay in a formal, structured, logical, nonemotional way, thus overcoming UDE nos. 2, 3, 4, 5, 7, 8, 9, and 10. The student identifies the hot button issues, the strengths and weaknesses of both positions, and at least one alternative action that would resolve the conflict. This process involves establishing facts, clarifying relevant values, and sequencing, forming, and stating conclusions and logical arguments. At this point, faculty expertise will overcome UDE nos. 1 and 6 as the student puts the Cloud and negative branch analysis into narrative form in step 7.

Step 7: Create an outline using a rubric for the persuasive essay.*

Of course, there are many ways to structure a persuasive essay, and this outline could certainly be improved with the instructor's assistance. If the outline is carefully prepared using complete sentences, the final paper will practically write itself. A similar TOC approach could also be used to prepare for a traditional debate.

3.7.2 Sample Outline of a Persuasive Essay Based on a Cloud Analysis

I. The central idea of this essay is that small amounts of marijuana should be decriminalized in favor of educational programs and treatment, as needed.
   A. Describe the nature of the problem: Describe the demographics of people being arrested and imprisoned for possession of small amounts of marijuana (taken from D in the Cloud).
      1. Define *small amounts*.
      2. Define *possession*.
      3. Give a brief history of the relevant law.
   B. Indicate that it's a serious problem: Criminalization is a serious problem because of all the negative consequences arising from incarcerating youthful marijuana users (UDEs from step 6; this could be further developed into a full-fledged negative branch if the UDEs were organized using sufficiency logic).

---

* For more information, see Polak, A. & Collins, J. Hamilton writing resources: Persuasive essays. http://www.hamilton.edu/writing/writing-resources/persuasive-essays.

1. Young people are sent to prison for unfairly long terms.
   a. Give data/examples*
2. Young people's education is disrupted.
   a. Give data/examples
3. Families are torn apart.
   a. Give data/examples
4. Whole communities are disrupted.
   a. Give data/examples
5. Young people have a criminal record.
6. Convicts can't get jobs when they are released.
   a. Give data/examples
7. Convicts can't vote.
   a. Give data/examples
8. Young people are negatively influenced by hardened criminals.
   a. Give data/examples
9. Upstate prisons are overcrowded.
   a. Give data/examples
10. The economic benefits are moved outside of the communities to the prison towns.
    a. Give data/examples

II. Show how this problem can be solved: Decriminalization will eliminate these negative consequences (trimming the negative branch).
   A. Establish common ground from which to argue.
      1. Both marijuana users and the authorities share the goal of wanting to have a harmonious society (taken from "A" in the Cloud).
   B. Show the flaws in the thinking of the authorities.
      1. State the opposition's position: The authorities might argue that they must remove all drug users, including small-time marijuana users, from the streets in order to have a harmonious society because of the following (assumptions for A and B):
         a. They are violent
            (1) Cite evidence against this argument: Evidence suggests that this is not true.
         b. They commit crimes
            (1) Cite evidence against this argument.

---

* The addition of data/examples should be extended to the entire outline.

    c. They don't contribute positively to society
      (1) Cite evidence against this argument.
    d. They disrupt communities
      (1) Cite evidence against this argument.

2. In order to get marijuana users off the streets, the authorities believe that we must criminalize possession of marijuana (and put offenders in jail) because of the following (assumptions for B–D):

    a. Marijuana users will always go on to use heavy drugs.*
      (1) Cite evidence against this argument.[†]
    b. If there are no users, there will never be dealers.
      (1) Cite evidence against this argument.
    c. There is no other way to get users off the street** (this is the assumption that led to the Bright Idea in the Cloud).
    d. By criminalizing marijuana use, there will be many people who can easily be sent to upstate prisons; there are economic incentives to feed the "prison–industrial complex."[‡]

3. The arguments used to support criminalization are not supported by facts, common sense, and/or logic.

C. Argue the position of those in favor of decriminalization.

1. We must maximize personal freedom in order to have a harmonious society because of the following:

    a. A society cannot be harmonious without it (taken from assumptions A–C).[§]

2. Marijuana use is an expression of personal freedom (taken from assumptions C and D′).[¶]

---

* For more information on this argument, see Golub, A. & Johnson, B.D. (1994, September). The shifting importance of alcohol and marijuana as gateway substances among serious drug abusers. *Journal of Studies on Alcohol and Drugs, 55.* Retrieved from http://www.jsad.com/jsad/article/The_Shifting_Importance_of_Alcohol_and_Marijuana_as_Gateway_Substances_amon/2059.html

[†] The study cited in support of the idea that marijuana is a gateway drug was a retrospective study showing that people who become hard drug users were more likely to have begun with marijuana than with alcohol. This does not mean that marijuana users are more likely to become hard drug users than are cigarette smokers or drinkers.

[‡] For more information, see Schlosser, E. (1998, December, Digital Archive). The prison-industrial complex. *The Atlantic.* Retrieved from http://www.theatlantic.com/magazine/toc/1998/12.

[§] As can be seen, many, but not all, of the assumptions and arguments developed by doing the Cloud were included by the writer in the final essay.

[¶] Note that the writer has decided to rephrase some of the questionable assumptions and to include them in his argument.

       a. Small amounts of marijuana are only for personal use.

       b. People should be allowed to ingest any nonpoisonous substances that they want to.

       c. People usually make good decisions about what is best for them.

       d. The government should never intrude on an individual's behavior that does not hurt others.

   3. Marijuana use is not a danger to society (taken from assumptions C and D').

       a. Marijuana is only a recreational drug, like alcohol.

       b. Marijuana is not always a gateway drug.

   4. Therefore, marijuana use should be decriminalized.

III. Conclusion—restate the what and how of the arguments, describe the implications, and offer some new insight: It is possible to satisfy both sides' *needs*:

   A. By decriminalizing small amounts of marijuana possession, the negative consequences of criminalization will be removed and personal freedom will be maximized.

   B. At the same time, the need of the authorities to get marijuana users off the street will be satisfied if marijuana (ab)users are put into treatment and educational programs, if warranted, instead of jail (Bright Idea from the Cloud).

      1. Give examples of successful programs.

   C. This would be a win–win solution for both sides, and a harmonious society would result.

3.8 Summary of How to Break a Conflict

We can summarize "breaking a conflict" Cloud in the following manner.

In any Cloud, make sure that want D' jeopardizes need B and want D jeopardizes need C. Since the needs are more general than wants, they should never clash with each other. There are four ways to break the conflict as shown in Figure 3.38.

   Method 1. Here, D is negated. D' fulfills both needs B and C. Surface the assumptions B–D, and argue why D' no longer jeopardizes B.

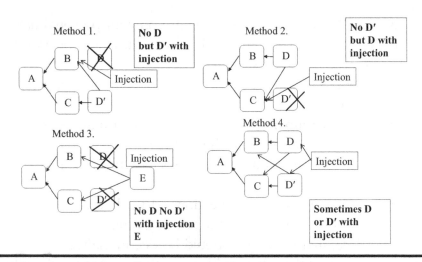

Figure 3.38 Conflict resolution: four ways of breaking the conflict. *From a presentation by Alan Barnard at the 10th International TOCfE Conference, 2007, Fort Walton Beach, FL.*

The following are examples:

1. Empowering a person at work (Example 3.6, Figure 3.17)
2. A student's dilemma—chronic conflict (Example 3.4, Figure 3.9)
3. Instructor's Communication Problem (Example 3.1)

Method 2. Here, D′ is negated. D fulfills both needs B and C. Argue why D no longer jeopardizes C.

The following are examples for empowerment Clouds:

Empowering a student to select a major (Example 3.5, Figure 3.17)

Method 3. Here, D and D′ are both allowed, but at different specific times and for specific purposes.

The following are examples:

1. Instructor's Cloud: "Talk, No Talk" (Example 3.3, Figure 3.10)

These examples indicate that a written or unwritten policy sometimes creates an UDE, and by changing the policy, a resolution of the resulting conflict can be achieved.

Method 4. Here, D and D′ are both negated, and an action E fulfills both needs B and C.

The following are examples:
1. Various clouds used in developing the CCRT (Example 3.7, Figures 3.22, 3.23, 3.24, 3.25)

3.9 Summary of Steps to Answer the Question, "What to Change?"

For an individual conflict, use an EC and surface the various assumptions underlying the connections: A ← B, A ← C, B ← D, C ← D′ and D ↔ D′ and propose injections.

For system-wide institutional problem solving, the next diagram (Figure 3.39) summarizes the steps that we follow to answer the first question of TOC:

0. Define the system, the areas of control and influence, and the goal. List issues as UDEs.

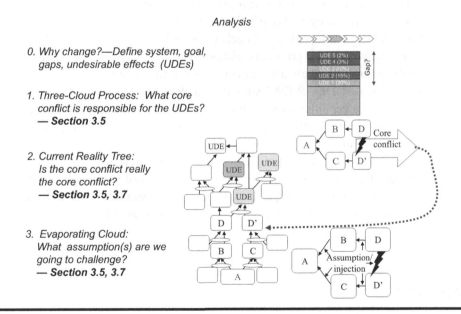

Figure 3.39 Answering question 1: what to change? In step 0, "Gap" represents expectations. Graphic for step 0 courtesy of Alan Barnard. Steps 1, 2, 3 and graphics courtesy of AGI.

1. Select three representative UDEs. Form an EC for each. Find the Core (Generic) Cloud.
2. Form a CCRT (Core Current Reality Tree) connecting the Core Cloud with all UDEs.
3. Surface the assumptions for each of the three Clouds, which should also work for the Core Cloud.
4. Provide a Bright Idea—an injection to break the core conflict.

Exercises

1. Select a case study on a Cloud from http://www.tocforeducation.com, and write it in your own words.
2. Write about your experiences in your chosen major. List all issues that you think get in the way of your graduating in your major. Write them as UDEs. Work with members of your group, and check the UDEs to see that they conform to the definition of an UDE.
3. Collect and write the various definitions of injections given in this chapter. We had to modify some definitions given in the TOCICO dictionary of terms, since the given definition did not cover all cases.
4. Pick one thing in everyday life that bothers you. Write a storyline using PowerPoint. Develop an EC. Check your logic to see whether it flows smoothly. Work with your classmates. Surface the assumptions underlying the arrows. Suggest injections to resolve the conflict.
5. Write a list of UDEs of the issues in your larger *system* from the points of view of three different stakeholders. From the most important three UDEs and their Clouds, prepare a Core Conflict Cloud. Surface the assumptions and suggest injections.
6. Write a summary of conflict resolution–decision making.
7. Consider the CRT developed based on the issues of basic skills courses instructors given in Example 2.2. Select three systemic UDEs and the core Cloud. Develop a Bright Idea to break the core Cloud.

References

Study guides and strategies: Persuasive or argumentative essays. (2012). Retrieved from http://www.studygs.net/wrtstr4.htm.

Cox III, J.F., Boyd, L.H., Sullivan, T.T., Reid, R.A., & Cartier, B. (2012). *The Theory of Constraints International Certification Organization Dictionary*, 2nd ed. NY: McGraw Hill.

Hetmanczyk-Bajer, H. (n.d.). The usage of the Theory of Constraints in the process of shaping social competencies of primary school pupils. Retrieved February 2, 2017, from http://www.TOCforEducation.com/research.html.

Nagarkatte, U. (2012). Motivational guide. Retrieved January 22, 2017, from www.TOCforCollege.com: http://www.tocforcollege.com/motivational-guide .html.

Schlosser, E. (1998). The prison-industrial complex. *The Atlantic*. Retrieved from http://www.theatlantic.com/magazine/toc/1998/12.

Chapter 4

What to Change to?

4.1 Overview

This chapter answers the second question: What to change to? The answer is the strategy of TOC solution. At this point, let us review what we have learned so far. In Chapter 1, we saw by way of an example why TOC can be called a theory of empowerment. TOC is based on conditional logic. There are two conditions: a necessary condition and a sufficient condition. A necessary condition requires the use of the connective "In order to … we must have. … " A sufficient condition involves the connective "If … then. … " We saw several examples of these. We also noted the categories of logical reservation for a sufficient condition statement. We saw how we routinely use sufficient condition logic in our day-to-day activities. People confuse necessary and sufficient conditions; this in itself becomes a cause for conflict. We defined *UDEs* and *DEs*, the logical opposites of UDEs. UDEs show us the current reality which may be miserable, and DEs show us what the positive future reality can be. In Chapter 2, we discussed sufficient condition logic in detail, the CRT (TP tool), and the branch. In several examples, we saw how powerful the branch is for resolving conflicts. We studied the negative branch TP tool, and the Negative Branch Reservation (NBR) that is developed by questioning the validity of a conditional statement. We also studied the TP tool intervention called an *injection* to trim the negative branch and the positive branch, where DEs are the results and injections are the causes. We showed how the positive branch becomes a logically robust tree. In Chapter 3, we studied a TP tool called the Evaporating Cloud (EC) or Cloud or Conflict Cloud, based on necessary condition logic. We saw in one application how to use EC to develop a persuasive essay. We studied various types of Clouds to resolve day-to-day and chronic conflicts. We saw how a Cloud can be used to empower people by challenging their confining assumptions, thus giving rise to an "out-of-the box" thinking and encouraging them to explore new horizons. In the earlier chapters, we thus developed three TOC/TP tools based on the two types of logic. In Chapter 4, we use another TP tool, the "Future Reality Tree (FRT)," to answer the second question of TOC, "What to change to?" This TP tool is based on sufficient condition logic. In Chapter 2, we touched on it briefly in terms of the positive branch.

If an UDE indicates a negative effect in a CRT, its logical opposite, a DE, (already considered in Chapter 2) indicates a positive effect in an FRT and tells us what to change to. All the DEs that arise from the core conflict, as discussed in Section 3.5, make up the FRT. But a DE by itself may be just wishful thinking or fantasy, popularly called by TOC people a "flying pig." Injections or interventions or actions must be introduced to make the DEs possible. In Section 4.2, we discuss a positive branch.

In Section 4.3, we again study half-baked solutions and the NBR. Some positive measures or injections being proposed to attain DEs might have negative consequences. Therefore, the entities of the FRT must be scrutinized using NBR.

In Section 4.4, we describe as an example the experience of the Department of Mathematics at Medgar Evers College of The City University of New York (CUNY). In Section 4.5, we discuss the FRT based on the DEs and strategic objectives (SOs) in the example.

The steps for answering the second question, "What to change to?," the theme of Chapter 4, are summarized in Section 4.6.

4.2 Positive Branch

Example 4.1: How Faculty and Counselors Can Reinforce a Student's Positive Experiences (Intervention to Sustain a Positive Branch)

We saw in Example 2.1 the following UDEs of a student:

1. I cannot follow the lecture.
2. I feel that I am not capable of doing mathematics.
3. I do not work hard in mathematics.
4. I don't do the homework or prepare for the course.
5. I do poorly on tests.

6. I feel that the exam is too hard.
7. I have difficulty learning the material (in math classes).
8. I have difficulty taking tests.

As shown in **Table 4.1**, from the UDEs, we can formulate desirable experiences by effects or DEs. These are the logical opposite of the experiences that he or she currently has.

Then, we use a branch to connect the DEs logically with if ... then ... logic. Figure 4.1 shows this positive branch or FRT. The FRT answers the question "What to change to?"

Table 4.1   Undesirable Effects (UDEs) and Desirable Effects (DEs)

UDEs	DEs
1. I cannot follow the lecture.	1. I follow the lecture.
2. I perceive that I am not capable of doing mathematics.	2. I am capable of doing mathematics.
3. I do not work hard in mathematics.	3. I work hard in mathematics.
4. I don't have time to do the homework or prepare for the course.	4. I find time to do the homework and prepare for the course.
5. I do poorly on tests.	5. I do well on tests.
6. I feel that the exam is too hard.	6. I feel that the exam is reasonable.
7. I have difficulty learning the material (in math classes).	7. I do not have difficulty in learning math.
8. I have difficulty taking tests.	8. I do not have difficulty taking tests.

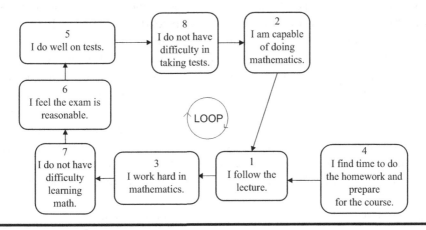

Figure 4.1   What to change to? (FRT).

The numbers refer to the original UDEs, not the order of entities. The loop in Figure 4.1 needs to be sustained. This branch seems to be only wishful thinking. In order to make it his/her actual experience, the student needs to take certain steps. This involves considering what is called the Prerequisite Tree (PRT) or Ambitious Target Tree (ATT). The PrT is discussed in detail in Chapter 5, but take a quick look at Example 5.3 for an idea of what this involves.

4.3 Half-Baked Solutions

A half-baked solution is a solution whose consequences have not been thought through completely. We discussed some half-baked solutions in Chapter 2. These solutions often lead to unanticipated negative results. Before taking any action, if you study the many possible consequence branches, you can avoid any potential negative consequences and find some actions which can reinforce the positive consequences. Using the NBR TP tool, your solutions to problems will not be half-baked solutions.

Example 4.2: A Realistic Course Load: Trimming a Negative Branch

The following example is one component of our effort to address student attrition in mathematics courses and college in general. We will consider the NBRs for a branch in an abbreviated FRT. The actual FRT is very long and beyond the scope of this text. The entity that we want to consider is the result in Figure 4.2 (realistic course load).

The scenario is as follows: Many students take a course load that they cannot manage due to their personal circumstances or course prerequisites. They come late and miss classes. For example, some students take a course load which is made up of all hard courses, instead of balancing their course load with some easy and some hard courses. The mentor's injection was to advise students to have a realistic course load. However, due to how the department schedules courses, it may be impossible for a student to sign up for a realistic load. Along with this injection, the department's injection was that "classes are scheduled to accommodate students." These injections led to the DE that students are punctual and attend all classes. The fact of life acknowledges the fact that a full-time student pays a flat fee per semester; however, the financial need of the student and need to work and earn money must be considered in a part-time student's workload (see Figure 4.2).

In Figure 4.3, we outline the negative consequences of the result: "Students have realistic schedules." We discussed this NBR in Section 2.5.1 in Chapter 2,

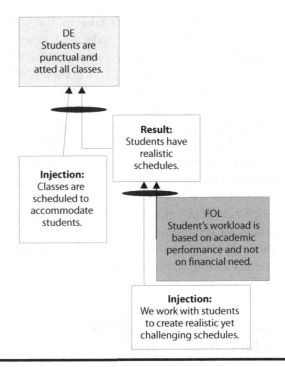

Figure 4.2   Realistic course load. FOL means fact of life.

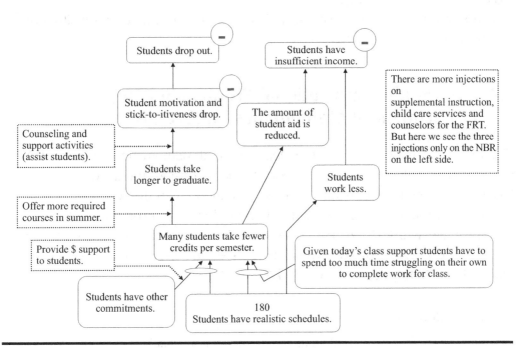

Figure 4.3   Example: NBRs on injection "Students have realistic schedules."

but here, we discuss it in detail. By realistic, we mean that science students balance their science and nonscience—hard and easy courses—in such a way that they can successfully carry out all of the course activities without overloading themselves. If a student has received an incomplete (INC) grade in a course taken during the previous semester/s, that course needs to be added to the course load, even though the student does not register for it. If a student has responsibility for his/her family, this time needs to be considered in developing the workload along with the time needed for homework.

Figure 4.3 shows how "Students having realistic schedules" could lead to negative effects such as reducing motivation, students having insufficient income, and students dropping out. We can trim this negative branch using various injections described by rectangles such as "Provide $ (monetary) support to students' to prevent the negative effects."

In short, the development of a positive branch must be accompanied by a NBR analysis. The positive loops which we usually find in an FRT need to be sustained.

4.3.1 Future Reality Tree (FRT) or Positive Branch as a Stand-Alone Tool

We have shown a Future Reality Tree (FRT) for a simple situation. If this satisfies your need, you can skip the rest of Chapter 4 and proceed to Chapter 5 (How to Cause a Change?).

If not, read on to learn how an FRT can be used in a complex situation to link injections to the DEs.

4.4 Case Study—Institutional Problem Solving: Department of Mathematics, MEC/CUNY

This material was presented by the Department of Mathematics at the 9th TOCfE International Conference, 2006, in Leon, Mexico. Consider the list of issues as UDEs in Chapter 1, Section 1.2.4, relisted here along with the respective DEs in Figures 4.4 through 4.6. Recall that the DEs are logical opposites of UDEs.

When we want Desirable Effects to be sustained and to become part of the culture of the institution, we call them Strategic Objectives (SOs), as in Figures 4.7 and 4.8.

Definition 4.1

SOs are the long-term goals that are attained automatically, as a result of consistent attainment of DEs.

Students' issues	Desired effects (DEs)
1. The instructor moves too fast for students.	1. **The instructor moves at a comfortable pace.**
2. The instructor cannot teach.	2. **Students are satisfied with the instructor's teaching style.**
3. Students are not capable of doing mathematics.	3. **Students do mathematics well.**
4. Students are not prepared for course (prerequisites for class).	4. **Students have all prerequisites for the course.**
5. I don't have time to do the homework.	5. **Students finish all homework on time.**
6. I don't see the importance/relevance of the mathematics.	6. **Students feel math is relevant for their career.**
7. I am unable to attend class regularly and/or on time.	7. **Students are punctual.**
8. Students do poorly on tests.	8. **Students do well on tests.**
9. I have to take care of my family/personal problems.	9. **I take care of my family/personal problems.**
11. The instructor does not care about me.	11. **The instructor helps me to keep up with the course.**
12. There isn't help outside of class when I'm free.	12. **There is adequate help when I need it.**
13. (I don't know how to graduate from college).	13. **I have sufficient knowledge/help to plan my college career.**
14. My course load is too heavy (I'm forced to be full time in order to get financial aid).	14. **I can handle my course load.**
15. I do not know how to get good grades in important courses.	15. **I get good grades in important courses.**
19. I cannot drop a class without jeopardizing my financial aid.	19. **I do not need to drop any class.**
20. I am forced to ask for incompletes.	20. **I am able to complete the course.**

Figure 4.4   Student's issues and DEs.

Faculty issues	Desired effects (DEs)
21. Students do not prepare for class.	
22. Students don't attend regularly or on time.	
23. Students do poorly on tests.	
24. There is not sufficient time to cover all material in the course.	24. There is sufficient time to cover all material in the course.
25. Students register late for the semester and don't start at the beginning of the semester.	25. All students begin at the start of the semester.
26. Students do not have prerequisites for class.	
Department chair issues	
27. There is a lack of cooperation by some faculty to carry out the departmental agenda.	
28. Too many students fail.	28. There is a high rate of passing.
29. There is insufficient input by some faculty to address major departmental issues.	
30. Some faculty are apathetic.	

Figure 4.5   Faculty and Chair issues and DEs.

Additional issues (reselected)	Desired effects (DEs)
33. There are too many incompletes.	**33. There are very few incompletes.**
35. Students don't graduate from college on time.	**35. Most students graduate on time.**
36. Dropout rates (in class) are too high.	**36. Few students drop out of classes.**
37. Level of achievement is too low in classes.	**37. Student achievement is high.**
38. The exams are too hard.	

Figure 4.6   Additional issues (reselected) and DEs.

Desired effects (DEs)	Strategic objectives (SOs) (examples)
24. There is sufficient time to cover all material in the course.	
25. All students begin at the start of the semester.	
28. There is a high rate of passing.	**28. Everyone passes.**
33. There are very few incompletes.	**33. There are absolutely no incompletes.**
34. Most students graduate on time.	
35. Few students drop out of classes.	
36. Student achievement is high.	**36. Retention in the department/program is high.**
37. Students perform well on exams.	

Figure 4.7   DEs and SOs.

The DEs and SOs along with appropriate injections form an FRT. The injections are called tactical objectives (TOs) in an FRT. The actual FRT and discussion are given in Section 4.5.

Desired effects (DEs)	Strategic objectives (SOs) (S—Student, D—Department, C—College)
1. The instructor moves at a comfortable pace.	1. The instructor allows time for review/enrichment (SD).
2. Students are satisfied with the instructor's teaching style	2. Students seek to take more courses in mathematics (D).
3. Students do mathematics well.	3. Students become math majors (DSC).
4. Students have all prerequisites for the course.	
5. Students finish all homework on time.	
6. Students feel math is relevant for their career.	6. Students incorporate math in their careers and in daily life (D).
7. Students are punctual.	
8. Students do well on tests.	8. More students pass the course (DC).
9. I have to take care of my family/personal problems.	9. I take care of my family/personal problems (S).
11. The instructor helps me to keep up with the course.	
12. There is adequate help when I need it.	
13. I have sufficient knowledge/help to plan my college career.	13. Students graduate on time/complete math course requirements (SDC).
14. I can handle my course load.	14. I can take extra credits (financial aid) (S).
15. I get good grades in important courses.	15. I get excellent grades in all courses (S).
19. I do not need to drop any class.	19. I can perform better in the course (S).
20. I am able to complete the course.	20. I ACE the course! (S).
	21. The department is a center of excellence (D).

Figure 4.8   DEs and SOs for students, department, and college.

4.5 Partial FRT for the Department of Mathematics

The base of the FRT shown in Figure 4.9 is the *Bright Idea* or *Great Idea* used to break the Core Cloud as discussed in Section 3.6. The Bright Idea is called the strategic injection (SI). The SI for the Department of Mathematics study was "The department offers programs tailored to the needs of its students." The SI, to begin with, is a general solution. We needed to expand it and make it specific. Thus, several specific injections were introduced.

The examples are as follows:

100: SI Bright Idea: department offers programs tailored to the needs of students.

105: We have ideal financial, academic, supplemental instruction, career, personal, and counseling support when needed.

110: The department provides faculty guidelines for instruction.

165: Advisors advise students to have realistic course loads.

The gray boxes in Figures 4.9 and 4.10 are DEs, and unshaded boxes are injections called Tactical Objectives (TOs), for the FRT. TOs become the goals or ambitious targets for PrTs to be discussed in Chapter 5.

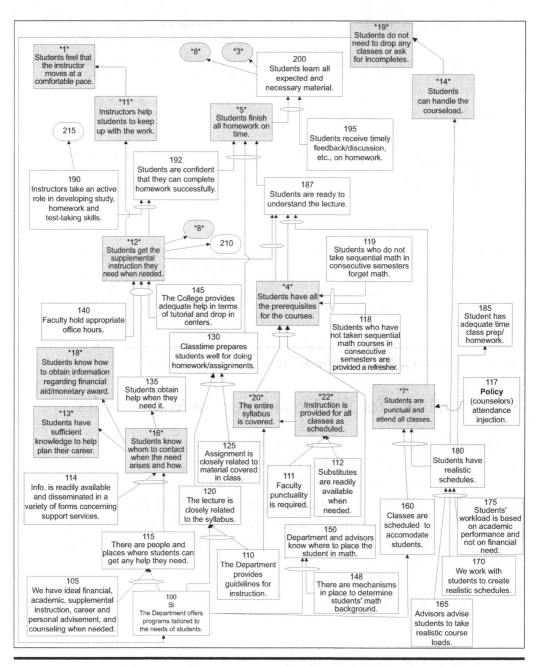

Figure 4.9   Part of the FRT.

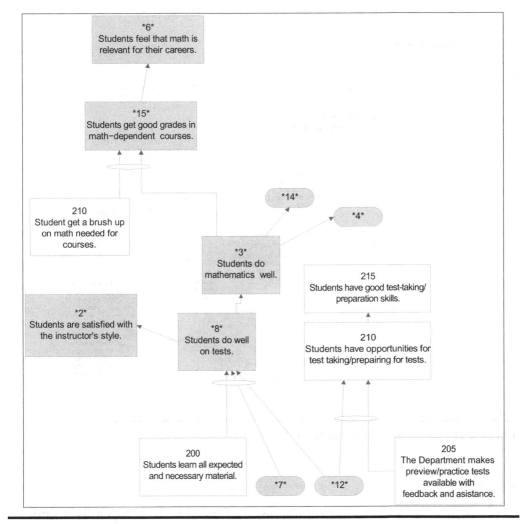

Figure 4.10   Students' part of FRT.

The interested reader can request the entire CRT and FRT from the first author.

We also looked for different sustaining loops in the FRT which could be reinforced as shown in Figure 4.11.

4.6 Summary of the Steps Needed to Answer the Second Basic Question: What to Change to?

The answer to this question is the Strategy for a TOC solution (Figure 4.12).

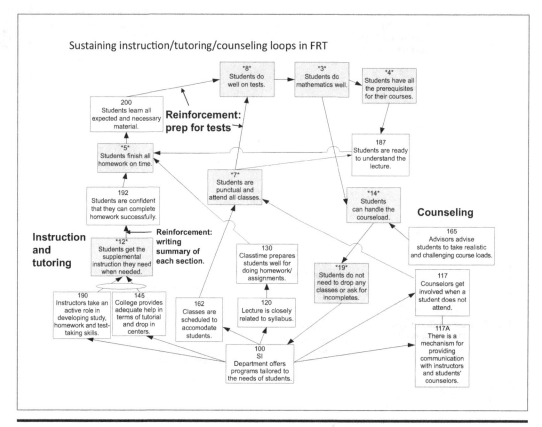

Figure 4.11 Sustaining loops in the FRT.

Exercises

1. Take any UDE to represent the issue of the day. Develop a list of negative consequences arising out of the UDE. This is a negative branch. Trim the negative branch with one or more injections.

2. Form a DE from your UDE. Develop a list of positive consequences from the DE. This is a positive branch. Describe one or more injections that will help to sustain the positive branch.

3. Form a set of DEs for the following set of UDEs:
   a. Students do not keep the area clean.
   b. Administrators do not respect me.
   c. The nonacademic challenges of students are often not addressed.
   d. The difference between an academic advisor and a counselor is not known.
   e. More and more students have mental health challenges.
   f. There are many turf wars among departments.

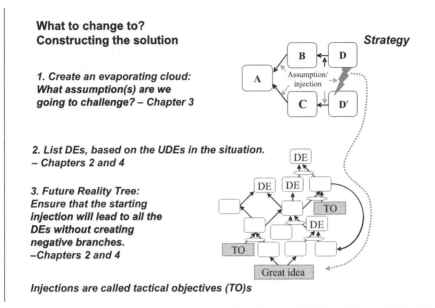

Figure 4.12   What to change to? (Courtesy of Avraham Goldratt Institute [AGI], New Haven, CT.)

g. Students don't see connections.

h. The student services department experiences many disruptions.

i. Students come to school hungry (no food, transportation, etc.)

j. College faculty are dismissive of students' personal issues.

k. Students who identify as lesbian, gay, bisexual or transgender are victimized.

l. Part-time faculty often do not attend to students' needs.

m. Some students fall between the cracks (e.g., first-year student seminar is not required of all students).

n. There is a large dropout rate in science classes.

o. There is inconsistency of outcomes from first-year student classes.

p. Staff morale is low.

4. Try to connect as many UDEs as possible and develop a CRT. Change the UDEs to DEs and then try to connect as many DEs as possible and develop an FRT.

Chapter 5

How to Cause the Change? Prerequisite Tree, Project Plan, and Transition Tree

5.1 Overview

This chapter answers the third basic question: How to cause the change? The answer provides the tactics of the theory of constraint (TOC) solution for a personal or institutional problem. The TP tools required here are the Prerequisite Tree (PrT), a project plan, and the Transition Tree (TrT). Recall that we developed a strategy in Chapters 2 through 4, by answering the first two questions of TOC: (a) what to change? and (b) what to change to? We can implement our strategy using tactics by learning the TP tools discussed in this chapter.

In Section 5.2, we develop the concept of a PrT. In order to achieve goals that at first glance seem unreachable, one needs to use the PrT, also known as the Ambitious Target Tree (ATT). A PrT is based on necessity condition logic and can be used as a stand-alone tool, for example, to construct a syllabus. We describe several simple examples of a PrT. In Section 5.3, we discuss how to plan a project once we have developed a PrT. Using a project plan, you will see how to do well in a course using a class lecture schedule. You will also see a game of multitasking. In Section 5.4, we discuss a case study. In Section 5.5, we will describe the concept of *Critical Chain Project*

Management (CCPM)* for managing a course successfully. In Section 5.5, we consider an institutional example of a PrT in a complex case derived from our institutional Future Reality Tree (FRT) discussed in Chapter 4. Section 5.7 deals with the TrT. The TrT gives a detailed step-by-step action plan without logical gaps. The difference between a project plan and an action plan is the amount of detail. Each task in a project plan gives rise to an action plan. Section 5.8 summarizes how to answer the third question, and Section 5.9 gives the complete TOC roadmap to resolve conflicts, make decisions, and solve problems, whether the problem is personal or institutional. Appendix 5.1 describes a TOC college course entitled, "The Creative Thinker's Toolkit."

5.2 Simple Examples

In overview, to develop a PrT or ATT, start with a simple statement of your goal or Ambitious Target (AT). Then, make a list of all the obstacles (Obs) to reaching that goal. Prepare a list of intermediate objectives (IOs) related to the Obs. An intermediate objective (IO) is usually the logical opposite of the obstacle, but not always. See Table 5.1. Logically connect the IOs using necessary condition logic: "Before I have this . . ., I must first have. . . ."

Step 1: State the AT and prepare a list of Obs.
There could be any number of Obs, not just 9 or 10.
We have observed in our teaching the ATT that our students find stating the IOs to be the hardest part. We want to make it clear that each obstacle needs at least one IO and that the IO is not a *specific* action but it is a state or condition that would exist if the obstacle had been overcome. A state does not take time. (Note that an IO is attained by performing an action which does take time). The actions not shown here are performed successively according to the logically listed IOs to achieve the ambitious target. To get an IO, make a statement logically opposite to the corresponding obstacle.

---

* For additional information on this topic, see Newbold, R. (2008). *The Billion Dollar Solution: Secrets of Prochain Project Management.* Lake Ridge, VA: Prochain Press.

Table 5.1   Step 1: Stating the AT and Preparing a List of Obs and IOs
AT: _____

Obstacle to Reaching Target (Obs)	Intermediate Objective (IO)
1	1
2	2
3	3
4	4
5	5
6	6
7	7
8	8
9	9
10 cont'd	10 cont'd

Step 2: Connect IOs (not Obs) logically, from bottom to top, using arrows to show the flow of the necessary condition logic in the PrT/ATT. Be attentive to the direction of the arrows!

The result is called an IO map. Drawing an IO map is optional, as long as the flow of logic is clear.

Step 3: Plan activities or actions to achieve each IO.

We have several examples of the ATT or PrT, starting with a very simple one.

Sometimes, we shorten this process by just listing the intermediate objectives and the respective activities to overcome them. Then, we connect the activities logically.

Example 5.1: AT: We Will Fry an Egg

This simple example (Table 5.2) was developed to help teach the PrT to Introductory Psychology students by Nancy Oley.

Sample PrT/ATT: We develop an IO map in Figure 5.1 by arranging the IOs (or activities in this simple example) in logical order.

We read the tree from top to bottom: Before I have 3, I must have 1 and 2. Thus, 1 and 2 are necessary conditions for 3. In other words, before we cook an egg, we must have/buy eggs and we must have oil. In order to develop a more complete ATT, however, we need to add in some details or missing steps as shown in Figure 5.2. They are numbered without the

Table 5.2 Example to Help Teach the PrT to Introductory Psychology Students
AT: We Will Fry an Egg

Obs	IOs
1. We do not have eggs.	1. We have eggs.
2. We do not have oil.	2. We have oil.
3. Eggs are not cooked.	3. Eggs are cooked.

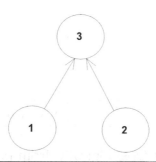

Figure 5.1   IO map for the activities.

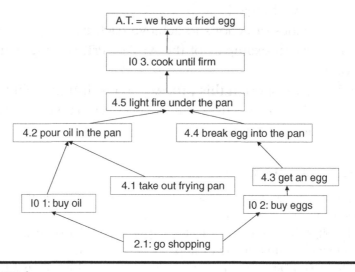

Figure 5.2   ATT: fry an egg.

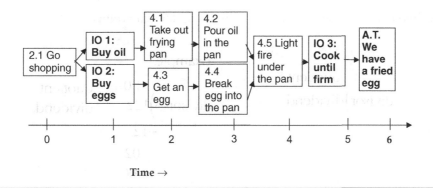

Figure 5.3   Project plan: fry an egg.

IO label. We do not use a banana in an IO map or ATT /PrT as we did in sufficiency logic, since both 1 and 2 are necessary and independent and not additional causes or prerequisites of 3.

The numbers in the previous ATT are for convenience only and have no meaning except that they relate to IO 3. The arbitrary numbers 4.1, 4.2, 4.3, 4.4, and 4.5 are added actions to achieve the goal 3, but some actions could be done before others, such as 4.5 before 4.4. Many people in fact do that.

As shown in Figure 5.3, if rotated 90° to the right and read from left to right with the first IO at time 0, the ATT/PrT also serves as a general time-line for a project plan, that is, a logical series of IOs. One or more specific actions may be required to achieve each IO. However, for simplicity's sake, we will call the IOs the *actions* in this context.*

On the time axis, note that once IO 3 is attained, we have reached the AT.

Example 5.2: Long Division of Whole Numbers

Students often have a difficult time in doing long division in arithmetic. The following ATT was developed to help students understand this topic.†
Suppose that Pat does not know how to perform long division of whole numbers. Jana, the teacher, and Pat worked together to come up with the following ATT and action plan. Note that one IO for each Ob is a must, but sometimes, several more IOs are necessary.

---

* Technically, an IO is a state or a condition.
† This example evolved in a breakout session of the 8th Annual International Conference of the TOCfE, Seattle, Washington, in August 2005.

We write a long division in the following traditional arrangement:

Example:

$$\frac{\text{quotient}}{\text{divisor}\big)\text{dividend}}$$

$$\text{divisor } 3\overline{)122} \quad \begin{array}{l}\text{quotient}\\ \text{dividend}\end{array}$$

$$\begin{array}{r} 4.0 \\ 3\overline{)122} \\ -12 \\ \hline 02 \\ -00 \\ \hline \end{array}$$

remainder

remainder 2

To create the ATT, the student first identified, with her teacher's help, the Obs or gaps in her knowledge about the topic. For each obstacle, they developed at least one IO, as shown in Table 5.3.

They then rearranged the IOs in logical order to create the Prt as shown in Figure 5.4. When just the numbers of IOs are arranged logically, we get an IO map.

Laying the PrT horizontally and renumbering it, the project plan to perform long division is shown in Figure 5.5. The plan also includes some specific actions that might be taken to achieve the IOs.

Table 5.3 ATT for Long Division
AT: We Do Long Division

Step 1: List the Obs	*Step 2: IOs*
1. I don't know what division means.	1. I know what division means.
2. I don't know where to start.	2. I know the long division template.
3. I don't know the terminology.	3. I know the terminology of division.
4. I don't know where to place the quotient at every step.	4. I know where to place the quotient at every step.
5. I have difficulty knowing where to use subtraction.	5. I know where to subtract.
6. I don't know multiplication tables.	6. I know multiplication tables.
7. I don't know how to use the multiplications tables.	7. I know how to use the multiplication tables.
8. I have difficulty with subtraction.	8. I know subtraction.
9. I do not know the relationship between multiplication and division.	9. I know the relationship of between multiplication and division.

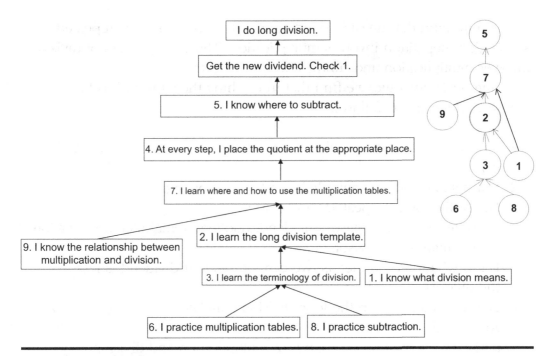

Figure 5.4   PrT for doing long division and IO map.

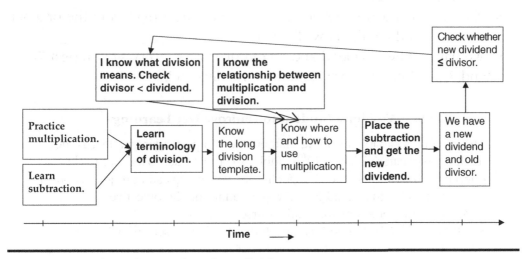

Figure 5.5   Project plan: perform long division.

Keep in mind that division of whole numbers is defined as repeated subtraction. Repetition involves multiplication. Thus, the process of division involves multiplication and subtraction.

Using necessity logic, we find that in teaching the subject, it is better to rearrange the steps as follows:

1. Practice multiplication tables—using recitation, video, songs, and flash cards.
2. Learn subtraction—single digits and by borrowing.
3. Learn division as repeated subtraction.
4. Learn terminology: divisor, dividend, quotient, remainder, and relationship: remainder < divisor.
5. Learn what division means (we cannot divide if dividend is less than the divisor).
6. Learn arrangement in the long division template.
7. Also, do the following:
   a. Learn the relationship between multiplication and division.
   b. When dividing the divisor into the dividend, first find the highest digit in the quotient. Then, multiply that quotient and divisor and put the answer under the dividend. Subtract.
8. Place the subtraction result, bring down the next digit from the original dividend, and get the new dividend.
9. We have a new dividend and an old divisor. At every step, repeat 7b and 8, until the divisor is less than the dividend.

Example 5.3: ATT for a Student to Improve Her Learning

The student is capable of doing mathematics. In particular, she learns the math course material. The ATT in Table 5.4 is a student's answer to the question, how to cause the change? To answer this question requires considering all the Obs that stand in the way of attaining the objective.

AT: The student learns the math course material.
She lists all the Obs (Table 5.4). Recall that the logic used for ATT is necessity logic.

This list of possible actions to attain the IOs with their Obs is arranged logically and renumbered (Table 5.5). Here, we have skipped the column of IOs—such as I have good study habits.

Read aloud: *Because* of Obs 1, before we can have action 3, we *must* first have action 1, and so on.

Table 5.4   List of Obstacles (Step 1)
AT: The Student Learns the Math Course Material (Step 1)

Obs	IOs (Left Blank)
1. I have forgotten/not taken prerequisite courses.	
2. I cannot get help outside of my classes.	
3. I have not formed logical connections between topics.	
4. I do not have good study habits.	
5. I do not know how to manage time.	
6. I do not know how to study for a test.	
7. I have test anxiety.	

Table 5.5   Logical Order of Possible Actions to Attain the IOs with Their Obs
AT: The Student Learns the Math Course Material (Step 2)

Obs	Action Plan
1. I do not have good study habits.	1. Take charge of directing my studies.
2. I do not know how to manage time.	2. Learn to use my time effectively.
3. I do not know the prerequisites.	3a. Learn the prerequisite material for each topic from the text or from consulting with instructor. 3b. Connect the prerequisite material logically to the present material.
4. I have not formed logical connections between topics.	4a. Form logical connections between current topics. 4b. Summarize important points. 4c. Read the material and note difficulties.
5. I cannot get help outside of class.	5a. Talk to the instructor/better students in class. 5b. Use the Internet to solve difficulties.
6. I do not know how to study for a test.	6a. Complete my assignments on time. 6b. Review the day before the test; do not cram.
7. I have test anxiety.	7a. Learn to relieve test anxiety. 7b. Take mock tests at home.

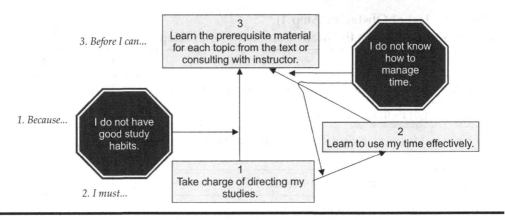

Figure 5.6   Part of ATT: Obstacles 1 and 2 are overcome by these IOs/actions.

Example: In Table 5.5, action 3a requires both action 1 and action 2. "*Because* I do not know the prerequisites, *I must* first take charge of directing my studies and *I must* learn to use my time effectively, *before* I can learn the prerequisite material. . . ." We show this graphically in Figure 5.6. Obstacles are put in *stop* signs.

Each of the IOs may involve several activities depending on the student and the situation. But it is clear that the ATT involves learning material logically and on time and performing well on the tests, a measure of learning the course material. This ATT also gives a roadmap for a sequence of activities to get better grades in any course: just turn the map 90° right and put in a timeline—dates/hours—for achieving the IOs.

In order for the student to sequence detailed activities to reach the IOs of the ATT without logical gaps, she can use a Transition Tree (TrT) for each IO as in Section 5.8.2.

Example 5.4: Use of the PrT and a Handout in a College Class

PrTs are currently being used in Psychology courses by Dr. Oley. The suggestion list in the following is handed out along with corrected PrT assignments.

PrT analysis handout (Dr. Oley)

Ambitious Target (AT):
   1. Ambitious Target—This is your goal and should appear at the top of your diagram. State it clearly so that there is no ambiguity.
Obstacles (Obs):

2. Obs—This is something that is standing in the way of your accomplishing your goal.
3. Obstacle numbers—Number the Obs; the order makes no difference.
4. Clarity—Check whether the meaning of your AT, Obs, or IO is unclear.

Intermediate Objectives (IOs):

5. Intermediate Objective—This is a general statement of what the situation would look like if the specific obstacles were overcome. For example, if the obstacle is that "I don't have the money," an appropriate IO might be "I will have the money" or "I will not need money." Do not assume that the IO is always just the opposite of the Obs. For example, a better IO might be "I have the resources that I need." Be creative in envisioning the IO.
6. Obs-IO parallels—For each obstacle, there should be at least one IO; for each, IO there should be one obstacle.
7. IO numbers—Each IO should be numbered according to the obstacle that it overcomes; the order of the numbers makes no difference. You should include these numbers in the PrT.
8. Complete sentences—Use a simple complete sentence to state the AT, Obs, or IO.
9. IO content—The IO should *not* explain *how* to overcome the Ob in specific terms. It should be more general. A specific solution comes later when you turn your PrT into an action plan.

Prerequisite Tree (PrT):

10. Tree structure—The tree should start at the bottom of the page and work toward the top.
11. Logic—To check the logic connecting these two IOs, use the test "In order to have the upper item, I *must first* have the lower item." Or, "If I don't have the lower item, I *can't* have the upper item."
12. Branches—Do you need another branch here? You can have many branches leading up to the AT.
13. Arrows—You need to use arrows to connect the items.

Example 5.5: Implementation of a PrT to Improve the Freshman Year Program Curriculum

ATT: We will implement TP tools of TOC in FYP to promote student success (see Table 5.6).*

* We would like to acknowledge this work done by a group of faculty from the Freshman Year Program and Department of Mathematics of MEC of CUNY at AGI, New Haven, Connecticut, in January 2007, with Women's Educational Equity Act (WEEA) funding from the U.S. Department of Education. Howard Meeks, AGI associate, retired professor from the Industrial and Manufacturing Systems Engineering Department, Iowa State University, served as the facilitator.

Table 5.6 PrT to Promote Student Success in the FYP
AT: We Will Implement TP Tools of TOC in FYP

Obs	IOs
1. The faculty have a workload that prevents any additional activities.	1. The faculty workload will allow for additional activities of any magnitude.
2. The faculty are not trained.	2. The faculty will be sufficiently trained.
3. There is no time to learn new ideas.	3. There is enough time to be receptive to new ideas.
4. The faculty are not open to the discussion of TOC.	4. The faculty will be open to the discussion of TOC.
5. Leadership at various levels has chronic conflicts that block collaboration.	5. Leadership at all levels of the college will resolve chronic conflicts that block collaboration.
6. TOC is not included in the college budget.	6. TOC is included in the college budget.
7. There is no faculty training in TOC.	7. The faculty will receive TOC training.
8. The curriculum is not coordinated between the FYP and academic departments.	8. The curriculum will be coordinated between the FYP and the academic departments.
9. The faculty do not receive support or want to participate in TOC training.	9a. The faculty will be reassured that they will have adequate support. 9b. The faculty will be willing to participate.
10. Part-time faculty do not get compensated for extra time spent (policy).	10. Part-time faculty will be compensated for extra time spent.
11. Students are not excited about TOC.	11. Students will be excited about TOC.
12. Leadership at some levels does not value problem solving.	12. Leadership at all levels will value problem solving.
13. TOC has not yet been proven to be an effective tool in education.	13. TOC has been proven to be an effective tool in education.

(Continued)

Table 5.6 (Continued) Implementation of TP Tools of TOC in FYP to Promote Student Success

AT: We Will Implement TP Tools of TOC in FYP

Obs	*IOs*
14. There is not enough time to teach TOC.	14. There will be sufficient time to teach TOC.
15. Faculty morale in the College is low.	15. Faculty morale in the College is high.
16. Some staff development programs are not meaningful.	16. All staff development programs will be meaningful.
17. FYP policies and practices are not strictly enforced.	17. Adherence to FYP policies and practices is strictly enforced.
18. There are no training programs available.	18. There are training programs available.
19. No trained help is available.	19. There is trained help available.
20. TP tools are not regarded as important in all programs.	20. TP tools are important in all programs.
21. We do not have a formal process of implementing new initiatives system-wide.	21. We will develop a formal process for implementing new initiatives system-wide.
22. Faculty/staff at some levels do not support the FYP.	22. Faculty/staff at all levels will support the FYP.
23. Workbooks are not available.	23. Workbooks are available.

The optional IO map was not developed, but a PrT was created directly using Post-it notes. Before writing the final draft of the PrT, we wrote each IO on the nonsticky side of a Post-it or similar item. The Post-its could then be stuck on a large sheet of paper or smooth wall and could easily be moved around to place them in a logical order. The final draft is shown in Figure 5.7.

A project plan for this PrT is shown in Figure 5.8. For a project plan, the activities in the PrT are sequenced on a flexible time axis.

A syllabus for a course that teaches TOC/TP tools to first-year students is in Appendix 5.1. This syllabus was generated using the PrT approach.

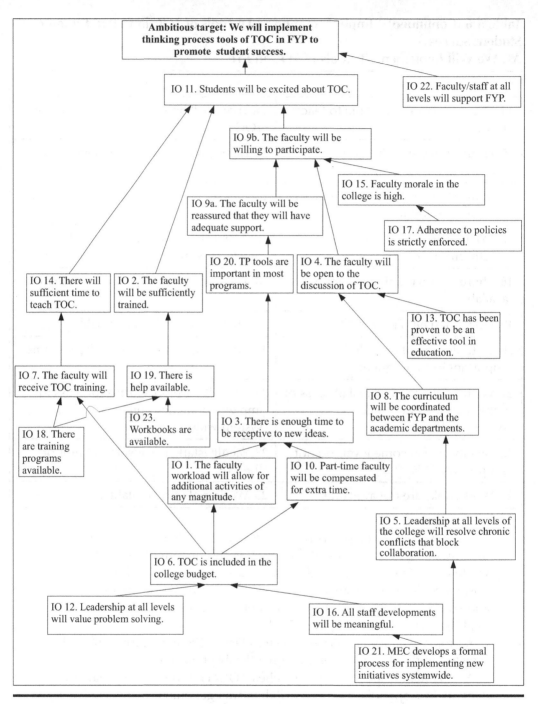

Figure 5.7   PrT: we will implement TP tools of TOC in FYP to promote student success.

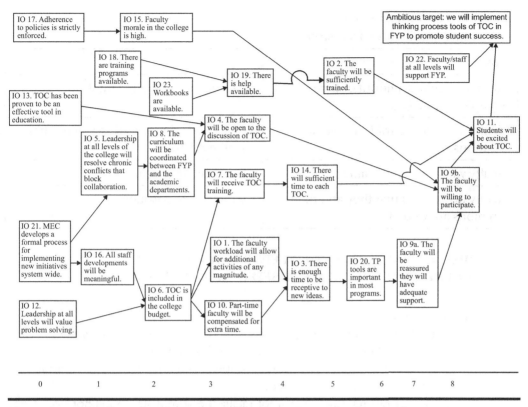

Figure 5.8 **Project plan for implementation of TOC in the Freshman Year Program.**

Example 5.6: Faculty Satisfaction in 90 Minutes

This example illustrates how the PrT can be used to uncover areas of dissatisfaction among college faculty in a way that avoids blame on any side and, by consensus, leads to the development of a logical plan for improving faculty satisfaction. This PrT/ATT was developed from a 90-minute discussion on improving faculty satisfaction that occurred during a Faculty Development Workshop held in January 2007, at MEC, and facilitated by Nancy Oley, chair of the Faculty Senate. Both faculty and administrators were present. Here we discuss the steps involved.

Discussion of faculty satisfaction: Table 5.7 shows the apprehension that the facilitator felt before holding the discussion. She used this table to build an ATT—a set of rules and actions that would permit a meaningful discussion.

**Table 5.7   Pre-discussion PrT
AT: Have a Meaningful Discussion**

Obs	IOs
Extremely limited amount of time to complete task.	Time will be used efficiently.
Faculty and administration have hostile relations.	Faculty and administration will not have hostile relations.
Faculty want to assign blame.	Blame will not occur.
Faculty do not feel that they and their opinions are valued.	Faculty will feel valued.

**IMPLEMENTATION OF THE STEPS TO BUILD A PrT
FOR THE AT "TO HAVE A SATISFIED FACULTY"**

1. Establish rules
    a. First, get the group to agree to use index cards to express issues (Obs) and desired outcomes (IOs). Define the terms.
    b. Ensure that each person can contribute as many ideas verbally and/ or on index cards as desired.
    c. Do not permit any criticism of ideas; the administration is not allowed to comment but can ask for clarification.
2. Reach a consensus on the appropriate AT or the common goal—"Have a satisfied faculty"—through open discussion.
3. List Obs: facilitator encourages faculty to state publicly or to write on index cards what they see as Obs to achieving the goal.
    a. Write ideas on the board.
    b. Go around the room until everyone has exhausted his/her list of unique Obs.
    c. Remind faculty and administrators, as needed, that no criticism or blame is allowed.
    d. Guide the group to develop IOs for each Ob on the index cards or verbally.
    e. Write down verbal IOs and collect index cards.
    Sample index cards are shown in Figures 5.9 and 5.10:
    Comment
        • Everyone quickly understood how to formulate Obs, although they tended to list them on a single card.
        • Not everyone understood how to formulate IOs versus specific solutions or actions.

- The discussion was respectful and low key.
- The administration took a lot of notes.
- Faculty expressed satisfaction with the discussion afterward.

4. After the faculty meeting
   a. The facilitator transcribes the ideas from index cards.
      – Many items were listed on the index cards but not mentioned publicly.
   b. Refine and combine IOs in order to
      – Create a first draft of complex logical trees (PrTs) to address the institutional climate, administrative and staff support, and the academic climate. See Figure 5.11 for an overview of the whole PrT, then a breakdown of the individual components in Figures 5.12 through Figure 5.16.

5. Follow-up
   a. Meet with Faculty Senate Executive Committee to review/revise the PrT.
   b. Present the PrT to the administration.

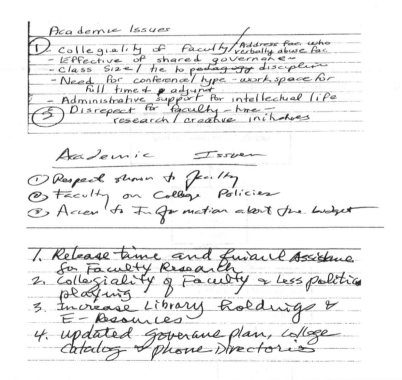

Figure 5.9   Sample index cards on academic issues.

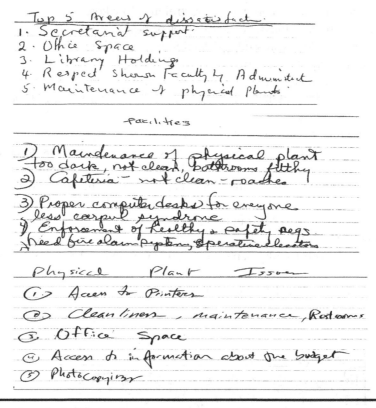

Figure 5.10 Sample index cards on resources.

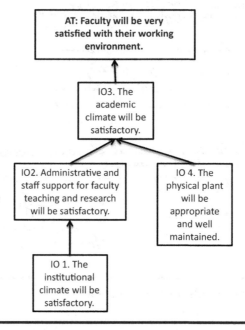

Figure 5.11 Faculty satisfaction in 90 minutes—overview.

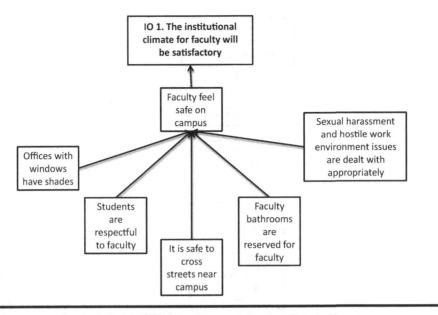

Figure 5.12 Faculty satisfaction in 90 minutes—institutional climate.

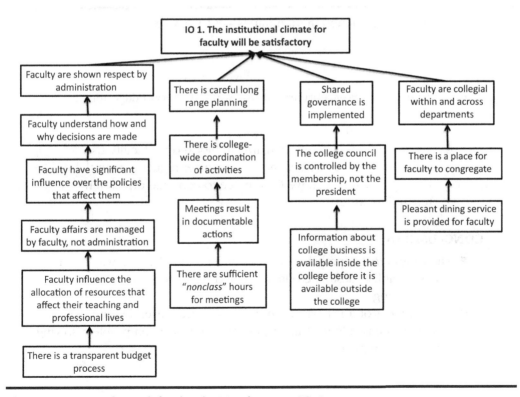

Figure 5.13 Faculty satisfaction in 90 minutes—IO 1.

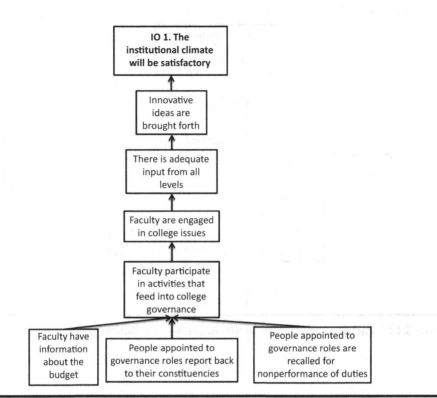

Figure 5.14 Faculty satisfaction in 90 minutes—IO 1 (contd.).

6. Corrective actions—February 2007—Administration takes steps to improve faculty satisfaction:
   a. Elevators are fixed.
   b. Bathrooms are cleaned regularly and locked for faculty use.
   c. Administration expresses the wish to meet regularly with the Faculty Senate Executive Committee to continue discussion of remaining issues.

CONCLUSIONS

- The *index card* approach is a very efficient and effective way to air issues, establish desirable outcomes, and promote teamwork in a university setting.
- Development of a PrT based on the index cards, even by one person, can help faculty/administration prioritize and focus on problem solving instead of complaining.

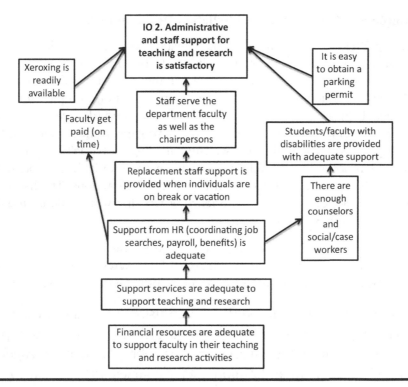

Figure 5.15   Faculty satisfaction in 90 minutes—administrative and staff support.

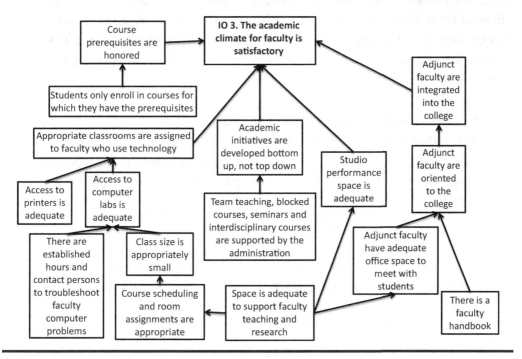

Figure 5.16   Faculty satisfaction in 90 minutes—academic climate.

Example 5.7: Curriculum and Syllabus Development

In Spring 2011, the Department of Mathematics decided to develop a seamless curriculum from Prealgebra to College Algebra (inclusive).* The purposes of this were to (a) ensure inclusion of any subtopics with which students have difficulty, (b) avoid unnecessary repetition of topics, (c) use more details in successive books on certain topics, and (d) develop a logical sequence of topics so that students do not have gaps in their understanding as they proceed through the course. The following partial PrT is a preliminary version of the curriculum on one mathematical topic, lines. Note that in Table 5.8, we have included a third column called Actions. The list of Obs was developed using our experience of working with students and the difficulties that they usually have.

Based on Table 5.8, the action plan in Table 5.9, discussed only in part, was developed using the YouTube videos of http://www.KhanAcademy.org. Some Obs have been reworded to use the resource more effectively.

A syllabus for any course can be developed using a PrT and turned into a project plan (e.g., lecture schedule) as discussed in the earlier examples. A PrT was used to unify the syllabus in Prealgebra, Elementary Algebra, and Intermediate Algebra and Trigonometry courses. PrTs similar to Table 5.8 on each topic in these courses and objectives were used to develop three textbooks: *Prealgebra* (Nagarkatte & Berenbom, 2014), *Elementary Algebra* (Nagarkatte & Berenbom, 2016a), and *Intermediate Algebra and Trigonometry* (Nagarkatte & Berenbom, 2016b). The syllabus for a TOC course for first-year students is given in Appendix 5.1. This syllabus was developed using a PrT approach.

Example 5.8: A PrT and Its Implementation in the Department of Mathematics

This example is a continuation of the institutional example in Chapter 4. It illustrates how the PrT can be used to implement an FRT in order to help a department reduce student attrition.

To recall, in January 2002, the Department of Mathematics analyzed student attrition in mathematics courses using TOC. From this analysis, they developed an elaborate Future Reality Tree (FRT) in which the departmental UDEs were converted into DEs as given in Chapter 4. The FRT requires various *injections* or actions taken to resolve a conflict or overcome an Ob. Injections in the FRT are called tactical objectives (TOs). A TO is the goal (AT) of the subordinate IOs. In order to achieve a TO, one must prepare a PrT.

* Team members included Joshua Berenbom, Tatyana Flesher, and Umesh Nagarkatte, in the Department of Mathematics at MEC.

Table 5.8 PrT on Lines
Student's AT: I can answer all questions about line equations

Obs	IOs	Actions
I do not know what a linear equation is.	I know what a linear equation is.	I learn what a linear equation is.
I do not know how to plot a point.	I know how to plot a point.	I learn how to plot a point.
I do not know how to plot a linear equation.	I know how to plot a linear equation.	I learn how to plot a linear equation.
I do not know what the intercepts of a line are.	I know what the intercepts of a line are.	I learn what x- and y-intercepts of a line are.
Given a graph of a line, I do not know how to find its intercepts.	Given a graph of a line, I know how to find its intercepts.	I learn how to find x- and y-intercepts of a graph of a line.
I do not know what a slope of a line is.	I know what a slope of a line is.	I learn what a slope of a line is.
Given a graph of a line, I do not know how to find its slope.	Given a graph of a line, I know how to find its slope.	I learn how to find the slope of the line from the graph.
I do not know the significance of the slope of a line.	I know the significance of the slope of a line.	I learn the significance of the slope of a line.
I do not know how to find the point-slope form of a line.	I know how to find the point-slope form of a line.	I learn how to find the point-slope form of a line.
I do not know how to find the slope-intercept form of a line.	I know how to find the slope-intercept form of a line.	I learn how to find the slope-intercept form of a line.
I do not know how to find the slope of a line from its equation.	I know how to find the slope of a line from its equation.	I learn how to find the slope of a line from its equation.
I do not know what the standard form is.	I know what the standard form is.	I learn what the standard form is.
Given a graph, I do not know how to find its equation.	Given a graph, I know how to find its equation.	I learn how to find the equation of the line given its graph.

(Continued)

Table 5.8 (Continued)   PrT on Lines
Student's AT: I can answer all questions about line equations

Obs	IOs	Actions
I do not know the relationships of slopes of parallel lines.	I know the relationships of slopes of parallel lines.	I learn the relationships of slopes of parallel lines.
I do not know the relationships of slopes of perpendicular lines.	I know the relationships of slopes of perpendicular lines.	I learn the relationships of slopes of perpendicular lines.
I do not know how to find an equation of a line that is parallel or perpendicular to a given line.	I know how to find an equation of a line that is parallel or perpendicular to a given line.	I learn how to find an equation of a line that is parallel or perpendicular to a given line.

Table 5.9   Action Plan Developed Using KhanAcademy.org PrT on Lines

	KhanAcademy.org videos
I do not know what the intercepts of a line are.	X and Y Intercepts (http://www.khanacademy.org /math/algebra/linear-equations-and-inequalitie/v/x --and-y-intercepts) X and Y Intercepts 2 (http://www.khanacademy.org /math/algebra/linear-equations-and-inequalitie/v/x -and-y-intercepts-2)
Given a graph of a line, I do not know how to find its intercepts.	Graphing Using Intercepts (http://www.khanacademy .org/math/algebra/linear-equations-and-inequalitie/v /graphing-using-intercepts) Graphing Using X and Y Intercepts (http://www .khanacademy.org/math/algebra/linear-equations -and-inequalitie/v/graphing-using-x-and-y-intercepts)
I do not know what a slope of a line is.	Slope of a Line (http://www.khanacademy.org/math /algebra/linear-equations-and-inequalitie/v/slope -of-a-line) Algebra: Slope and Y-Intercept Intuition (http://www .khanacademy.org/math/algebra/linear-equations -and-inequalitie/v/algebra--slope-and-y-intercept -intuition)

(Continued)

Table 5.9 (Continued)   Action Plan Developed Using KhanAcademy.org PrT on Lines

	KhanAcademy.org videos
I do not know how to find the slope of a line from its equation.	Graphs Using Slope-Intercept Form (http://www .khanacademy.org/math/algebra/linear-equations -and-inequalitie/v/graphs-using-slope-intercept -form)
I do not know what the standard form is.	Linear Equations in Standard Form (http://www .khanacademy.org/math/algebra/linear-equations -and-inequalitie/v/linear-equations-in-standard-form) Point-Slope and Standard Form (http://www .khanacademy.org/math/algebra/linear-equations -and-inequalitie/v/point-slope-and-standard-form)
Given a graph, I do not know how to find its equation.	Algebra: Equation of a Line (http://www.khanacademy .org/math/algebra/linear-equations-and-inequalitie/v /algebra--equation-of-a-line)
I do not know the relationship between slopes of parallel lines.	Parallel Lines (http://www.khanacademy.org/math /algebra/linear-equations-and-inequalitie/v /parallel-lines) Parallel Lines 2 (http://www.khanacademy.org/math /algebra/linear-equations-and-inequalitie/v /parallel-lines-2) Parallel Lines 3 (http://www.khanacademy.org/math /algebra/linear-equations-and-inequalitie/v /parallel-lines-3)
I do not know the relationship of slopes of perpendicular lines.	Perpendicular Lines (http://www.khanacademy.org /math/algebra/linear-equations-and-inequalitie/v /perpendicular-lines) Perpendicular lines 2 (http://www.khanacademy.org /math/algebra/linear-equations-and-inequalitie/v /perpendicular-lines-2)
I do not know how to find an equation of a line that is parallel or perpendicular to a given line.	Equations of Parallel and Perpendicular Lines (http:// www.khanacademy.org/math/algebra/linear -equations-and-inequalitie/v/equations-of-parallel -and-perpendicular-lines) Word Problem Solving 4 (http://www.khanacademy .org/math/algebra/linear-equations-and-inequalitie/v /word-problem-solving-4)

Note: The may links change as the website is updated.

As mentioned before, the *stop signs* are the Obs. The way to read this tree is shown in Figure 5.17. This tree which deals with tutors' less than ideal behavior is only a small part of a huge tree covering all aspects of student success.

Figure 5.18 illustrates how a PrT can be used to create departmental guidelines to promote student success. Stop signs are used to list the various Obs, and the logic to overcome the Obs is shown. A copy of the *Departmental Guidelines* (2002, 2007, 2013), first introduced in 2002 and approved by the president of the college, is available from the first author. The following paragraph from the guidelines indicates the significance of the document:

> As part of our goal of continually improving the instruction that the Mathematics Department provides, we have found it sensible to provide a written statement of departmental goals and the guidelines for implementing these goals. The purpose in doing this is to implement policies that will lead to improved student performance, which in turn will lead to a higher rate of students' passing mathematics courses and an overall improvement in student retention. Many of the guidelines in this document are longstanding informal policies, but they may have been carried out haphazardly or inconsistently

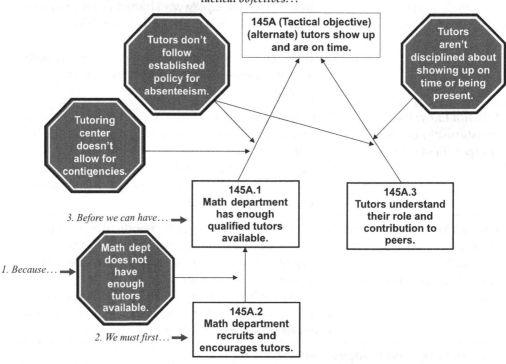

Prerequisite tree (PRT) example no. 1
Concerns that there are obstacles that will block us from achieving the solutions' tactical objectives...

Figure 5.17 PrT—tutors show up and are on time. *Developed in a Jonah course, January, 2002, Abraham Y. Goldratt Academy, facilitator—Steve Simpliciano.*

Identifying what we need to get cooperation

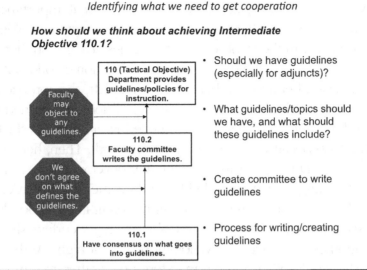

How should we think about achieving Intermediate Objective 110.1?

Figure 5.18 **Active collaboration on departmental guidelines.** *Developed in Jonah course, January 2002, Abraham Y. Goldratt Academy, facilitator—Steve Simpliciano.*

> from instructor to instructor. This set of departmental guidelines attempts to clarify and reiterate these policies so that the department can speak with a uniform voice. These guidelines are especially important for adjuncts who are often unaware of accepted procedures and do not have extensive contacts with full-time department members. (*Departmental Guidelines*, 2002, 2007, 2013. p. 1)

A TOC analysis of students' academic and nonacademic UDEs leads to the synchronization of instructional activities, support activities, instructional support, and college support to attain the goal: *to offer instruction and programs tailored to the needs of the student.* The detailed PrT, not given here, clarifies how the TOC analysis synchronizes all the resources.

If you are working with children, go to the section on TOCfE. If you want to know how to manage a project, read on. If not, go to Section 5.6 on the TrT.

5.3 Case Study: A Student in an Introductory Psychology Class

Nancy Oley

I first introduced the concept of the PrT in an Introductory Psychology class made up mostly of first-year students. Students had done small exercises using sufficiency and necessity logic before I discussed the PrT. Their first rigorous assignment was to create a PrT to reach a goal of personal importance, for example, passing the class. There was one woman student, a bit older than the rest, who typically sat in the front row. As the semester wore on, her attendance became quite variable, and she didn't turn in the PrT homework. But then, on the last day of class, after all the other students had left, she approached me. She explained why she had been absent. Her apartment had burned down, forcing her and her 9-year-old daughter to move into a homeless shelter. She lost her $40,000 job because of her absence from work. Then, her laptop was stolen at the shelter. During all this, her daughter developed an ear infection, which, through improper treatment, led her to become deaf. In order to deal with her daughter's disability, she had to visit her daughter's school during the day, thus missing my class. Because of the shelter's night curfew, she was unable to switch to another Introductory Psychology section at night. At this point, I thought that she would be asking for an extension or other accommodation (which she deserved!). Instead, she thanked me for having taught her the PrT, which she said was the only thing that had helped her to navigate the minefield of her life successfully during this difficult time, and assured me that she would be back the next semester to pick up where she had left off.

5.4 Managing a Project

5.4.1 How to Pass a Course with a High Grade

Definition 5.1

A project—A set of finite-duration tasks that must be performed in a specified sequence to produce a desired result within a prescribed time and budget. . . ." (Ricketts, 2007, p. 25)

Recall from Chapter 1 that a project plan is an application of the sufficient condition, "if . . . then . . ." logic.

Project Plan*

A project plan looks at the whole sequence of tasks. For instance, if the goal is to get a degree, we must consider the whole series of courses that

---

* Thanks to Jim Cox, professor emeritus, Industrial Engineering Department, University of Georgia, for the stimulating discussions in October–November 2007. For more information, see Newbold, R. (2008). *The Billion Dollar Solution: Secrets of Prochain Project Management*. Lake Ridge, Virginia: Prochain Press.

we need to take. But at the same time, we should not be overwhelmed by any project. We should not think, "Oh, when am I going to finish all this?" No one has asked us to do everything in one day, or this moment, and by our own effort alone. We must relax and enjoy what we are doing; we must concentrate fully on what has to be done at this moment; we must relate to people surrounding us in a friendly manner. That will make our time working on the task meaningful. We have to know that people such as our teachers, our friends, and our relatives want us to succeed in whatever we are doing and are ready to help in whatever way they can. Even strangers come to help a person in need.

First of all, we need to be proactive. This means that we have to remain in charge of our own project. In a huge institutional or company project, we play many roles. Our role and the tasks that we need to do constitute our project plan.

Academic Success

We need to take many courses. We should aspire to get an "A" in each course. We should take charge and make a commitment to finish the course syllabus. For each course, there are many lessons. If a lesson-wise syllabus is not available, work with the instructor to find out how he or she will emphasize topics in terms of the time to be allocated for each topic. Lessons can be bunched as weekly tasks. Figure 5.19 describes a course as a project. Let's assume that there are four tests and that they are announced at least a week or two beforehand.

For each project, there are various human resources—our family, employers, mentors, teachers, tutors, classmates, and colleagues—to help us carry out our project. Our family, job, scholarships, and student loans help us keep working toward our goals without worry and in a protected environment by providing our financial and comfort resources.

In a course, the instructor is the primary resource; the tutors are supplementary resources. There are print materials and web materials to help

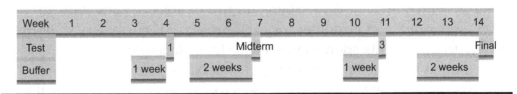

Figure 5.19　Taking a course as a project.

us that are our secondary resources. We should make timely use of these resources to the best of our ability. We must respect all our resources and acknowledge from time to time the people we get our help from. Acknowledgment and recognition encourage everyone to improve. It brings satisfaction and happiness to all parties involved.

In any project, we must consider changes or setbacks due to unseen factors. We must know Murphy's law: "Anything that can go wrong, will go wrong." When we plan a project, we should take into account Murphy's law and include enough flexibility so that we can change our course of action if needed. Being aware of all these factors enables us to take a systematic approach to finishing a project.

A course, as a project, has a definite duration, a set path, and a fixed program. Finishing it successfully will give you practice in finishing your entire academic course of study as a series of projects. It will also give you practice in completing more complicated projects in your career and life and will help you to live a meaningful life.

To become educated, we must take a number of courses and carry out each course as a project. You will learn in Section 5.6 how to manage a project using what is called a *critical chain*.

In order to use our time meaningfully, we must not multitask; we must carry out a single project in a focused manner.

5.4.2 Game of Multitasking

Let us play a game of multitasking. I owe this game to Alan Barnard, a TOC teacher from South Africa (Barnard, 2007). Let us assume that you have a portfolio of three projects to finish. Play this game and experience the feeling you have. It teaches us that it takes longer to finish a project if you multitask. While being *proactive*, you will have to make sure that you are not multitasking.

The assumption behind multitasking is that the sooner we start a project, the sooner we finish.

You will need a stopwatch or the equivalent and a data collection sheet as shown in Table 5.10. There are three projects, each with 20 tasks, and a different customer for each project. All customers want their project to be done as soon as possible. The *task* is to copy each item from the left-hand column of a project to a blank column to its right. The *task time* is how long in general it takes to complete each individual task.

Table 5.10 Multitasking Game

	Project 1	*Project 1*	*Project 1*	*Project 2*	*Project 2*	*Project 2*	*Project 3*	*Project 3*	*Project 3*
1			A			Δ			
2			B			O			
3			C			◊			
4			D			Δ			
5			E			O			
6			F			◊			
7			G			Δ			
8			H			O			
9			I			◊			
10			J			Δ			
11			K			O			
12			L			◊			
13			M			Δ			
14			N			O			
15			O			◊			
16			P			Δ			
17			Q			O			
18			R			◊			
19			S			Δ			
20			T			O			
58 seconds	___	___	59 seconds	___	___	1 minute	___	___	

A project consists of the list of tasks. The *expected project time* (lead time) is how much time it *should* take to complete a single project. *Safety* refers to extra time allowed for errors, problems, and delays—the buffer. The *typical project time* is how long it generally takes to complete each project by itself.

Starting Conditions

Each task time = ½ second (1 second with 100% safety)
Expected project time (called lead time) = 20 seconds

Typical project time is given in the bottom left-hand column for each project: 58, 59, and 60 seconds.

Promised portfolio of three projects lead time = 60 seconds
First, play the game as follows by completing project 1, then project 2, and then project 3. Be sure to note your actual project time in the bottom box for each project:

Project 1: Write 1–20 vertically in column 2.
Project 2: Write A through T vertically in column 5.
Project 3: Draw the associated triangle (Δ), a circle (○), and a diamond (◊) vertically in column 8.

Then, play the game again, this time doing task 1 from project 1, task 1 from project 2, and task 1 from project 3, etc. (*multitasking*). Note your actual project time in the bottom box for each project:

Start with task 1 project 1; that is, write 1 in column 3.
Task 1 project 2; that is, write A in column 6.
Task 1 project 3; that is, draw triangle (Δ) in column 9.
Then, go on to the task 2 of each project and so on.

The point of the game is to convince you that constant shifting from one task to another takes away speed and concentration. If we move from the first project of numbers to writing letters, we must think about which letter to write, and after that, if we move to the third project, we must decide which figure needs to be drawn—a triangle, a circle, or a diamond. These decisions take some time. If you do the three projects without multitasking, it would take you at most 3 minutes, which is the project time. But if we multitask, we move constantly from one task of one project to a task of another, taking considerably longer to finish all three tasks. Bad multitasking makes each project longer and should never be done.

If so, then how do we carry out multiple tasks that we need to accomplish during the day? If it is so boring to do just one project all day, the key is to *divide and conquer.* Divide the project into small parts or tasks, and make a flexible mental marker called a *milestone* at the end of a set of tasks. We should reward ourselves in some way—take an exercise break, eat, or entertain ourselves for some time. We may do this intuitively in many projects, but we should explicitly plan how to execute our projects.

Exercise: If you are an instructor, ask your students to read the two topics of this section and write a summary of each topic.

If you are satisfied with this discussion of project management, go to Section 5.8, on the TrT. If you want to know how to manage a complex project, read on.

5.5 Critical Chain Project Management (CCPM) of a Course: Student's *Critical Chain*

Definition 5.2

A *critical chain* is the particular set of tasks which determine when a project can finish. They are critical because improvement anywhere in the critical chain means that the project can get done earlier and/or better. It requires taking resource* capacity into account. Resource capacity is typically regarded as the constraint or leverage point of the project. A leverage point is an area where a small change can have a big positive impact on a student's performance. Finding the constraint or leverage point is the function of TOC.

For Critical Chain Project Management (CCPM) of a course, the constraint is the student, since a proactive student can make a rapid individual improvement using all resources. Students' study habits and academic preparation determine how difficult a syllabus topic is and play an important role. The most difficult topic in the course, the one that takes longer to grasp and uses more resources, is a constraint for the student. With the help of CCPM, once the syllabus is handed out, you, the proactive student, can be vigilant in mastering the course topics with or before the instructor covers them.

If you finish a project on time or early, you will build confidence in doing projects and credibility with those who wanted you to carry out the project. For a course, finishing early provides time for revisiting the ideas and getting a deeper understanding. Sometimes, a mechanism is in place at your college

---

* This is discussed in detail after Table 5.11 for a course. Basically, resources are those people, including the student, or items that support a student's study or in short "a student's support team and supplemental software."

for you to accelerate your program and/or get a waiver or credit by studying material from the next course, at the same time as the current course.

5.5.1 Implementation of CCPM in Mathematics Tutoring

The following example shows increased accountability and effectiveness of faculty and staff that resulted in fostering better communication among the students, instructors, and tutors. The discussion continues in Section 5.5.2.

Although the course syllabus (Table 5.11) and the following discussion is related to mathematics, this discussion is relevant wherever a lesson-wise syllabus is available.

Basic goal: The Department of Mathematics offers academic programs that are tailored to the needs of the students of the college.

Departmental assumptions: The working assumptions on which this discussion is based are as follows:

1. All persons engaged with the department (students, faculty, and staff) want to improve themselves.
2. External recognition of a person's efforts at self-improvement can frequently lead an individual to make greater and more sustained efforts toward improved performance.
3. Leading students to regard each of their course syllabi as a 14-week long project, putting responsibility on them to finish, and helping them to finish will develop their confidence and give them training in how to finish projects. Then, they will also be able to complete other more complicated projects in life.
4. Students regard their teachers as a primary resource, the tutors as a supplementary resource, and computer web-based materials as secondary resources, which they can use to finish the project at hand.
5. In any course syllabus, there is plenty of "buffer"* time allocated which doesn't necessarily have to be used on all topics. However, students should try to finish as many lessons as they can and use the usual 1 week buffer before a test only for mastering the difficult topics (see Figure 5.19).

---

* A buffer is an amount of time put into the schedule systematically in order to protect against unanticipated delays and to allow for early starts. Buffers are essential parts of the schedule. These ideas are also discussed after the Table 5.11 is discussed.

Table 5.11   Lecture Schedule for College Algebra and Trigonometry—MTH 138

NAME:_____ **Name of Instructor:** _____

Lesson	Topic	Section/s	Student/Date	Tutor	Instructor
1	Linear inequalities, compound inequalities	1.7, 1.8			
2	Functions	2.2, 2.4			
3	Absolute value equations and inequalities	2.6			
4	Slope, distance, and linear functions	2.7, 2.8			
5	Systems of equations in two variables	3.1			
6	Systems of equations in three variables	3.2			
7	Introduction to trigonometry	4.1			
8	Right angle trigonometry	4.2			
9	Trigonometric functions of any angle	4.3			
10	Trigonometric equations	4.4			
11	TEST 1	Score			
12	Review of factoring	5.1, 5.2			
13	Solving polynomial equations	5.3			
14	Review of arithmetic with rational functions	5.4, 5.5			
15	Complex fractions	5.6			
16	Division with polynomials	5.7			
17	Equations with fractions	5.8			
18	Radicals	6.1			
19	Rational exponents	6.2			
20	Computations with radicals	6.3			
21	Further computations with radicals	6.4			
22	DEPARTMENTAL MIDTERM	Score			
23	Complex numbers	6.5			
24	Completion of the square	7.1			
25	Quadratic formula	7.2			
26	Discriminant, word problems	7.2			
27	Equations that lead to quadratic equations	7.3			
28	Parabolas	7.5			
29	Circles	7.6			
30	Ellipses and hyperbolas	7.7			
31	Nonlinear systems of equations	7.8			
32	Test 3	Score	Safe zone		
33	Exponential functions	8.1			
34	Inverse functions	8.2			
35	Logarithms	8.3			
36	Properties of logarithms	8.4			
37	Logarithmic and exponential equations	8.5			
38	Applications of e	8.6			
39	Sequences	10.1			
40	Series	10.2			
41	Infinite series	10.3			
42	Test 4	Score			

DEPARTMENTAL FINAL EXAM Score

Each student coming for tutoring is given the list of tasks or topics from the syllabus for the appropriate course (See the Detailed Lecture Schedule... in Appendix 5.1).

Copies of all syllabi from Intermediate Algebra to Calculus are available in the department. In the sample Lecture Schedule for College Algebra and Trigonometry in the following (Table 5.11), the last three columns are for the signatures of the student, tutor, and instructor after completion of a set of topics. Students and tutors must also have the scores of various class tests when they complete an appropriate set of topics.

To develop the three zones, a tutor draws an inclined line from lecture 1 to the last lecture in the student/date column (line in Table 5.11 is broken at the tests). The tutor marks the 1-week point before each test, joining these points with a line (line below the broken line in Table 5.11). That gives the beginning of the 1-week buffer (medium gray). On the opposite side of the first line at the same distance, a tutor draws a parallel line showing the end of 1 week late buffer (line above the broken line in Table 5.11). Below the beginning of the buffer (medium gray), there is a light gray safe zone and on the other side is the dark gray zone.

After a student finishes a topic, he or she makes a point in the safe area if he or she has finished it before the instructor does, in the medium dark area if he or she finishes it with the instructor or within 1 week after the instructor, and in the dark gray area if he or she finishes more than 1 week after the instructor does. The points are connected as the weeks go by. If the curve is completely in the safe area, then he/she proceeding through your course effectively. Otherwise, she/he should go to the help area as early as possible. This plot shows student's visual progress curve during the semester. See a student's progress at the end of this discussion.

The instructor is provided with these copies as well, so as to get an idea of what service the tutors are offering to their students. The instructor knows that he or she is the primary facilitator for the course and the tutors are supplementary facilitators. The instructor makes an effort to contact several tutors for his/her course and to acknowledge that the tutor's service in individualizing help for the students is valuable. This will help to maintain communication between the student, the tutor(s), and the instructor. The instructor communicates the *Departmental Assumptions* stated at the beginning to students.

The department measures (a) the pass rate of the class, (b) the class average score on each test, and (c) the ratio of passing rates to tutorial expenses for a course. It keeps track of these numbers using a computer database along with the number and list of students in courses taking tutoring, all tutors, and instructors.

It usually happens that a student comes for the first time right *before a test* to get a sample test solved by the tutor. The tutor should not solve the problem but help the student solve the problem by asking questions—in order to understand the steps where the student has difficulty. This pinpoints the student's difficulty. The tutor then should take out the *problem set* for the course; if the student has not been given one, and along with helping the student on a particular problem, get several problems on the given topic from the problem set. This should continue until all problems related to the sample test are solved. The department has more tutors available during the week before, after the midterm, and 2 weeks before the final.

The instructor and tutor emphasize to the students that sample tests are given for the students to develop their test taking skill, so instead of solving that sample test first, they should use the problem set to do a lot of problems, get ready for the test, and then take the sample test as a mock test at home while timing themselves without looking at any text or notes. To finish more or all questions on any test in a given time period, the student should look at the entire test first, do the easy problems, and then go on to difficult problems, even going out of the sequence in which problems on the test are given.

Along with the scores on a test, the instructor indicates to the student which topics the student had difficulty with. If an error is made, it is so indicated to the student and whether the error is due to not understanding the topic, carelessness, or lack of time. If students come to tutoring the first time *after a test* bringing their tests with them, the tutor should ask them to mark the topics from their list of syllabus topics where they made their mistakes. The tutor should require them to do that problem again and check where they have difficulty. The tutor should then help students do more problems on the topic in question from the problem set. As far as possible, the effort should be more that of the student than of the tutor.

About 10% of the students do well in a course and are bored by the pace of the course. They must be given a choice: (a) work with students who are not doing well in their class, even outside of class time, because by helping others, they will improve their own understanding, or (b) if some students want to finish all topics early, they are encouraged to work with a tutor on a regular basis, studying the topics from the book by themselves, showing the tutor his/her work on the problem sets. They must attend classes, since an instructor provides insight into or easy methods of working on a topic which they might not get by studying themselves. They take their tests along with other students in the class. In addition, if the students are basically finished with all lessons from a course, arrangements should be made for the students to get in touch with an instructor of the next course, complete the set of lessons from that course, and take tests in the tutorial area from the instructor. They should take their finals with the appropriate instructors. Students who do this should be given an exemption (not credit for the course not taken) from the next course by the chair and should be placed in a more advanced class. We have examples of students in the past finishing two sequential courses in one semester.

In each of the two choices, a lecture schedule is carried by a student attending tutoring. The student initials in front of the topics and gets the initials of the tutor on the topic(s) and shows it to his/her instructor who initials the form at the appropriate places and gives it back to the student. This classification can yield the number of students who are ahead, on time, or falling behind for the student database and focuses on students who need intervention from tutors, instructor, and counselors. For a record of progress of all students coming for tutoring, the tutorial coordinator, with the help of an assistant, enters the number of students lagging behind, absent/about to fall behind, and going ahead of the course schedule into a database once a week.*

A sample progress curve for a student as shown in Table 5.12 is given at the end of this section.

---

* Thanks to Jim Cox, professor emeritus, Industrial Engineering Department, University of Georgia, and James Holt, professor emeritus of Engineering & Technology Management, Washington State University, for stimulating discussions in 2007–2008 about designing CCPM for a course syllabus as a project.

Table 5.12 College Algebra and Trigonometry—MTH 138 Section

NAME:_____ Name of Instructor:_____

Lesson	Topic	Section/s	Student/Date	Tutor	Instructor
1	Linear inequalities, compound inequalities	1.7, 1.8	SH. 2/1	PA. 2/1	TB. 2/4
2	Functions	2.2, 2.4			
3	Absolute value equations and inequalities	2.6			
4	Slope, distance, and linear functions	2.7, 2.8			
5	Systems of equations in two variables	3.1	SH. 2//10	PA. 2/10	TB. 2/11
6	Systems of equations in three variables	3.2			
7	Introduction to trigonometry	4.1			
8	Right angle trigonometry	4.2			
9	Trigonometric functions of any angle	4.3			
10	Trigonometric equations	4.4			
11	*TEST 1*	Score	75 2/25		
12	Review of factoring	5.1, 5.2			
13	Solving polynomial equations	5.3			
14	Review of arithmetic with rational functions	5.4, 5.5			
15	Complex fractions	5.6			
16	Division with polynomials	5.7			
17	Equations with fractions	5.8	SH. 3/15	PA.3/15	TB. 3/17
18	Radicals	6.1			
19	Rational exponents	6.2			
20	Computations with radicals	6.3			
21	Further computations with radicals	6.4			
22	*DEPARTMENTAL MIDTERM*	Score	85 3/18		
23	Complex numbers	6.5	SH. 3/31	PA.3/31	TB. 4/1
24	Completion of the square	7.1			
25	Quadratic formula	7.2			
26	Discriminant, word problems	7.2			
27	Equations that lead to quadratic equations	7.3			
28	Parabolas	7.5			
29	Circles	7.6			
30	Ellipses and hyperbolas	7.7	SH. 4//12	PA.4/13	TB. 4/15
31	Nonlinear systems of equations	7.8			
32	*Test 3*	Score	96 4/18		
33	Exponential functions	8.1			
34	Inverse functions	8.2			
35	Logarithms	8.3			
36	Properties of logarithms	8.4			
37	Logarithmic and exponential equations	8.5			
38	Applications of e	8.6	SH. 5//10	PA.5/10	TB. 5/12
39	Sequences	10.1			
40	Series	10.2			
41	Infinite series	10.3			
42	*Test 4*	Score	84 5/19		

DEPARTMENTAL FINAL EXAM   Score 92

5.5.2 Details of Technical Terms Used in CCPM for a Mathematics (or Any Other) Course

Tasks: A student receives a lecture schedule for the course listing the topics he or she is responsible for. This is the *set of tasks*. The student should know the goal of the course and how it is relevant for his/her career/specialization, and should seek clarification from his/her instructor/tutor, since it is not possible to list all relevancies in the syllabus.

An important goal of students taking a mathematics course is to master the concepts and skills listed in the syllabus so as to use the knowledge immediately in their own lives and in the next courses for which a particular course is a prerequisite. The goal while learning a course is to link the ideas logically so as to form a mental picture of the course and not a set of isolated facts or rules. The long-term goal of mastering mathematics is to develop a logical way of thinking for studying any subject and in life.

The collection of sequential topics to be learned is the *critical chain* for each student, which means that the student has to know his role, the instructor's role, and the tutor's role along with syllabus topics. The student has to also know if there are supplementary materials available on the web. The instructor and tutor must understand their roles as facilitators.

Resources: The instructor is the primary resource, and the tutor is a supplemental resource to facilitate mastery of the course. Every tutor and instructor must make it clear to the student that they are only facilitators and that it is the student's responsibility to acquire this knowledge, and it is to his/her benefit to make use of them on a regular basis and to follow up on their directives.

Project tracking: We monitor the status of the project—What is being covered and how much has yet to be covered? We also evaluate the status of the project—What are the difficulties that students had with current and past topics? What is the score on the class exam/s and the midterm? What exactly are the mistakes made on a sample test, the actual test, etc.?

Importance of tutor: The instructor does not have sufficient time to individualize the process of learning, as he or she has the main responsibility of presenting the course content. But the tutor can help the individual student manage the project. He or she can help him/her track the project and focus on the student's particular test errors and correct the student's understanding.

Scheduling critical tasks: Topics such as trigonometry, exponential functions, and logarithms are important in college algebra/trigonometry and precalculus. However, if the instructor puts them at the end of the syllabus, they are often presented in a hurried manner with no deep understanding on students' part. They have to be covered early in the syllabus. Some instructors make sure that they cover these topics as early as possible. By doing this, if a student has not understood the concepts, there is time to help him/her. In any course, the instructor can review the syllabus in order to identify the high-risk tasks and place them early in the semester.

Buffer management: A buffer is time put into a schedule systematically in order to protect against unanticipated delays and in order to allow for early starts (studying before the instructor covers a topic). Buffers are a standard component of the schedule. Buffers are not slack time. Slack is free time available to postpone a task to do later on. Buffers are an extremely valuable tool for monitoring the status of projects and determining whether drastic actions are required to keep a project on track.

Every course lecture schedule has built-in buffers—based on the average time to complete a topic. Although these buffers cannot always be arranged ahead of time, they allow for flexibility on the part of the instructor to cover a certain topic faster or more slowly than indicated in the syllabus. Experience shows that an instructor typically finishes topics for a test about a week before the test. If an instructor is absent on a certain day, there is a time buffer (not advertised) to cover the topic and the rest in the remaining periods. Similarly, if the student is absent for a particular class, he or she can cover the missed topic in a reasonable time on his/her own or with the help of the resources available.

There are four types of buffers: project buffers, feeding buffers, resource buffers, and strategic resource buffers (not discussed here).

Project buffers: If the buffers are arranged in a more systematic manner (according to the difficulty of a topic) as with a project buffer, instead of placing the buffers throughout the syllabus, the student can complete the topics on his/her own or with the help of the resources. From this point of view, the student should allow *project buffers* of 1 week (or usually half the time allocated to the tasks) before the test. That is, the student should finish all tasks—studying the prescribed topics—1 week before a class test, ideally in half the time allocated for covering the topics in the syllabus. In the week(s) leading up to the test, the student should take various sample and old tests and work on the areas that are perceived as difficult. For the final exam, the student should have a 2-week buffer. In this manner, the procrastinating student avoids the *student syndrome*, where he or she starts studying a day or two before a test. If a student does not have difficulties and is finished, the instructor can make available to the student reinforcement/enrichment material to study. In the past, for at least ten students at different times, some instructors have given the topics of the next course in the course sequence, and most of the students have finished and ended up taking the final exam for the next course also. The department gave them a waiver, but no credit, for the next course. Most of them did "A" level work in both courses! Thus, a student was not restricted by the policy constraint of taking only one course per semester. This requires constant communication between student, tutor, and instructor. The project buffer needs to be checked, and if it is being used up doing certain tasks, extra help in terms of instructor and tutor intervention has to be given so that the tasks are finished before the project buffers are used up.

Feeding buffers: These buffers make sure that supplemental work is available if a student needs it. Thus, giving the students a departmental selection of test preparation problems is adequate. If a large variety of problems is available, the course becomes richer and the student has more practice materials. From that point of view, faculty should keep continuously adding to the set of available problems.

Resource buffers: If a student needs extra help/time to finish the task before the project buffer begins, the instructor/tutor should make more help/time available as the need arises. Invoking the resource buffer is a wake-up call to alert all the stakeholders to impending problems, since it shows that more time is being taken than anticipated.

Information flow: The information flow to manage buffers is illustrated in Figure 5.20. It is nothing new. We do this checking already. What is different here is the introduction of the three buffers and making the student aware of his/her responsibility.

Suggestions for dealing with multiple courses: Students should develop a "realistic schedule" by approaching counselors and advisors to help them.

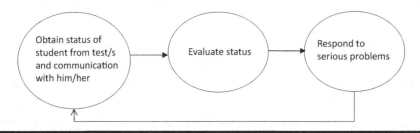

Figure 5.20   Information flow.

Students should take a balanced set of courses—some technical and some not, but not all hard or all easy. They should manage the project and resource buffers by using the days when the course does not meet and weekends to complete the various tasks of each course.

If they practice the principles discussed here, they will enjoy every course. Students might also be able to complete more courses and finish their required courses earlier.

5.6 Developing a Prerequisite Tree (PrT) and Project Plan from a Future Reality Tree (FRT) Institutional Example

In this section, we show how to develop a complex PrT and project plan for an institutional problem. We used each of the injections or Tactical Objectives (TOs) discussed in Chapter 4 as an Ambitious Target (AT) and developed a PrT for each. We put all these individual PrTs together to make a humongous PrT. Here, the top of the tree is the strategic injection which is also the Bright Idea from the FRT (see Section 3.6). Once we started to develop the various PrTs for the TOs, we discovered that TOC touches all stakeholders concerned with student success. The PrT is not limited only to instruction, but includes tutoring, advisement, counseling, and financial support of the student, thus providing a *holistic* approach to the student. We had to reach out to tutors, counselors, advisors, etc., and get their support to implement our reforms.

In many colleges/universities, because of departments operating as isolated "silos," it is hard to communicate with other colleagues in their specialized areas, for example, counseling. So, improvements are made only in terms of students' academic needs, while overlooking their nonacademic needs. A TOC analysis of student attrition in mathematics courses made us aware of how important the other stakeholders are for student success and retention. We had to make a special effort to get agreement or "buy in" from the administration to reach out to the other stakeholders. In that sense, the theory of constraints (TOC) is a Theory of Communication. We give an example of a sub-Future Reality Tree for the Math Department in Figure 5.21 and the project plan related to tutoring and instruction in Figure 5.22 (time is on the *x*-axis).

A complete PrT and a project plan are given in Figures 5.23 and 5.24. It is heartening to note that the project plan developed in 2002 is robust and still viable and being implemented, thanks to the many stakeholders. The project plan is, of course, not static but is part of the Process Of OnGoing

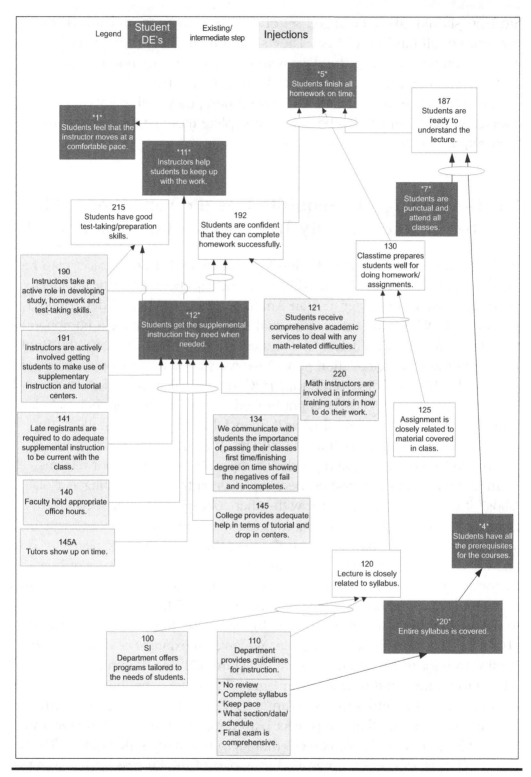

Figure 5.21   Partial FRT of the Math Department.

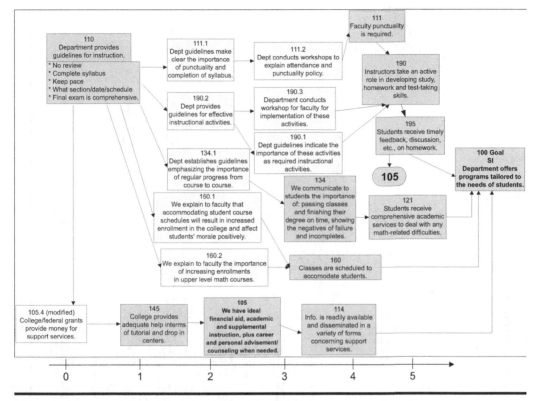

Figure 5.22 Partial project plan for achieving a departmental goal.

Improvement (POOGI) discussed in Chapter 6. An interested reader of the PrT can get an enlarged print copy from the first author.

Figures 5.25 through 5.27 describe the project plan for department and adjuncts, counselors, supplemental instruction, and tutors, respectively.

5.7 Transition Tree (TrT): A Stand-Alone Tool

5.7.1 General Discussion of a TrT

In any presentation, lecture, or procedure, one has to lay down various steps in a logical manner. How do you make sure that there is no logical gap? TOC provides a tool called the Transition Tree (TrT or TT) to do this. It is a powerful empowerment tool that uses sufficient condition logic.

Every TrT starts with a goal or an objective to be attained and a clear set of actions. An ATT or PrT, discussed in previous sections, is the starting point if the objective to be attained is known, but a clear set of logical

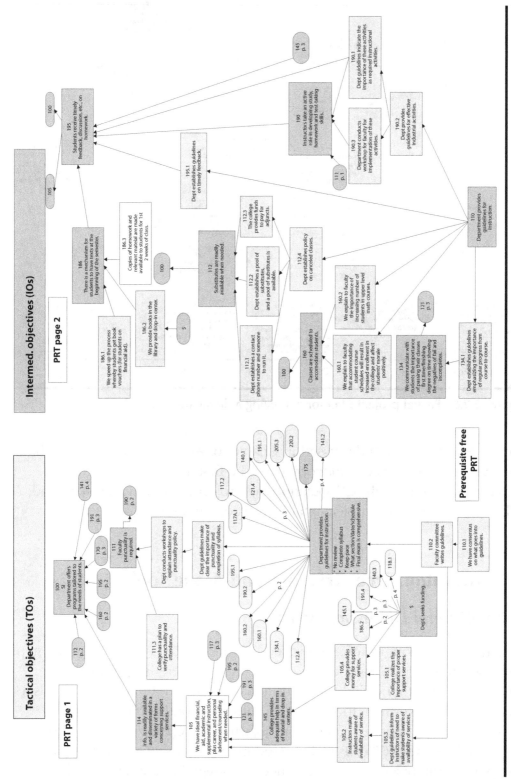

Figure 5.23   PrT for the Department of Mathematics pages 1 and 2 (January, 2002).

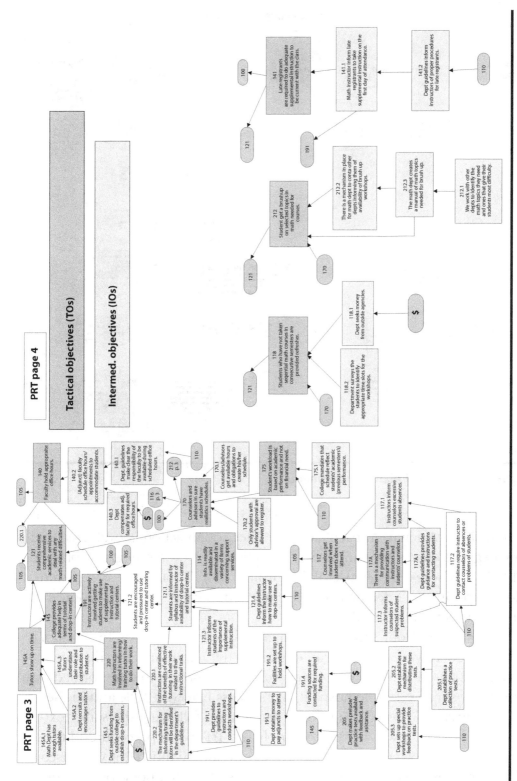

Figure 5.24 PrT for the Department of Mathematics pages 3 and 4 (January, 2002).

Project plan – (page 1 - department)

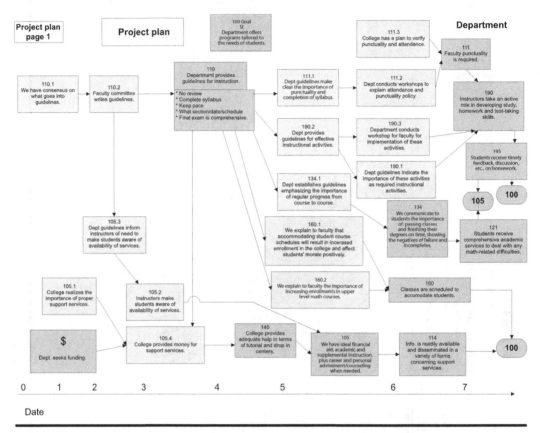

Figure 5.25 Project plan—department.

actions is not known. At each step, the effect of an action is evaluated and any negative effects are trimmed (see Section 2.5.1 on the negative branch). The TrT is also extremely useful for turning an ATT into an action plan that clearly specifies the detailed activities needed to carry out each action in the plan to achieve an IO of the ATT.

Tracy Burton-Houle, the TOC facilitator for the team of the first author at AGI, New Haven, Connecticut, explained the importance of this tree in January 2002. In South Africa, there were two hospitals that performed heart transplant surgery. In one hospital, the success rate was 90%, and in the other, it was 10%, even though both teams were following the same textbook procedure. It was decided to apply the TrT to the procedure in the hospital with a lower success rate. While developing the TrT, it was discovered that there was a logical gap in the steps of the textbook procedure.

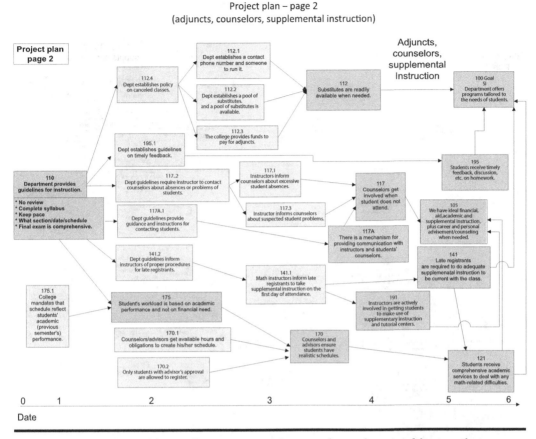

Figure 5.26   Project plan—adjuncts, counselors, and supplemental instruction.

They asked the successful surgeon in the other hospital about how he filled in this gap. The surgeon told what he did, which was not published anywhere in literature, and the logical gap was filled. From that time forward, the success rate in the other hospital equaled that of the more successful hospital. Thus, the TrT or TT is useful filling in any logical gaps.

TrTs are also used to give a clear set of directions. The constructed TrT is a good tool to use for training newly hired workers. This provides a clear way for people to learn duties and *why*. To add clarity: The only thing needed for the new hires to do is to learn how to read the TrT. Another way to accomplish the new hire training is to list the set of actions and the entities that explain why the actions must occur. It is not as concise, but may be satisfactory.

The TrT can be used in developing action plans to implement a strategic plan. TrTs have been used to create emergency evacuation manuals by industries such as airline manufacturers.

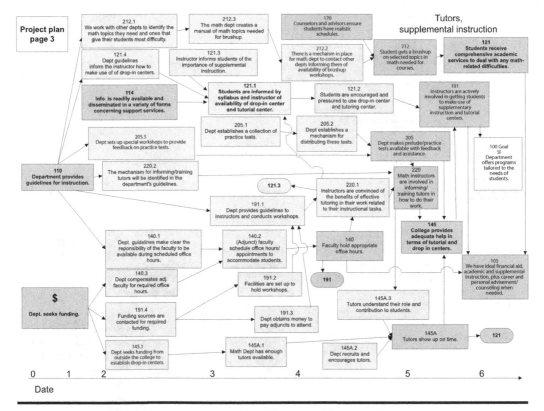

Figure 5.27 Project plan—tutors and supplemental instruction.

5.7.2 Structure of a TrT

This tree has a repeated entity structure as shown in Figure 5.28.* Each action is supported by four entities to make it logically sound. Sometimes, the five entities are listed differently, but we will follow the procedure outlined here. In brief, first narrate the storyline that demands some actions to achieve an objective or overcome an obstacle. Then, list all actions according to their logical order of execution. Fill in the steps numbered 2, 3, 4, and 5 in the following as necessary for each action. The action causes effect 2, the new reality. The cause (action) is justified by need 3 for the action. Up to this point, it looks like a negative or positive branch: if . . . then . . . because . . . . The TrT further needs the action to be supported by the fact of life 4. The fact

---

* This general TrT structure is based on a course in Constraints Management given by Dr. James Holt, professor emeritus of Engineering & Technology Management, Washington State University.

5 describes details of the when, where, and how of the action. The entities 5 and 2 cause the next step—the next need—to finally achieve the objective.

Sometimes, the order of actions is modified while developing the TrT.

General steps to developing a TrT: List all actions to be taken according to their logical order.

Example: Storyline: An instructor has important new ideas to introduce to the class and he wants students to participate in the discussion. He is troubled by the fact that the students do not listen to him and talk among themselves.

1. Write down the objective (this may be the top entity in the TrT block in Figures 5.28 and 5.29 or the final goal of the series of actions planned).

    The objective in Figure 5.29 is taken from the classroom example.
2. Write down the *action* entity no. 1 in the TrT of Figure 5.29. Try to answer questions such as the following:
    – "What should I do in order to achieve the objective?"
    – "What should I do in order to satisfy the need" (or overcome the Ob)?

    Example continued: Action: Make the material relevant to their lives. (In this simple example, we are dealing with only one action. More complex situations will be addressed later).
3. Write the obstacle or need in entity no. 3 in the TrT.

    If it is an obstacle, write the words "I need to overcome the obstacle that…"

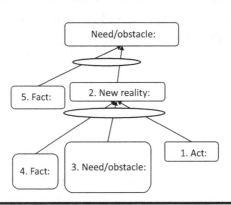

Transition tree—block structure

Figure 5.28 Repetitive nature of TrT.

Transition tree—goal: Students participate in the discussion.

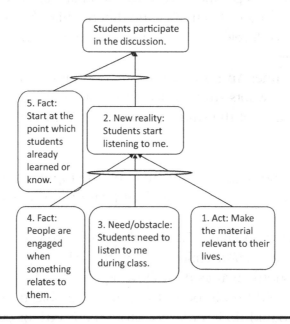

Figure 5.29 TrT for an instructor.

To continue the previous example: The instructor's need is "Students listen to me during class" or "I need to overcome the obstacle that students do not listen to me."

Ask the following questions to flesh out the need:

– What is the need to take this action?

– Why is this action important? In order to. . . .

– Why take this action? In order to. . . .

Do not confuse this need with the need entity B or C in a Cloud. In a Cloud, there is a set of opposite wants/or two opposing actions. In TrT, there is no such pair!

4. Write the *fact* entity no. 4 in the TrT. Ask questions such as the following:

– "Why will taking this action achieve the objective?"

– "Why will taking this action satisfy the need/overcome the Ob?"

– "What do you assume when you claim that this action satisfies this need"

A fact for the previous example: "People are engaged when something relates to them." This fact is a fact of life, an assumption, a general statement or a rationale.

5. Write the *new reality* no. 2 needed after the execution of the current action.

This is a new state or condition—a definite change or IO in a PrT. Answer questions such as the following:

– What new ability do you have after taking action 1 that enables you to take the next action? Verbalize the new ability/reality.

– What negative effects will be caused by the next action unless this action is taken? Verbalize that they will not be created.

New reality: Students start listening to me.

Example continued: Start with the information that students have already learned or know. Relate the new topic to known facts. A prolonged discussion of a totally unfamiliar topic will bore students and they will not participate.

6. Write the fact no. 5 needed for the place/time/details to execute the current action.

Answer questions such as the following:

– When/where/how should the execution of the action take place?

– Verbalize the new ability/reality for which the fact is required.

7. The goal is attained. Otherwise, keep repeating the TrT block structure.

The TrT for the example is in Figure 5.29.

There might be more actions necessary for the instructor, which will be clear once the instructor starts to look at entities 1 and 2. Entities 3 and 4 help the presenter to ascertain that there are no negative effects and no logical gaps. This short tree, with small changes, can be used to prepare a classroom presentation.

Example 5.9: TrT to Help a Student Modify Behavior (To Cause a Change in a Troubled First-Year Student's Behavior)*

The overall objective: "The first-year student changes his/her behavior."

Storyline: Kim is a 17-year-old first-year student who behaves in a way that leads to significant negative effects. You, the authority, want Kim to change his behavior. The problem is that you have had the prior bad experience that Kim is aware of the negative consequences of his behavior, but will continue to behave in a negative way, even if he will be sanctioned. This happens for two reasons:

---

* Guidance for this example was received from Dr. Howard Meeks, AGI, New Haven, Connecticut, retired professor of Industrial and Manufacturing Systems Engineering Department, Iowa State University, Ames, Iowa, January 2006.

1. Kim wants to maintain and show his independence.
2. Kim wants to satisfy the original need that led him to act this way to begin with.

List your actions in logical order: This is the plan you are thinking about.

Action no. 1: I initiate a discussion with Kim in a relaxed atmosphere, away from his peers who might provoke him to show his independence.

Action no. 2: I mention to Kim his behavior (or bring him to mention it) and ask him about its outcomes:

"What will happen then?" And then what might happen?"

I continue to ask Kim these kinds of questions about every outcome that he mentions, until we form a negative branch that starts with Kim's behavior and ends up with a meaningful outcome for Kim.

I ask Kim to write out the negative branch by himself.

Action no. 3: I ask Kim to examine the negative branch and think it over. I don't tell Kim to change his behavior.

Action no. 4: I ask Kim to consider the logical opposites of statements in the negative branch and to construct a positive branch by himself without any further comment about his behavior (these branches might be needed later to provide injections for correction of behavior).

Action no. 5: At a later time, I examine Kim's behavior for signs that will tell me whether Kim has or has not changed his behavior.

Action no. 6: If, after a few days, his behavior has not changed in response to action no. 5, I figure out what Kim's original need is, using questions such as the following:

1. Why are you behaving in this way? For what?
2. What are you trying to achieve in this way?
3. What prevents you from changing this behavior?

Action no. 7: I direct Kim to find an alternative way to satisfy his need, using questions such as the following:

4. Can you achieve this in another way?
5. Can we do something else to achieve this?

I work on injections to continue to work on his needs (this part may not be needed).

We will construct the TrT using the repeated structure as shown in Figures 5.30 through 5.34.

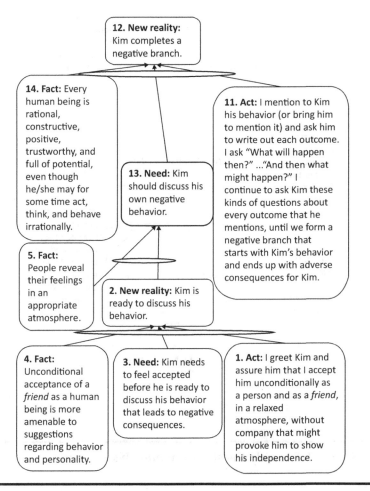

Figure 5.30   Page 1 TrT to help the student modify his behavior.

The facts are quite complex in the above TrT. They are based on "Treatment—12 principles" from the Muktangan Rehabilitation Center, Pune, India (http://www.muktangan.org).

5.7.2.1 TrT as a Stand-Alone Tool

If this satisfies your need and if you are working with children, go to TOCfE. If you are interested in applying TrT to word problems in mathematics, read on. If not, review the different stand-alone tools given in the Appendix on TOCfE. The websites http://www.tocforeducation.com and http://www.TOCforCollege.com have examples of several applications of the stand-alone tools of TOC to community work.

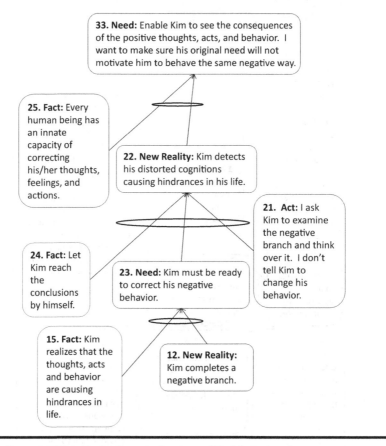

33. Need: Enable Kim to see the consequences of the positive thoughts, acts, and behavior. I want to make sure his original need will not motivate him to behave the same negative way.

25. Fact: Every human being has an innate capacity of correcting his/her thoughts, feelings, and actions.

22. New Reality: Kim detects his distorted cognitions causing hindrances in his life.

21. Act: I ask Kim to examine the negative branch and think over it. I don't tell Kim to change his behavior.

24. Fact: Let Kim reach the conclusions by himself.

23. Need: Kim must be ready to correct his negative behavior.

15. Fact: Kim realizes that the thoughts, acts and behavior are causing hindrances in life.

12. New Reality: Kim completes a negative branch.

Figure 5.31   Page 2 TrT to help the student modify his behavior.

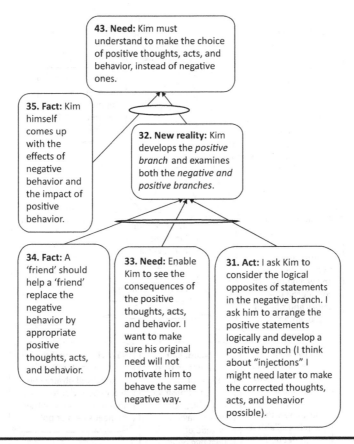

Figure 5.32   Page 3 TrT to help student modify behavior.

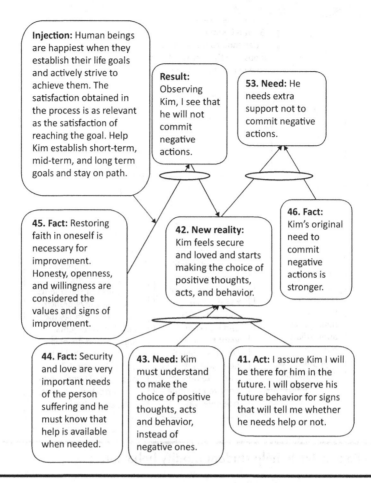

Figure 5.33   Page 4 TrT to help the student modify his behavior.

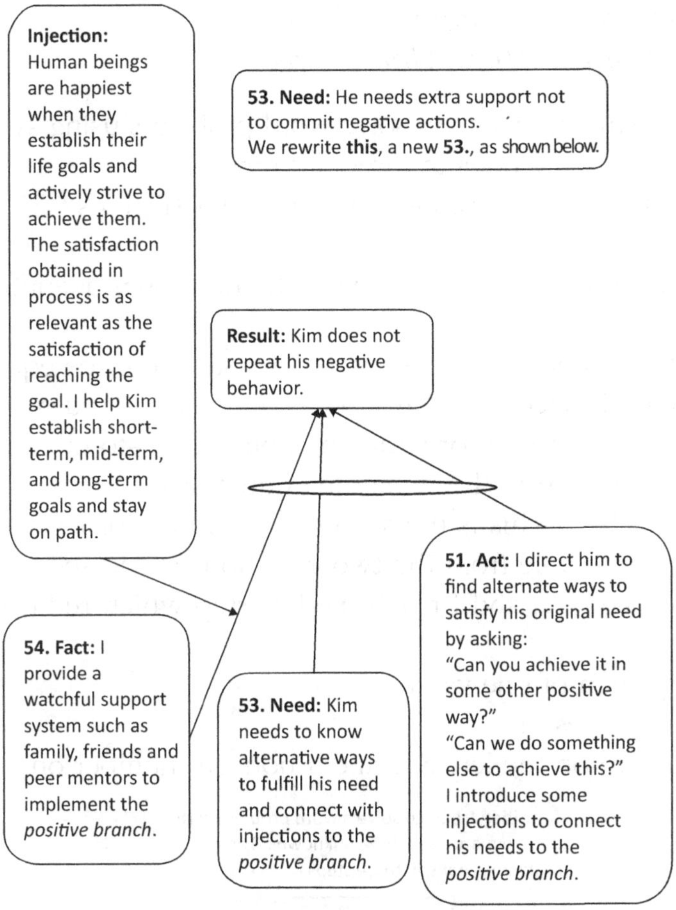

Injection: Human beings are happiest when they establish their life goals and actively strive to achieve them. The satisfaction obtained in process is as relevant as the satisfaction of reaching the goal. I help Kim establish short-term, mid-term, and long-term goals and stay on path.

53. Need: He needs extra support not to commit negative actions. We rewrite **this**, a new **53.**, as shown below.

Result: Kim does not repeat his negative behavior.

51. Act: I direct him to find alternate ways to satisfy his original need by asking: "Can you achieve it in some other positive way?" "Can we do something else to achieve this?" I introduce some injections to connect his needs to the *positive branch*.

54. Fact: I provide a watchful support system such as family, friends and peer mentors to implement the *positive branch*.

53. Need: Kim needs to know alternative ways to fulfill his need and connect with injections to the *positive branch*.

Figure 5.34 Page 5 TrT to help the student modify his behavior.

5.7.2.2 TrT to Solve a System of Three Equations in Three Unknowns

Suppose that a student wants to solve word problems using systems of three linear or nonlinear equations in three unknowns.

Here is a set of actions used to construct a TrT (Figures 5.35 through 5.37).

1. I read the word problem identifying the unknown quantities such as x, y, and z.
2. I translate sentences into equations. I must have three equations.
3. Rearranging if necessary, I use the first equation and one of the methods—substitution or addition/subtraction—to eliminate one variable (x, y, or z) from the remaining equations. I get two equations in two variables. This is the second step. I now proceed to eliminate the second variable from the two equations at the second step repeating the procedure, and I reach the last step which reduces to the following:
   - An equation of one variable
   - Has all zeroes or
   - Has a zero on the left side and a nonzero number on the right side

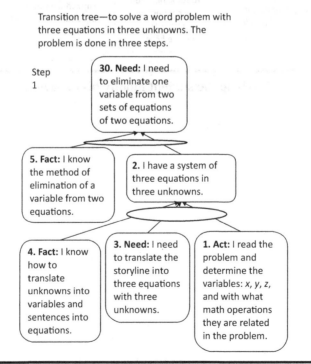

Transition tree—to solve a word problem with three equations in three unknowns. The problem is done in three steps.

Step 1

30. Need: I need to eliminate one variable from two sets of equations of two equations.

5. Fact: I know the method of elimination of a variable from two equations.

2. I have a system of three equations in three unknowns.

4. Fact: I know how to translate unknowns into variables and sentences into equations.

3. Need: I need to translate the storyline into three equations with three unknowns.

1. Act: I read the problem and determine the variables: x, y, z, and with what math operations they are related in the problem.

Figure 5.35 TrT to solve a system of three equations in three unknowns—step 1.

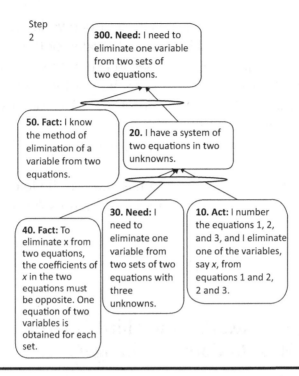

Figure 5.36 TrT to solve a system of three equations in three unknowns—step 2.

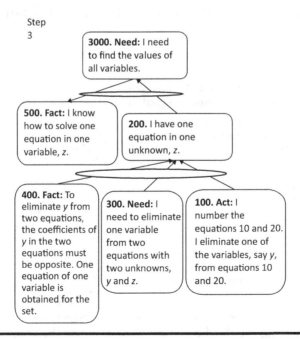

Figure 5.37 TrT to solve a system of three equations in three unknowns—step 3.

4. At the last step, if I have - an equation of one variable, I solve it and use the value of that variable to find the value of the second variable from one of the equations at the second step. I use the two values of the two variables to find the value of the third variable. I have a unique solution for each variable. Once I find the values of all variables, I interpret the meaning in the given context.

If, in the last step, the last equation has all zeroes, then the system has infinitely many solutions.

In the third step, if an equation has zero on the left side and a non-zero number on the right side, then there is no solution and the system is called inconsistent.

In this problem, 2, 20, and 200 are new realities.

5.8 Summary: Answering the Third Question of TOC: How to Cause a Change?

The PrT, the project plan, and various TrTs answer the third question of TOC: How to cause the change? The required steps are summarized in Figure 5.38. The tactics of a TOC solution to a problem is the answer to the third question, "How to cause the change?" in order to make the future reality into actual reality.

3. How to cause a change?
Designing the implementation   *Tactics*

5. *Future reality tree: ensures that the starting injection will lead to all the DEs without creating negative branches.*

6. *Prerequisite tree: in what order do we implement the TOs and what blocks their implementation?*

7. *Project plan*

8. *Transition trees: what actions must we take to implement the prerequisite tree?*

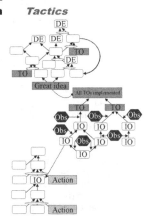

Figure 5.38   Answering the third question: how to cause the change? (Courtesy: AGI, New Haven, CT.)

We studied the Future Reality Trees in Chapter 4 and the tactics for change in this chapter.

Note that the action described as the last entity in the TrTs in Figure 5.38 is here placed in the middle and the working assumptions to the right. This is one variation of the TrT.

5.9 TOC Roadmap: Summary of All Steps of TOC

Key terms

UDE: undesirable effect

DE: desirable effect

Obs: obstacle

IO: intermediate objective

TO: tactical objective

We employ the following logical steps, as summarized in Figure 5.39: define the problem, list the issues and UDEs related to the problem, and select three important UDEs. "Define a problem precisely and you are half way to a solution" (Goldratt, 1990).

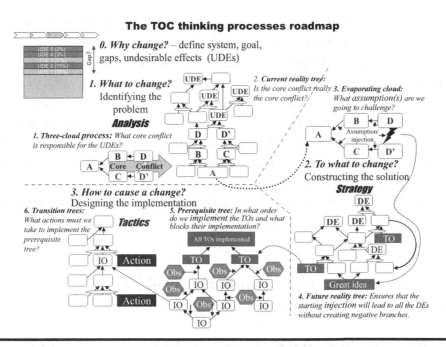

Figure 5.39   TOC roadmap. (Courtesy: Part 0. Why change? - Alan Barnard, Parts 1 through 6 AGI, New Haven, CT.)

Consider three Clouds to develop the generic Cloud root cause.

1. Create the CRT (branch).
2. Identify negative feedback loops in the CRT.
3. Create the FRT (branch).
4. Create positive loops in the FRT.
5. Identify NBRs. This topic answers, "What could possibly go wrong with the proposed solution?"

These steps are discussed in Chapters 2 and 4.

6. Develop a PrT/ATT.
7. Create a project plan.
8. Develop TrTs to execute the activities of the project plan.

These steps are discussed in Chapter 5.

We also observed that the Cloud tool (Chapter 3) and ATT/PrT in Chapter 5 require necessary condition logic, while the branch tool (Chapter 2) and TrT require sufficient condition logic.

Exercises

1. Select a case study on an Ambitious Target Study from http://www .tocforeducation.com, and rewrite it in your own words.
2. Using a problem assigned in a course as an AT, list all the Obs you have to overcome to attain the AT in PrT format.
3. For a course in your chosen major, a day-to-day lecture schedule given by an instructor is the project plan that he or she will be using for the semester. Based on that plan, decide what Obs you personally feel that you have and devise a PrT and project plan for the course. Discuss the project plan with your instructor or counselor.
4. Using the goal of your graduating from college as an AT, develop an ATT and a project plan based on Example 5.3.5.

Appendix 5.1 Creative Thinker's Toolkit: A Freshman Year Course

COR 100: Creative Thinker's Toolkit: Thinking and Acting
Fall/Spring

1. **Course:** COR 100, Creative Thinker's Toolkit: Thinking and Acting, 3 Cr. 3 Hr.
2. **Textbook (initial):** TOC: Creative Problem Solving—Umesh Nagarkatte and Nancy Oley
3. **Objectives:** This course supports "Thinking across the Curriculum." The course empowers students to think effectively, solve problems, make responsible decisions, and reach their academic and personal goals.

   The course has been developed to bring students in contact with the academic faculty of their chosen major in their first year or as early as possible in their academic career. This is an interdisciplinary course taught by various instructors in students' chosen major: Science/ Mathematics, Business, Social and Behavioral Sciences, and Liberal Arts/ undecided.

Learning Competencies:

Students will be able to do the following:

1. Solve complex problems.
2. Resolve conflicts at home and at work: work out daily conflicts.
3. Articulate personal, academic, and vocational goals.
4. Learn virtually anything.
5. Think creatively.
6. Make win–win decisions.
7. "Read between the lines" and "connect the dots."
8. Manage their time.
9. Approach tasks confidently.
10. Clarify values.
11. Identify wants and needs.
12. Think about consequences.
13. Communicate effectively.
14. Argue persuasively.

Topics/Content Areas:

- Conceptualization: how to state and shape a problem
- Problem solving: hypotheses, algorithms, and heuristics
- Creativity: brainstorming with convergent/divergent thinking
- Decision making
- Argumentation and evidence
- Argument mapping and reconstruction
- Making logical inferences: normative patterns for deduction and induction
- Basic research methods

4. **Learning Activities**
   - Developing a plan.
   - Articulating obstacles.
   - Visualizing and rendering problems/issues graphically.
   - Collaborating on team-based community projects (students of a particular major will be divided into several groups of four or five students for semester-long collaborative work).
   - Writing intensively—using journals, blogs, and wikis to develop storylines, surface assumptions, summarize topics, and describe ongoing projects.
   - Faculty workshops several times each semester to share findings and discuss instructional issues. Examples will be provided from appropriate disciplines that use the thinking process tools.
   - As assessment, the student will prepare several small and large PowerPoint projects and at least 10 examples resolving their own daily conflicts during the semester, and a final project plan for their career as the summative assessment in the course. In addition, the faculty in various disciplines will assign other projects in their disciplines.
5. **Instructor/s:** Various from different disciplines
   Office:
   Telephone:
   Hours:
   Appointment:
   E-mail:
6. **Prerequisites:** None
7. **Software:** Students will use Microsoft WORD and Powerpoint to construct various diagrams involved in the course. No previous knowledge of software is assumed.
8. **Resources:**
   - **Faculty:** In addition to working with the Freshman Year Program instructor as the key resource, students will work concurrently with other academic instructors of the course. All faculty will first participate in a workshop on TOC and topics related to their areas of professional expertise, facilitated by Drs. Nancy Oley of the Department of Psychology and Umesh Nagarkatte of the Department of Mathematics, assisted by Dr. Michael Fitzgerald of the Department of Philosophy.
   - **Students:** Fellow students are another important resource. Students will study with three to four other students, discussing the ideas

with them twice a week on a regular basis to motivate them and to improve performance. Students are expected to attend all classes. Any absences from the class create a gap in understanding, since there is no substitute for firsthand knowledge obtained in the interaction with the classroom instructor and fellow students.

– **Other resources:**

Reading Materials:

- Lahey, B.B. (2011). *Psychology: An Introduction*, or newest edition. New York: McGraw Hill. Selected chapters. Any introductory psychology textbook of the appropriate reading level could be used.
- Vaughn, L. (2010). *The Power of Critical Thinking*, 3rd ed. New York: Oxford University Press. An introductory text that guides students through the basics of reasoning, argumentation, and explanation.
- The first author has developed a *Motivational Guide* introducing various effective tools and strategies that students can use to understand life and to achieve success in personal and academic work.

There are additional help materials on the following websites:

- http://www.TOCforEducation.com
- http://www.tocforcollege.com

Other useful TOC websites will be identified as the instructor becomes aware of them.

9. **Strategies for the Learning Outcomes**

 a. Faculty in various disciplines teaching the course will communicate with each other frequently and meet formally prior to teaching the course and every 4 weeks during the semester. They will also work with Student Academic Success Service (SASS) counselors or similar counselors/advisors formally before the course starts and then as the need arises.

 b. Use all available technical resources. Each class will be equipped with a smart cart.

 c. Topics will be presented with concepts and algorithms in a logical fashion, informally and formally, using examples from various sources including newspapers and websites. The course schedule is attached at the end of the document.

 d. Confidence will be instilled in students through their active participation in instruction. Consistent individual and group work will lead to success.

e. Students will prepare a word-processed summary in their own words of each section using the examples from their discipline in a structured format: goal and concept or concepts with example/s linked in a logical order. This will give them practice with writing, reflection, and test review. The writing will be collected as a portfolio at the end of the semester.

f. Students will be assigned homework to turn in and will receive feedback within a week.

g. Students will complete several projects, and the instructor will select some for class presentation.

h. Instructors will always available through office hours and by appointment and by e-mail.

10. **Assessment Methodology**

The grade will be determined as follows:

1. Assignments: All assignments must be completed and handed in by the date announced. The deadlines for turning in the projects are listed in the syllabus. Students who do not hand in all their assignments will not receive a passing grade, regardless of their other work.

2. The summaries of each chapter will constitute 25% of the course grade.

3. Student PowerPoint presentations and various logic trees developed by the student:
   • 10 Conflict Resolution Clouds (25%)
   • Ambitious Target Tree to attain student's academic goal (25%)
   • Collaborative community project (25%)

11. **Expected Outcomes**

1. The strategies will guarantee that students perform A or B quality work.

2. Students will be able to use computers and use software to do their homework.

3. Students will learn how to apply the concepts and skills of the course to practical situations.

4. Students will develop communication skills.

5. With their cooperation, it is expected that 100% of the students will pass the course.

6. Most students will develop an ability to handle credit-bearing courses in their disciplines systematically.

12. **Syllabus for Creative Thinker's Toolkit**

Detailed Lecture Schedule for COR 100–Creative Thinker's Toolkit: Thinking and Acting

Fall/Spring

14 weeks, 27–28 meetings, 1.5 class hours/meeting

Lecture	Date	Topic	Chapter/ section
1		What are TPs? Underlying logic—logic twigs.	1
		Create groups of students in the class for collaborative work. Discussion of examples of logic from the academic disciplines	1
2		*Argumentation and evidence*—graphical method of resolving conflicts—Evaporating Cloud—creating a simple personal Cloud. *Identifying wants and needs. Clarifying values*; identify and resolve day-to-day conflicts, multitasking game	2–1, 2 Slides 2–6
		Number game—finding order in chaos. Examples from the academic disciplines— academic class Project—list of UDEs	Slide nos. 7, 8
	Assignments due	2 personal Clouds, Chapter 1 summary	
3		Addressing chronic conflicts. *Resolving conflicts at home and at work.* Working out daily conflicts	2–3
		Examples in the disciplines—writing about your experiences in mathematics/ disciplines—listing UDEs and making Clouds from three chosen UDEs	
4		Approach tasks confidently; empowerment Clouds	2–4
		Examples from the academic disciplines	
5		3-Cloud process; summary of Clouds	2–5

(Continued)

Lecture	Date	Topic	Chapter/ section
6		Making the Core Conflict Cloud and surfacing assumptions, suggesting injections. *Constructing persuasive arguments*; examples from the academic disciplines	
	Assignments due	4 personal Clouds, Chapter 2 summary, academic project Core Conflict Cloud	
7		*Communicating effectively; how to debate*; student individual/group presentations on Core Conflicts	
8		*Argument mapping and logical connections—* the branch—checking if . . . then . . . logic	3–1
		Examples of the branch from the academic disciplines	
9		*Learning how to read between the lines; making decisions*	3–2
10		Examples from the academic disciplines	
		Negative branch reservations and positive branches	3–3
11		*Solving complex problems*; examples from the academic disciplines	
12		Half-baked solutions; *thinking about consequences*	3–4
		Examples from the academic disciplines	
	Assignments due	4 personal Clouds, Chapter 3, 1–6 summary, academic project; CRT	
13		*Inferential patterns: deduction and induction*—CRT	3–5, 6
		Discussion of students' academic CRTs	
14		Student individual/group presentations on CRTs	
15		FRT	3–7, 8
16		Student's academic FRT	

(*Continued*)

Lecture	Date	Topic	Chapter/section
		Examples from academic disciplines	
17		*"Connecting the dots,"* TrT	3–9
18		Solving a system of equations—Science and Business example	
	Assignment due	Rework previous 10 personal Clouds, Chapter 3 summary, academic project list of DEs and FRT	
19		ATT	4–1, 2
		Examples from the academic disciplines	
20		*Envisioning your goals*; students prepare their ATTs	4–3, 7
21		Examples to solve problems in academic disciplines using ATTs	4–8
22		*Time management*: how to develop a project plan and use the TrT to bring it into action.	4–9
	Assignment due	Chapter 4 summary	
23		*Becoming more creative thinkers*; student individual/group presentations on ATTs	
24		Student individual/group presentations on ATTs	
25		Presentations	
26		Summary of TPs	4–11
27		*Learn virtually anything*; examples in academic disciplines	

Note: Italicized phrases identify 15 learning competencies.

References

Barnard, A. (2007, October 10–13). *How to SEE and UNLOCK inherent potential within each of ourselves and others*. 10th Theory of Constraints in Education International Conference, Fort Walton Beach, FL.

Berenbom, J., & Nagarkatte, U. (2013). *Departmental Guidelines*. Unpublished report, Department of Mathematics, Medgar Evers College, Brooklyn, NY.

Goldratt, E. (1990). *Theory of Constraints.* Great Barrington, MA: North River Press.

Nagarkatte, U., & Berenbom, J. (2014). *Prealgebra.* Ronkonkoma, NY: Linus Learning.

Nagarkatte, U., & Berenbom, J. (2016a). *Elementary Algebra.* Ronkonkoma, NY: Linus Learning.

Nagarkatte, U., & Berenbom, J. (2016b). *Intermediate Algebra and Trigonometry.* Ronkonkoma, NY: Linus Learning.

Ricketts, J.A. (2007). *Reaching the Goal: How Managers Improve a Services Business Using Goldratt's Theory of Constraints.* Indianapolis, IN: IBM Press.

Chapter 6

Five Focusing Steps in the Process of OnGoing Improvement (POOGI): Institutional Problem Solving

6.1 Overview

The purpose of this chapter is to bring together TOC concepts introduced in previous chapters in order to show how they can be used to solve systemic institutional problems. Institutional problem solving or systemic problem solving requires us to traverse the entire TOC roadmap. This chapter is important for administrators and leaders who want to make rapid continued progress in their institutions. To ensure the Process Of OnGoing Improvement (POOGI), institutions use five focusing steps, discussed starting in Section 6.2.

At the outset, we recall from Chapter 1 some technical terms: A *system* in academia consists of students, faculty, services, staff, administration, and their interactions related to a goal. A system for an institution is all departments and personnel related to the goal. A system for a person is all people related to an interpersonal or personal issue. *Performance* is measured in terms of learning, passing rates, graduation rates, number of students who enter graduate school or employment, being *more* successful in achieving goals, etc. A *constraint* is something which hinders attaining a goal and which should be removed.

> Paradigms are sets of assumptions we believe are valid. We go through a "paradigm shift" when we realise one or more of our assumptions are no longer valid. (Cox & Goldratt, 1986)

System performance improves due to a *paradigm shift* in how we view the underlying issues (our attitude about the situation) and results in changing various behaviors, measurements, and policies that are restricting or constraining that improvement.

In Section 6.2, we define the five focusing steps of the Process Of OnGoing Improvement (POOGI) and relate them to constraints in academia. In Section 6.3, we relate in detail these steps as they applied to the institutional study at MEC. In Section 6.4, we illustrate numeric measures of the system *throughput* in terms of graduating students and students progressing toward a degree. In Section 6.5, we discuss how institutions or departments can use TOC to carry out a program review or self-study. In Section 6.6, we discuss strategic planning in a higher education institution. We also compare the the popular Strengths, Weaknesses, Opportunities and Threats (SWOT) analysis to the POOGI of TOC in Sections 6.5 and 6.6.

6.2 Five Focusing Steps of the POOGI

These steps are adapted from Ricketts (2007).

Step 1: *Identify* the system constraint. (Apply TOC to find where the constraints are.)

Step 2: *Exploit* the system constraint. (Utilize the constraint to the fullest extent. Help the constraint work better.)

Step 3: *Subordinate* everything else to the constraint. (Nonconstraint links must keep the constraint busy. Otherwise, stay out of the constraint's way.)

Step 4: *Elevate* the constraint. (Apply TOC to improve the productivity of the constraint. Expand the capacity of the constraint.)

Step 5: Do not let the inertia set in! (Find the next system constraint and repeat the previous four steps.)

In step 4, we provide appropriate resources using TOC techniques so that the constraint can produce more. This is different from step 2, where we only focus on the functioning of the existing conditions of the constraint.

The following discussion summarizes the roles of the various tools given in Chapters 2 through 5.

Before beginning to solve a problem, it is necessary to define the problem. Depending on the educational institution, improvement can only be made in the area of one's responsibility and in the area under one's control. This is illustrated in Figure 6.1; see also Sections 1.4.1 and 1.4.2.

No institution with many totally isolated entities (units) like the one shown in Figure 6.2A exists in nature. If it existed, to improve the institution A, each entity in A would need to exert an independent effort which is an enormous undertaking. But, in nature, there exist only institutions such as shown in Figure 6.2B. In this case, no entities in the institution are isolated. They are always logically connected to one another by cause-and-effect relationships. Experience has shown that improving every entity individually does not lead to overall improvement of the institution, since the weakest component will always remain weak and hold back the overall

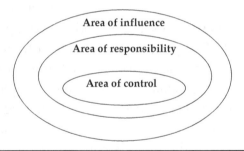

Figure 6.1   Span of control.

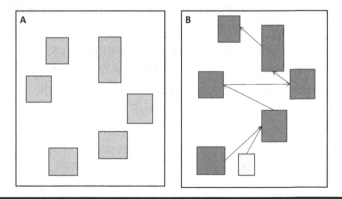

Figure 6.2   Systems/institutions.

improvement. Institution B can be improved by improving *just the two bottom entities*. Using TOC to address the issues related to a constraint, for example, the two bottom entities in institution B, leads to a harmonious resolution of the systemic problem and improvement of the whole institution. TOC with its TPs uncovers such bottom entries or constraints and by improving them, improves the whole institution.

The institution A does not exist. The institution B has interrelated entities. Arrows indicate cause-and-effect relationships between entities.

An educational institution is a service organization. Its customers are the students, industries, and graduate schools: some students want to be entrepreneurs, some want to teach in schools, some want to just graduate and enrich themselves, and some industries employ its students; some higher education institutions, such as graduate or professional schools, will further develop the academic knowledge of the students. The institution has to be sensitive to both students' needs and other customers' needs. If students' needs are not met, they will look to other institutions to meet their needs. Similarly, employers, colleges, universities, businesses, and professional schools look for quality graduates from other educational institutions. Thus, the survival and reputation of an educational institution depends upon recognizing and meeting its students' needs and delivering a quality education.

With the single goal of helping students to meet their needs and graduate, the administration, staff, and faculty of an institution can come together and resolve any issues that arise. Stakeholders should not get trapped emotionally in any one point of view. For those used to making ad hoc decisions, a systemic analysis might seem tedious, since it does take time to flesh out the assumptions underlying the various issues which can then be addressed in a way that has a long-lasting effect. TOC analysis gives definitive answers to such questions and provides methods to anticipate all the likely consequences of these decisions.

Most institutional initiatives start as a reaction to pressure from outside influences such as changes in laws, or arise internally from a troublesome written or unwritten *policy, measurement, or behavior* within the institution. Policies are monitored using measurements, and people behave according to the way they are measured; there are no measurements that are not associated with policies, implicit or explicit. Initiatives may also depend on public funding that reflects legislative policy. For example, for college recruiters or recruitment departments, the pressure (policy) is to enroll as many students as possible, since in some cases, public funding of the institution may depend on enrollment (measurement). For the admissions department, the pressure is to select students who exceed the minimum requirement of academic preparation. For program and curriculum developers in the institution, the pressure is to do the development work in the shortest possible time. For advisement, the pressure is to place the students correctly. For academic departments, there is pressure to maintain quality of instruction and assessment standards and, at the same time, to accommodate students with various skill levels and deficiencies. For career advisement personnel, there is pressure to place as many graduates as possible. For counseling, library, and other services, there is pressure to work within various state or university regulations and available funding and to meet student and faculty demands. The various entities tend to react mostly to their particular pressures, treat the symptoms, and fail to address the causes. The "silos" of these various departments create conflicts as given in Figure 6.3.

The partial organizational chart for an educational institution in Figure 6.4 shows selected departments. This figure summarizes the silo mentality of most institutions. Each department or functional area is working in isolation. Each department operates within its own silo and with its own issues.

The problems that arise from this silo mentality are further illustrated in Figure 6.3, which shows the institution from the larger perspective of input/output relationships and processes associated with the departments in Figure 6.4.

Each area in Figure 6.3 represented by a silo has a particular function to perform or *job* to do, criteria for success or agenda (goal), undesirable

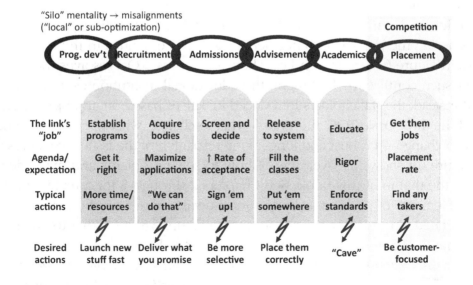

Figure 6.3 Institutional flowchart detailing the functions of each silo.

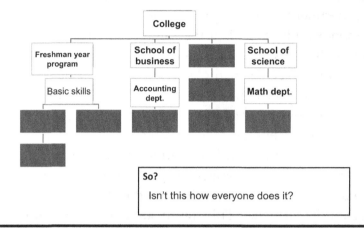

Why "TOC"?

Most of us view what we're doing via thinking of the organization as "the chart"… and focusing our efforts on our responsibilities in our individual departments

So?

Isn't this how everyone does it?

Figure 6.4   Partial organizational chart.

actions that it takes (UDEs), and actions that it would prefer to take (DEs). For example, the faculty needs to educate students. They do this typically by enforcing strict academic standards. But in order for the program to continue, the faculty is under pressure to let a sufficient number of students pass, thus accommodating students by lowering academic standards. This creates a dilemma.

Different departments strive to excel in their own functions without considering the impact on other departments. The entities in the lower two rows in Figure 6.3 are in conflict. They act as silos. TOC resolves these and other such conflicts by looking at the educational institution as a system.

If instead, the stakeholders introduced initiatives based on an objective analysis of the three basic TOC questions—what to change, what to change to, and how to change—a robust and long-lasting resolution of the issues would result.

Figure 6.5 shows an overview of how to solve problems and make decisions, the theme of this book. See Chapters 2 through 5 for a review of the main elements of problem solving. Good decisions rest on the three elements needed to make improvements (see Figure 6.5): (a) What to change, (b) what to change to, and (c) how to cause the change.

Our discussion shows the importance of administrators making decisions after collecting the required data, using these questions, and considering consequences of their decisions. If they succumb to misinformation or incomplete

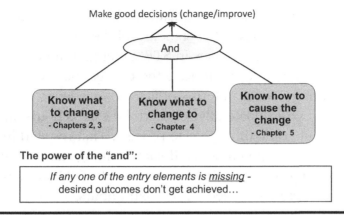

Figure 6.5 Importance of the three questions.

information and biases, then the institution, faculty, students, and community suffer.

Examples of making changes while ignoring the first of the three questions abound. We will consider three examples.

Improvements made on the basis of symptoms without the systematic analysis of the three questions lead to only temporary solutions and conflicts between the different entities (units). Ignoring any one of these questions in the given sequence leads to adverse consequences.

1. Because of the policy issued by a college/university administrator, every degree-granting department in a college had to present a 3-year plan of course offerings. No academic department was consulted in developing this policy. When the departments strictly adhered to this policy, many students had to wait several semesters until a given course was offered according to the plan, which delayed their graduation. There was no flexibility to offer courses according to student need.
2. Most departments work like silos and do not communicate with other departments on a regular basis. If two courses that are required as corequisites for each other are scheduled at the same time in two related departments, students' graduation is delayed.
3. State Regents and university administrators made a rule without input from faculty that a student could have no more than 120 credits to graduate, regardless of whether a course was developmental and prerequisite to college-level courses or carried credit toward the student's degree program. The consequence of this action was that some upper-level courses that the student was supposed to have in a recognized degree

program could not be accommodated within the 120-credit limit, thus potentially watering down the standard of the university degree.

4. A college had gateway courses in STEM that had more hours than the number of credits. In order to save the college money, without considering the consequences in terms of faculty's academic rights or student attrition, a provost unilaterally reduced the excess hours and assigned credits without going through due process. That resulted in faculty outrage and legal repercussions. If such a ruling stands, it would result in lower passing scores in these courses and STEM attrition, since the preparation of students needs those extra hours.

Many decision makers like to make changes in a hurry without analyzing "what to change" (discussed in the Chapters 2 and 3) and do it so quickly that they ignore the possible UDEs. Many do not involve all the stakeholders and their issues. Many administrators bring in consultants, who do not have the complete picture of the college scene and waste money because their recommendations cannot be implemented. Decisions made in this way might not address the needs of some stakeholders or might create UDEs for the stakeholders. For example, administrators of a college decided to lower the exorbitant costs of teaching basic skills in the English and mathematics departments by separating these areas from their home disciplines and employing instructors who were not completely trained in the regular disciplines. An unanticipated consequence of this was that the standards of instruction were lowered and students could pass the exit exam but were not "college ready." Although operating expenses were lowered, thousands of students dropped out due to the lowered quality of instruction, thus costing the college millions of dollars in students' fees had the students continued and lowering the number of graduating students.

In Chapter 2, we studied how to describe issues as UDEs by removing the emotion from them.

> Recall that an UDE should "be serious, be a condition not a lack of an activity, not blame anyone, happen frequently, have a serious negative outcome, [and] not incorporate the solution within the statement." (Cox III et al., 2012)
>
> The UDE should state what bothers you in a simple, clear, complete sentence, not a compound sentence using *but, and,* or *because.* It is not a negative effect or a symptom. It should be a *benign* statement; that is, it should not hurt anyone. It should have

no emotion. It should focus on a current fact. The UDE should focus on an *action/activity* or *want*.

Chapters 2 and 3 especially deal with the CRT and illustrate the use of negative branches to analyze the harmful consequences that a policy decision might cause. A TOC analysis of what to change begins with listing all issues, expressing them as UDEs, and logically linking them to form a CRT, discussed in Chapter 2. You can develop the root or the Core Conflict, by the three-Cloud process as discussed in the later sections of Chapter 3. The Core Conflict is the constraint in the system at that point in time.

TOC practitioners observe that often we don't improve because we're stuck in a chronic conflict that causes most of the problems that we struggle with on a day-to-day basis.

Definition 6.1

Chronic conflict: A conflict for an individual is a chronic conflict if the person feels trapped, does not see any other choice, and feels powerless to remove the conflict. The individual submits to the reality unwillingly. The issue is long term, highly emotional, with little effort being given to addressing the issue. The issue may be personal or interpersonal. (AGI*, Maintenance Skills Workshop [MSW] booklet 3)

Any conflict not addressed directly has a tendency to become a chronic conflict, unless, because of the passage of time or change in the situation or maturity, the issue no longer exists. Chronic conflicts were discussed in Chapter 3. How can we identify a chronic conflict or a constraint? We review how to identify the constraint from a set of issues that we want to resolve (see also Section 3.6).

In the TOC approach, no party is blamed; we have active participation of all stakeholders and analyze the current situation in terms of policy, measurements, and behavior and not in terms of the particular people sitting there or reacting to them. No changes for change sake are to be made. If we want to improve some system, as seen earlier, improving every entity separately in the system does not improve the system; rather, by addressing the weakest link in the chain of entities in the system, we bring about rapid systemic improvement.

---

* Avraham Goldratt Institute (AGI), Haven, Connecticut. The authors had their Jonah training in TOC at AGI in 2001–2002 and 2005 with funding from two US Department of Education grants.

Using TOC, an institution is able to identify the weakest link, bottleneck, or constraint in a systematic fashion. To do this, list all the issues. Define UDEs, each of which is an objective, simple statement that describes a current negative situation and does not blame anyone. Select three important UDEs from the set. Form an Evoporating Cloud for each of the three UDEs, as in Chapter 2, and a Core Cloud (Conflict) that represents the three Evoporating Clouds as in Chapter 3. Just three important systemic UDEs are sufficient to identify the constraint. In order to convince ourselves that the Core Conflict is indeed so, we have to show that most of the UDEs are logically linked to the Core Conflict. In other words, a Current Reality Tree (CRT) with the Core Conflict as the root must be formed. If a CRT does not include all important UDEs, then one must reanalyze the three statements selected and check whether the UDEs can in fact be connected by adding intermediate logical statements. This answers the question, what to change? See the detailed discussion in Chapters 2 and 3. The dilemma or opposing wants in the boxes D-D′ in a Core Cloud is the *conflict*, constraint, or problem. **This process IDENTIFIES the bottleneck or constraint of the system (step 1).**

By analyzing the assumptions underlying the Core Cloud, we obtain a resolution (injection) to break or resolve the conflict which considers the needs of both involved parties and transcends the opposing wants that cause the conflict. That resolution is popularly called the *Bright or Great Idea*, or *strategic or starting injection (SI)* in TOC. All stakeholders must agree that it is indeed the bright idea that would resolve the conflict. That is the first step in figuring out *what to change to*.

The detailed answer to the question, *what to change to?* lies in considering the logical opposites of UDEs. These are called Desired Effects (DEs). When these are logically connected, one gets the skeleton of a Future Reality Tree (FRT). The effort or intervention or a Tactical Objective (TO) that has to be taken up as an "injection" to bring each DE into reality must be added along with the DE to develop a complete FRT. The root of the FRT is the SI. The FRT answers the question, *what to change to?* This is explained in detail in Chapter 4. It shows logically that by addressing the *Great Idea* or "SI," we can turn the DEs into reality. **This process implements step 2, that is, how to make maximum use of the constraint or how to EXPLOIT the constraint.**

When we want to answer the question, *how to cause the change?* we work with the listed injections of the FRT, the TOs. For each TO, an *Ambitious Target Tree (ATT)* is developed using Intermediate Objectives (IOs) as discussed in Chapter 5. All the ATTs combined make a humongous

Prerequisite Tree (PrT). The top of the PrT is the Great Idea discussed earlier. **One should SUBORDINATE everything else to the decisions about how to handle the constraint in order to realize the Bright Idea or achieve the main objective.** In other words, nonconstraint links must keep the constraint busy. All resources should be directed toward resolving the Core Conflict—the weakest link—using the Great Idea. In this way, the currently available resources do not get wasted on improvement of each individual entity in the system but are used to improve the system (see Figure 6.6) as a whole. This is done using the PrT and other concepts in Chapter 5 to answer the third question, *how to cause the change?*

In order to implement the proposed changes, Chapter 5 gives a step-by-step plan with TrTs for each IO of the PrT, so that the hurdles and obstacles to implementation of the SI have already been anticipated and dealt with. Extra resources may be needed to increase the capacity of the constraint. **This indicates how to ELEVATE the constraint.** The word *elevate* involves action to implement the Great Idea, using all resources in a synchronized manner, as shown by the project plan (based on the PrT). In this step are expenditures, actual services, tangible results, and the tangible part of the answer to the question *How to cause the change?* You will see long-term improvements and a paradigm change (change in attitude). In that sense, the weakest point in the logical chain of the system has been elevated in strength and is no longer a constraint.

For the Process Of OnGoing Improvement (POOGI), elevating the constraint automatically leads to the next step. Once the constraint is unblocked, find the next system constraint and repeat the previous four steps. **Do not let the inertia set in! Go back to step 1** to identify the new weakest link. These steps will be further explained with a case study.

The *throughput* is the ultimate product or outcome of the educational institutional processes, also called the throughput chain, such as the number of well-qualified students graduating from an educational institution. The products of a higher educational institution are not inert, having just monetary values as in industry, but have intangible value—education or knowledge—which is priceless.

Figure 6.6 shows the educational institution from a systems point of view. In this simplified example, the throughput is the number of graduating students and those placed in industry and graduate schools; the types of careers achieved; the school's reputation; and the school's income from alumni donations and performance-based grants, etc. The processing of students forms the throughput chain.

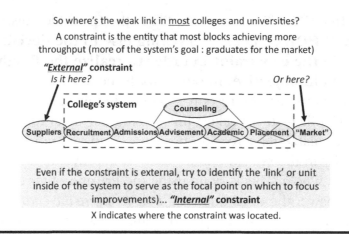

So where's the weak link in <u>most</u> colleges and universities?

A constraint is the entity that most blocks achieving more throughput (more of the system's goal : graduates for the market)

Even if the constraint is external, try to identify the 'link' or unit inside of the system to serve as the focal point on which to focus improvements)... *"**Internal**"* constraint

X indicates where the constraint was located.

Figure 6.6 Colleges and universities from a system point of view.

TOC emphasizes that we should concentrate on the *weakest* link or constraint in the chain leading to the goal. There can be only one weakest link at any given time. We have discussed how to identify the constraint in a chain in earlier paragraphs.

Since the student is the most important customer for an educational institution, the system has to be geared toward meeting the needs of the student and graduating her/him with a quality education in the shortest possible time. A typical incoming student at a college moves through the system in the sequence shown in Figure 6.7. A student desirous of graduating with a degree enters the college enrolled in a Freshman Year Program (FYP). Meeting the basic skills requirement is his/her first concern. Or, as a transfer student, the student might need some or none of the FYP and basic skills courses. The student might also be able to take some credit-bearing courses while fulfilling the basic skills requirements. Then, the student needs to go through college-level English and mathematics requirements, which can be taken concurrently and as prerequisites to a degree program in a specific discipline. The student finishes the course track of years Y_1, Y_2, Y_3, and Y_4 in sequence and graduates. There are students who drop out or cannot be placed in a specific year because of failure, absenteeism, personal and family problems, courses not being offered when the students are ready, and many other problems. If any college wants to improve its throughput (graduation rate), these students' concerns must be addressed, so as to expedite their passage through the system.

In most liberal arts colleges, Departments of Mathematics and English play a dual role. They are *service* departments to other departments (the *client*

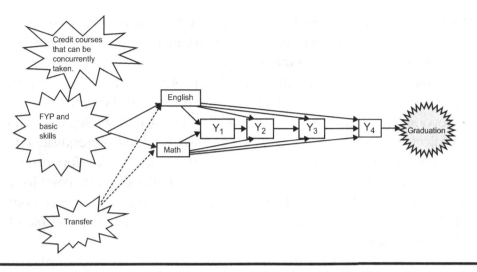

Figure 6.7 Students' progression through an educational institution.

disciplines) and are also "provider" departments. A provider department offers courses for its own majors. The English and math departments, in particular, draw inputs—most importantly, students—from the clients (other departments) and the providers (the math and English Departments). Their inputs (resources) are the students who require a service such as pre- or corequisite courses in mathematics or English and the students who are majoring in mathematics or English, respectively. Some service departments that do not have degree programs of their own, such as the FYP, basic skills instruction, counseling, library, and computing services, are purely service departments and draw their resources from clients only. In Figure 6.7, the arrows from English and math departments to years 2 through 4 indicated extra math or English courses taken by students of client disciplines as well as by English or math majors. Those arrows do not apply to all students of the liberal arts colleges.

Sometimes, conflicts may arise between the resources, e.g., courses offered, and the resource constraints, e.g., times that the courses are offered, of two departments. For example, as mentioned earlier, suppose that a student with a biology major requires a calculus and a physics course and the physics course has the calculus course as a pre- or corequisite. If the mathematics department schedules the calculus course at the same time that the physics course is offered, it can delay the student's graduation. Thus, service projects (courses or projects of service departments) such as course scheduling, need to incorporate communication methods to coordinate constrained resources across the two departments (i.e., need to coordinate the two courses for clients and providers). They need quality assurance methods that identify conflicts without unduly interfering with curricula/disciplines, that are trouble-free (do not generate ill will), that diagnose the cause of the trouble, and that apply a suitable remedy.

It should be apparent that the impact of problems with a service project (e.g., course scheduling) can affect both the client and the service provider well beyond the duration of the project. For instance, if we regard a course as a project, as discussed in Chapter 5, a student taking prerequisite courses in a certain service provider's area, such as the mathematics department, must be equipped with concepts, skills, and confidence to succeed in the courses offered by the client departments, e.g., the physical sciences department. If the student is not so equipped, then he or she is not capable of handling the course in the client discipline.

Clearly, service departments such as mathematics and English play a very important role in the college, since every college student must take at least one course in each of these departments. Considering the importance of writing and communication and the need for prerequisite mathematics courses in other science, business, and social sciences courses, the sooner students complete the college requirements in mathematics and English departments, the sooner they are on the way to graduation. <u>In that sense, in the language of TOC, mathematics and English departments play the role of a *constraint* in the throughput chain.</u>

Moreover, the departments feeding students to the mathematics and English departments such as the FYP or Accelerated Study in Associated Programs (ASAP) have a responsibility to build confidence and prepare students in credit-bearing courses in terms of content and process. The Departments of Mathematics and English, in turn, have to be extremely sensitive to the client departments', e.g., psychology, business, and biology, needs.

Communication among stakeholders and arrangement for the smooth flow of students into and through the *constraints* is an essential condition for steadily increasing the supply of graduates. One implication of this is that an adequate number of well-prepared students should be supplied to the English and mathematics departments and that, unless the two departments themselves offer further formal preparation for college-level courses, i.e., basic skills, these departments should not be overloaded with weakly prepared students.

In some colleges and universities, basic skills service departments are housed literally or figuratively outside of the respective disciplines as a *cost-saving* measure, without thinking through all the consequences. For example, as discussed in the consequences of not analyzing the question *What to change*, by separating basic skills from the Department of Mathematics and by sometimes employing faculty without advanced degrees in math to teach these courses at a lower pay rate, administrators may overlook the fact that there is a sophisticated side to elementary mathematics (Wu, 2009). Unfortunately, faculty from nonmathematics disciplines often know only how to manipulate symbols and do not take the advanced calculus/mathematical analysis required of mathematics majors. Thus, the students of basic skills departments who are taught by nonmathematicians do not receive a deep, college-level understanding of basic mathematics.

The only goal for basic skills service departments that are isolated from their respective disciplines is to ensure that a maximum number of students pass the remedial math/English *exit* tests and are qualified to take the lowest level of mathematics or English courses in the respective departments. Having to take basic skills is often demoralizing, since these courses are the ones that they were supposed to have passed in high school. If, instead, the basic skills courses in English and mathematics are offered within their respective disciplines, then first-time first-year students automatically land in these departments. Preparing students becomes the responsibility of and an opportunity for the two departments. Students' morale is raised when they come into early, daily contact with faculty in credit-bearing courses and tutors in the same department. Students have one less link to pass through to graduate. The mathematics and English departments have the higher goal of graduating students with a degree and not just of having students pass some university-mandated exit test. They can exercise flexibility in terms of placing students in higher-level courses by direct observation of students' capabilities, thus potentially lessening the time needed for graduation, and consequently increasing the throughput. First-year students also work toward the higher goal of graduating with a degree, rather than just passing the exit tests. In conjunction with the FYP advisors and resources, the mathematics and English departments are well placed to fulfill their responsibility of instilling confidence in students with a focus on graduating students with any major of the student's choice.

The two departments also have responsibility for the students in client disciplines, of course, including their own majors. As shown in Figure 6.6, in general, the advisement and counseling departments play a critical supporting role, and academic departments deliver the courses for the main throughput or *T*. Considering the goal of increasing throughput, the various departments in an educational institution can come together and brainstorm, using the systematic TOC approach to resolve any conflicts that may arise from time to time.

In the following, we discuss in detail the five focusing steps of TOC for an educational institution's ongoing improvement.

6.3 The Process Of OnGoing Improvement (POOGI)

Step 0: Agree on the system goal. Define the *constraint* and the *problem*.

In order to agree on a common goal, a brainstorming session is necessary, where people are free to express their issues and understand their roles in terms of the college's goal of graduating more and more qualified students. We need to focus on throughput (T) in Figure 6.6. We may not be sure how our issues are related to T and each other, but we feel that they are related. If we do not focus on the constraint resulting in a lower T and instead focus on symptomatic issues, we will only have made a misaligned effort and end up with the effect depicted in Figure 6.8: we will not find out why we don't graduate more students.

Recall that the TOC analysis done in the Department of Mathematics at MEC* and discussed in earlier chapters considered the goal, "*To reduce student attrition.*" To confine it to the faculty's area of responsibility, the mathematics team restricted itself to the more specific goal, "To reduce student attrition in mathematics courses." As previously mentioned, a team of three mathematics faculty members including the chair developed all the steps during a Jonah Program at AGI.[†] This case study[‡] will be used as our example for the following discussions. After defining the goal of the system and the fact of a constraint, we were ready to consider the five focusing steps as a process to get the most out of the system in terms of the system goal. Here, *the system* includes the stakeholders involved in the process of graduating students: full-time and part-time faculty, students, and tutors in the Department of Mathematics, as well as the counselors and advisors working with the department. In the following, we will use TOC terms, assuming that the reader is familiar with the terms from the discussion of thinking process (TP) tools in earlier chapters.

---

* As far as the authors know, MEC of CUNY is the first college to use TOC to address the problem of student attrition.
† Dedicated Jonah Course at AGI, New Haven, Connecticut, January, 2002.
‡ Details of this research were presented at the international conferences of TOCfE in 2006 and 2007 and at TOCICO in 2007.

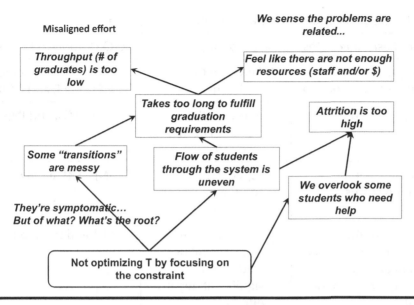

Figure 6.8 **Logical relationships among concerns expressed during a brainstorming session.**

6.3.1 *Levels of Resistance, Levels of Buy-In, and TOC/TP*

Before any initiative is introduced by the leadership team, it is necessary to know the "layers of resistance" and "levels of buy-in" of stakeholders. The reason for this is that the perceived resistance to adopting any initiative can be turned into a positive force using the TOC and TP tools in a systematic fashion, level by level. The process of obtaining stakeholder "buy-in" is explained in Table 6.1. The reader can see that Table 6.1 is a PrT on how to introduce any initiative in a system.

The mathematics department team developed buy-in using the following steps. These steps were introduced in Chapter 1 and are repeated here for relevance. Some steps need to be repeated from time to time since faculty, administrators, and counselors keep changing for personal or institutional reasons. Some administrators ignore the work done and introduce their own half-baked initiatives.

Our buy-in steps were as follows: informally train team members who did not participate in the formal training (Spring 2002); introduce issues (UDEs) and findings (DEs) informally to department faculty (Spring 2002); prepare departmental guidelines and get departmental consensus (Summer and Fall 2002); have trainer Dean Steve Simpliciano of the Avraham Goldratt Institute make a presentation to the college president and his cabinet (May 2005);

Table 6.1   Steps for Introducing an Initiative in a System

Layers of Resistance (Obs)	Levels of Buy-In (IO)	TOC/TP Tools to Use (Actions)
1. Disagree on the nature of the problem.	1. Agree on the problem	1. UDEs, UDE Clouds, the CCC, CRT, and CCRTs
2. Disagree on the direction of the solution.	2. Agree on the direction of the solution	2. CCC, ECs, and INJs
3. Disagree that the solution solves the problem.	3. Agree that the solution solves the problem	3. INJs, FRT, and DEs
4. It will solve the problem, but there are potential negative consequences to the solution.	4. Agree that the solution will not lead to any significant negative effects	4. FRT and trimmed NBRs
5. It will solve the problem, but there are obstacles to implementing the solution.	5. Agree on the way to overcome any obstacles that might block or distort implementation of the solution	5. INJs, PRT, IO map, and TrTs
6. Unverbalized fears.	6. Overcome unverbalized fears	6. Committed leadership, TrTs, and individual TrT branches

Abbreviations: CCC, Core Conflict Cloud; CCRT, Communication Current Reality Tree; CRT, Current Reality Tree; DE, desirable effect; EC, Evaporating Cloud; FRT, Future Reality Tree; INJ, injection; IO, intermediate objective; Obs, obstacles; PrT, Prerequisite Tree; NBR, Negative Branch Reservation; TrT, Transition Tree; UDE, undesirable effect.

provide a Management Skills Workshop for other personnel and directors of the FYP and Post Secondary Readiness Center (December 2005); provide a TOC workshop for tutors and counselors (April 2006); provide a refresher TOC workshop for tutors (March 2007); provide a TOC workshop for the new FYP director and academic advisors, FYP counselors, and Women's Center counselors (April 2007); develop a TOC course at the first-year student level: Creative Thinkers Toolkit (2010–2011); conduct workshops to train advisors and counselors to teach the course and establish communication with academic faculty (July 2011); launch the TOC website for a college-level audiences (http://www.tocforcollege.com) (July 2011); present research to the college faculty, staff, and new administration (November 2011, February 2014, February 2015); arrange for MEC faculty and counselors to attend the TOCfE conference (February 2012); and hold TOC mentors' workshops for all stakeholders (July 2012, December 2013, January 2015, January 2016). Several first-year student advisors received credentials as TOC facilitators to guide students and colleagues.

The Cloud tool was not initially introduced to all of the full-time Department of Mathematics faculty members. Only the UDEs and DEs described in Chapters 2 and 3 for the institutional example were presented. The faculty of the department and various stakeholders at the college agreed with the UDEs, since they were selected from students' academic and non-academic issues and faculty issues developed by the college-wide faculty senate. The agreement of long-time college employees to participate in the various workshops was gained through PowerPoint presentations of various CRTs, FRTs, PrTs, and other presentations made at various TOC conferences and at special meetings with different departments, similar to the steps which are included for overcoming layers of resistance.

The Department of Mathematics faculty easily accepted the logical approach, since the discipline itself is based on logic, and it was not necessary to describe to them *necessary* and *sufficient* condition logic. The MEC president insisted that the trainer should present what we had learned. The difficulty of finding a convenient time for both the facilitator and the president played a role in the delay in elevating the solution/problem to the college level. Once the facilitator/trainer gave a 20-minute presentation using the basics of TOC, the CRT, UDE-DE chart, and FRT, the president congratulated the team and the chair's leadership, saying, "Conflict Resolution, Problem Solving, Decision Making! I have never seen anything like this. Everyone in the College, starting with the FYP advisors, counselors, Academic Foundations, and middle management, should implement TOC." Finding appropriate facilitators for the workshops was a major task, since there are very few TOC experts who have intuition and experience with a college environment. Funding from several competitive federal grants provided the muscle and credibility for acceptance and the resources for holding workshops. These steps were in line with the five focusing steps and the POOGI. To prepare this book for publication, we looked through the PrTs produced in the Jonah Program in January 2002 as discussed in Chapter 5. It was gratifying to see that activities where funding ($) was an injection were implemented over the years. For this, we thank the US Department of

Education and the grant reviewers who awarded our department competitive grants worth about four million dollars. The project plan completed in 2002 could not be fully carried out mainly due to the arrival of a new administration unsympathetic to the department initiatives, but it is still evolving. Our accomplishments show the robustness of TOC. The five steps are discussed in detail in the following sections.

6.3.2 Step 1: Identify the System Constraint (the Weakest Link)

1. Ensure that each problem or issue is stated as an UDE.
2. Position the UDEs (use Post-its) on a wall or a table so that causes are below and effects are above.
3. Create a Cloud for three systemic or key UDEs (be sure to check the logic).
4. Integrate all three Clouds into a more Generic Cloud or (Core) Conflict and assure that it is logically sound. This defines the constraint in terms of a conflict in D and D',—two opposing actions.
5. Use simple cause-and-effect relationships to link the identified Core Conflict to all the UDEs.

If the Core Cloud does not connect to all the UDEs, the Generic Cloud or Core Cloud is not generic enough and we must go back and find other key UDEs, and go through the process again. Even after forming a Generic Cloud, before connecting the UDEs, it is good practice to work out some additional Clouds to determine for ourselves that we will arrive at the same Generic Cloud. In our experience, most of the UDEs can be connected to the D entity of the Generic Cloud. See Chapters 2 through 4 and Sections 3.6 and 4.6 for more guidance on steps 1 to 5.

Thus, this step requires three TOC tools: ECs, the Core Cloud, and the CRT. It answers the question 1 of TOC: "What to change?" While developing the CRT, the team must use the *categories of legitimate reservations (CLR)* to make the logic robust. A discussion of the CLR is given in Section 1.8. This part of the MEC case study has already been discussed in detail in Chapters 2 and 3.

Figure 6.9 shows an example of the Core Conflict Cloud, the final result of the three-Cloud process for students in the case study. Comment: When our students' issues (UDEs) and Clouds were presented in Leon, Mexico, at the 10th International Conference of TOCfE in 2006, a faculty member from a college

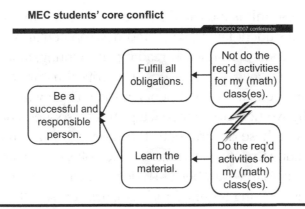

Figure 6.9   MEC students' core conflict.

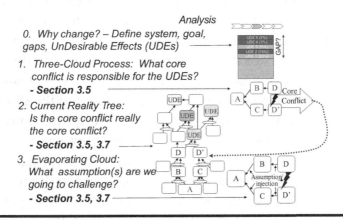

Figure 6.10   TOC question 1 and three TP tools. Graphics on Step 0 courtesy of Alan Barnard, Steps 1, 2, and 3 and graphics courtesy of AGI, New Haven, CT (Figure 3.40 reproduced here for continuity of discussion).

in Mexico remarked that our team was discussing *their* students' issues! The material was also presented at the 2007 Theory of Constraints International Certificating Organization (TOCICO) 6th International Conference, Las Vegas, Nevada, and is reprinted here with the permission of TOCICO.

Figure 6.10 summarizes the processes involved in identifying and linking the UDEs to a Core Cloud.

6.3.3 Step 2: Exploit the System Constraint

Utilize the Constraint to Fullest Extent. Help the Constraint Work Better.

This step requires getting the most out of the weakest link of the system chain, that is, help the constraint work better and utilize the constraint to the fullest extent. The weakest link is indicated by the Core Cloud. In our case, the constraint was the student failing basic and developmental courses in mathematics and basic courses in English reading and writing, along with her/his other academic and nonacademic issues. The critical nature of the roles played by English and mathematics departments in the college was discussed prior to discussing why we need to change (step 0). The sooner students complete the requirements in these departments, the sooner they advance to complete their discipline requirements. For example, the college's constraint is usually *mathematics*, since a large number of students enter needing math remediation and have difficulty passing required mathematics courses. If so, then in order to remove the constraint, much work has to take place in the mathematics department itself in order to have the best possible instruction, tutoring, interpersonal relationships, and the learning environment for faculty and students.

Even after finishing the core requirements in English and mathematics, more work is necessary for the college system to bring the throughput to a higher level. We must, for example, address the concerns of students who have completed their coursework. As in Figure 6.7, and the discussion following it, it is necessary to assure that college policies maximize use of the *constraints* or departments where students' constraint resides and where a large number of students with the Core Conflict are studying, in order to reach the goal of graduating more students now and in the future. As discussed in an earlier paragraph, one way to improve throughput is to change the way that the students are fed into the *constraints*: the constraints are neither starved for *well-prepared* students nor overloaded with *weakly prepared* students. This could be achieved by placing the basic skills courses within the constraint departments. In this way, the preparation of students becomes the responsibility of the bottleneck or constraint, and resources will be concentrated there instead of scattering them among the three departments (basic skills, English, and mathematics). Otherwise, all the various provider and client departments and their disciplines will have fewer students finishing their requirements and graduating. This ideal situation was created in many educational institutions by merging the basic skills courses with their respective departments, even though they had been separated earlier. Such a solution exploits the system constraint—students' weakness in mathematics.

At this point, we continue with another example from the case study that looks at the TOC work done by the Department of Mathematics to address the college's constraint, student attrition. With course instruction, tutoring, and the learning environment in the department as areas under their direct control, the department studied Step 2. This second step, illustrated

What to change to?
Constructing the solution   *Strategy*

1. Create an evaporating cloud:
What assumption(s) are we
going to challenge? - Chapter 3

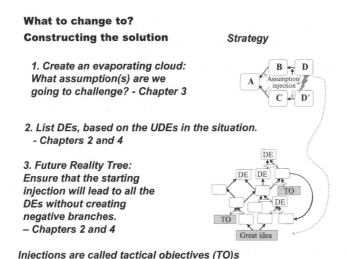

2. List DEs, based on the UDEs in the situation.
  - Chapters 2 and 4

3. Future Reality Tree:
Ensure that the starting
injection will lead to all the
DEs without creating
negative branches.
– Chapters 2 and 4

Injections are called tactical objectives (TO)s

Figure 6.11   Processes needed to eliminate the conflict and build a positive future reality. Courtesy of AGI, New Haven, CT (Figure 4.12 reproduced here for continuity of discussion).

in Figure 6.11, helps us to *break* the Core Conflict or resolve the dilemma in the Core Cloud. The TOC steps needed for this are find the *Bright Idea/Great Idea or Startig Injection* to break the conflict, develop DEs and the FRT, and eliminate NBRs. These ideas have been presented in Chapters 2 through 4

In the case study, the Bright Idea was "The department offers programs tailored to the needs of its students." The injections are part of the FRT. They suggest the measures or initiatives to be implemented. Much TOC application work was accomplished around the college over the course of 6 years. This shows the long-lasting effectiveness of our TOC analysis in sustaining continuous progress.

6.3.4 Step 3: Subordinate Everything Else to the Constraint

Nonconstraint Links Must Keep the Constraint Busy. Otherwise,
Stay Out of the Constraint's Way.

The key here is to make sure that the nonconstraint links keep the constraint busy and otherwise stay out of the constraint's way. This is the crucial step in institutional problem solving and is the first step in answering the third question "How to cause a change?" In this step, while doing work on the conflict/constraint, we might discover that there are several system UDEs that might seem to keep us from reaching the goal. However, we should maintain focus on the constraint itself. In our case, analysis of the constraint, that is, the work of the department (for example, mathematics or

English) where the constraint resides, is the necessary work for student success in credit-bearing mathematics or English courses.

The case study of MEC and the Department of Mathematics continues. When it came to Mathematics, a large number of students needed basic skills and/or personal counseling, and helping them was important. However, developing those areas under the direct control of the department was even more important and allowed the Department of Mathematics to continue to focus on its credit-bearing courses. We approached the FYP advisors and basic skills instructors and included them in mentoring workshops to motivate and prepare more students in the credit-bearing courses.

6.3.5 Step 4: Elevate the Constraint

> Apply TOC to Improve the Productivity of the Constraint. Expand the Capacity of the Constraint.

Here we apply TOC to expand the capacity of the constraint and improve its productivity. This is the step where the plan that was developed using the PrT/ATT needed to be implemented in order to answer the question, "How to cause the change?"

At MEC, this step showed that the process involved increasing student support resources: implementing improvements in instruction through curriculum development and pedagogy; enchancing support services such as tutoring; developing online and print test preparation materials; and finally, continuously monitoring of these efforts as suggested by the injections of the FRT or the IOs of the PrT, project plan, and TrT. This is the tangible or action part of how to cause the change. The project plan created in 2002 is so robust that it is still unfolding.

Steps 3 and 4 are summarized in Figure 6.12. The detailed PrTs and Project plan are presented in Chapter 5.

In order to implement these changes, the stakeholders must accept that the proposed changes are indeed the ones needed to resolve the issues. This buy-in process can be difficult. A higher educational institution is a bastion of academic freedom. The following discussion makes the difficulties of implementation clear. These difficulties are also discussed in Chapter 1.

In industry or government, a directive given by superiors is explicitly followed by subordinates. In primary or secondary school, the Board of Education or principal decides on new initiatives and teachers are expected to adopt them. At the college level, no professor will change behavior or adopt

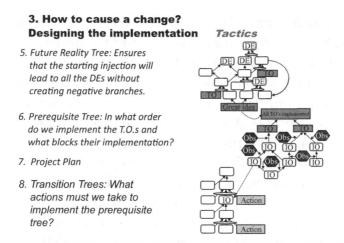

3. How to cause a change?
Designing the implementation *Tactics*

5. *Future Reality Tree: Ensures*
   that the starting injection will
   lead to all the DEs without
   creating negative branches.

6. *Prerequisite Tree: In what order*
   do we implement the T.O.s and
   what blocks their implementation?

7. *Project Plan*

8. *Transition Trees: What*
   actions must we take to
   implement the prerequisite
   tree?

Figure 6.12   Processes needed to cause a change. Courtesy of AGI, New Haven, CT (Figure 5.38 reproduced here for continuity of discussion).

new pedagogical strategies, however wonderful, by decree of the department chair or a college administrator. Considering union regulations and academic freedom, senior faculty do not feel obliged to accept any modifications in their normal activities or changes in the curriculum. Any perceived activity extraneous to instruction is usually regarded as an impediment. Thus, faculty acceptance of any new initiative is of paramount importance in a college setting.

In our case study, the mathematics department faculty came to a consensus as to how to implement the plan developed in TOC training. However, this required the chair's taking time out in monthly department meetings to discuss the issues faced by all the faculty and the team's proposed solution. After four months of discussion, in Spring 2002, an agreement was reached among all the mathematics department faculty members regarding the plan. The entire TOC roadmap was used for implementation. A project plan was developed from the PrT during the winter break, and TOC-inspired activities currently taking place around the college still follow the dynamic 15-year-old plan. The Future Reality Tree (FRT) allowed us to create a series of faculty guidelines (*Departmental Guidelines*, 2013) which outline the roles of instructors, tutors, and counselors. The guidelines are still enforced in the department.

Significant progress in the functioning of the department and progress toward attaining the goal of *reducing attrition* over 15 years are detailed in the document *A TOC Initiative at MEC* adapted in Chapter 7 (Nagarkatte, 2007). Major external funding played an important part. Within 2 years of the birth of the bachelor's degree program in the department and because of the learning environment created by the open discussion of student issues, the number of math majors went from 7 to 29. Over the next 12 years, the department increased the number of majors to 50, graduated about 70 math majors, and recruited 40 students to the newly minted math minor. A holistically oriented *Motivational Guide* (Nagarkatte, 2013) was developed to teach students introductory TOC concepts along with how to achieve academic success, how to regard a course as a project with Critical Chain Project Management (CCPM), how to study any subject, how and why to study mathematics, how to study using a team approach, and techniques for achieving tranquility.

After working within the math department, the team needed to approach the service departments who shared or fed resources (well-prepared students) to the mathematics department. Those are the FYP; Academic Foundations Division (AFD—basic skills); and personal counselors from the Student Advisory and Student Support (SASS) Department and the Center for Women's Development (CWD). Their cooperation was required in order to improve the quality of students entering credit-bearing courses in the Department of Mathematics. However, the math department had little leverage with these departments. Progress was made only after the president of the college, Dr. Edison O. Jackson, accepted the faculty guidelines, and the facilitator of the math team, Steve Simpliciano of the Goldratt Institute (AGI), gave him and his cabinet a presentation about TOC in May, 2005. As a result of the presentation, the president indicated that everyone in the college should learn this theory for conflict resolution, problem solving, and decision making, starting with the FYP and AFD. The president acknowledged that the Department of Mathematics had addressed not only the department's major issue but the entire college's issue of student attrition. Thus, he was the one who took responsibility for raising the constraint to the college level. *This is elevating the constraint.* It is because of his leadership and encouragement that efforts were able to continue vigorously.

From 2005 to 2007, approximately 250 members of the college community, including students, staff, counselors, faculty, and members of administration, were exposed to TOC: Funding from the department was provided through U.S. Department of Education grant funds for a Management Skills Workshop course for the grant personnel and directors of the programs cited earlier, and TOC workshops and refresher workshops for tutors, counselors, and academic advisors.

To elevate the constraint, another effort on the part of any administration is essential, and that is to maintain an adequate number of satisfied qualified faculty in the constraint departments: mathematics and English.

6.3.6 Step 5: Warning!!! Do Not Let Inertia Set In!

Do Not Let Inertia Become the Constraint. Find the Next System Constraint and Repeat the Previous Four Steps.

One should never let inertia itself become the constraint; always look for the next system constraint and repeat the previous four steps. For the POOGI, it is necessary to focus on the current constraint. Once the leadership has become committed to POOGI, the system's continuous progress is guaranteed for the working teams.

Once improvements had been made in teaching and learning in such things as administration of departmental exams, streamlined course offerings, and introduction of writing components, etc., within the mathematics department, the college's focus could then be shifted to improvement in the feeder departments as the constraint departments. The president took the initiative in spring, 2008, to hold a retreat to resolve all issues of the FYP and basic skills, both housed in the College of Freshman Studies, a constraint department. This process showed all the participants that administrators and faculty could work together. A few months after these workshops, the president decided to merge the basic skills courses and faculty into their respective Departments of Mathematics and English. By merging the basic skills departments, he raised the expectation for students: their goal would not be just to qualify for credit-bearing courses—a short-term goal—but to focus on graduating with a degree—a long-term goal.

In summary, TOC and the five focusing steps constitute an objective, logical procedure which transcends all personalities involved in decision making and allows an educational institution to resolve all institutional and departmental issues. This concludes the discussion on how an educational institution can address a systemic problem using the five focusing steps.

6.4 Numerical Measures of Performance in Educational Institutions

Administrators use reports of performance, enrollment, pass rates, D/F/W rates, attrition rates, and graduation rates over several years to judge the effectiveness of various initiatives. But educational institutions lack a single, useful numerical measurement of improvement. The reader may have come across the term *throughput* in Section 6.1, the number of graduates as a measure of the performance of an educational institution. The following discussion develops a single measurement for a more effective throughput and is a collaboration of the first author with Eva Chan, director of the Office of Institutional Research and Assessment at MEC. This section has also been reviewed by Janice Cerveny, our facilitator for many faculty and advisor workshops at MEC.

How can we measure and improve the success of an educational system in the context of TOC? As in industry, TOC offers us numerical measures appropriate for higher education to quantify and analyze the impact of attrition, success, return on investment, cost per student, and inventory turns. In business, however (see Ricketts, 2007), throughput (T) is commonly measured in terms of money made by selling the product; inventory (I) is the money tied up in terms of the number of units finished but not sold plus the money spent to finish the product; and operating expense (OE) is all of the money you spent to produce the throughput. A successful business runs by focusing the system effort on achieving the goal "Make money now and in the future." In order to do this, the business keeps on improving T, while reducing I and OE. Reducing OE or reducing I alone has a limited effect on making money, whereas increasing T has unbounded potential.

In TOC, the measures in a business's success (Ricketts, 2007) are defined in terms of the following:

Net profit (NP), where NP = T − OE
Return on investment: ROI = NP/I
Productivity: $P = T$/OE
Inventory turns: $i = T/I$.

This section redefines throughput and shows how TOC concepts can be applied to the measurement and analysis of a higher education system.

If we add some new variables and apply some of these business measures to a not-for-profit 4-year educational institution, we have a broader definition of T_i as *not just* the number of graduates placed in industry, professional, or graduate schools, but also the number of students *moving up to the next level*, that is, going from first-year students to sophomores, etc. There is some intrinsic and extrinsic value in completing 1, 2, 3, or 4 years of college in terms of earning power for a student. But for institutions, we define throughput, T, as the number of students advancing from one academic level (*graduating*) to the next. After they complete year 4, they are graduates with a degree in a major. Thus, the number of students making up T has four components: T_1, T_2, T_3, and T_4.

$$T = T_1 + T_2 + T_3 + T_4.$$

Although we do not show this formally in the following, we might also want to include in T_i the number of students who did not graduate but were placed in industry as interns or who were promoted within industry due to the quality of their work during their college years, since this is also a measure of student *advancement* and thus success for the college.

T_i is the number of students moving up from level i to the next academic level.

T_1 is the number of first-year students who are qualified to become sophomores at the start of the next academic year.

T_4 is the number of graduates with a degree in a major.

No exact dollar amount can be placed on T. T does produce income for the institutions as well as students. But we do not consider this fact here.

N is the number of students who are registered in the college. N has five components: N_0, N_1, N_2, N_3, and N_4.

$$N = N_0 + N_1 + N_2 + N_3 + N_4,$$

where N_0 is the number of students taking courses, but not matriculated or classified (nonmatriculated), and N_i is the number enrolled in the year $i = 1$, 2, 3, and 4.

I is the inventory defined as the number of students in the first-year student class and up who completed their respective academic year with *passing grades* and who are eligible to continue their studies in the college the next semester but have not yet *moved up to the next level*, that is, not yet changed their class standing, because, for example, they did not complete a sufficient number of credits. One might think of them as *extended* first-year students, etc. Thus, I has four components I_1, I_2, I_3, and I_4. I_1 is the number of extended first-year students. I_4 is the number who have completed the 120 credits required for graduation but have not graduated (i.e., they will have to take more than 120 credits to graduate with a major, perhaps due to having missed or needing to repeat a required major or other course).

$$I = I_1 + I_2 + I_3 + I_4.$$

SA_i is the student attrition in the year i which consists of the number of students who did not move into the next year's class due to certain specific issues—failure in a course, official and unofficial withdrawal, or incomplete work—and those who received a passing grade in a required course but did not advance in standing. (The latter might occur, for example, if the student needed a C in a course to proceed to the next one in a sequence as required in some mathematics courses but, having gotten a D, will have to repeat the course, as with an F.) SA, then, is the total number of students in all classes who attrited or who did not advance in an academic year, measured over a 4-year period:

$$SA = SA_1 + SA_2 + SA_3 + SA_4$$

Intuitively, given a fixed N, if student attrition, SA, increases, then T decreases, and eventually fewer students are placed in industry, professional, or graduate schools.

OE is the operating expense, that is, the money spent to educate all N students over 4 years.

Based on the previous discussion, the net throughput (T) for an undergraduate 4-year educational institution over 4 years is defined as follows:

$$
\begin{aligned}
T &= \text{(total number of students, including tranfers, in each class)} \\
&\quad - \text{(student attriters)} - \text{(inventory)} \\
&= (N_1 - SA_1 - I_1) + (N_2 - SA_2 - I_2) + (N_3 - SA_3 - I_3) + (N_4 - SA_4 - I_4) \\
&= T_1 + T_2 + T_3 + T_4.
\end{aligned}
$$

We can now redefine some business terms within an educational context in the following:

Productivity: $P = T/OE$ (measured in units of number of students/\$ calculated over 4 years). This is only roughly equivalent to the usage in business but useful for academic administration.

Cost per student: CPS = OE/N

Return on investment: ROI = $(T + I)$/OE = (Number moving up or graduating + number continuing in a specific year, that is, in the *pipeline*, but lacking appropriate credits to move to the next level in their major)/OE.

Inventory turns: $i = T/I$. This is a pure ratio of the number of students graduating or moving up, compared to those in the pipeline and are not graduating to the next level. This is a (positive) fraction less than or equal to 1. The larger the fraction, the larger the throughput.

If an educational institution is successful, first of all, it should have high throughput, T. T increases by increasing N and by reducing both the number of students in inventory, I (by making them count in T), and by reducing the loss due to student attrition, SA.

These measures do not take into account the intangible qualities such as knowledge, friendships, mentorship, and the values that a college education offers a student to succeed in life or the community contributions, creative work, research, and publications of the college faculty and grants received by them. However, high student attrition (SA) with the consequent reduction in throughput (T) can be easily seen to have a drastic impact on P, ROI, and i.

6.5 TOC and the Program Review

6.5.1 Overview

Program reviews and institutional self-studies are important for obtaining resources and earning accreditation from the evaluating or regulating regional or national associations.

This section describes an unsatisfying and perhaps typical college/ university program review/self-study experience and suggests how TOC can be used to improve it for the long-term benefit of the stakeholders (faculty, staff, students, administration) and the institution, taking into account the subjective as well as objective factors involved in the process. We argue that a thorough program review requires consideration of the three core questions of TOC: what to change, what to change to, and how to cause the change. These questions can be answered by a systematic TOC analysis of the current situation at the college, the college's future goals and objectives, and an efficient and effective strategy and tactics for reaching those goals and objectives. The TOC process, by providing a holistic view of the institution and involving stakeholders and their subjectivity at all levels, seems better able to engender cooperation than the usual process and provides a logical and dynamic roadmap to their collective future that stakeholders can understand and support (POOGI).

6.5.2 What's Wrong with Program Reviews?

Program review (or at least the preliminary aspect, the self-study, which forms the basis for the external evaluator's review) is an unwelcome rite of passage for the college community. It is often treated as a crisis situation, an institutional emergency that must be dealt with urgently, at the expense of all other activities: Entire administrative offices are retasked to produce the review, and faculty are redirected from their teaching and research to collect departmental data and to self-reflect in writing. Once the review is complete, the institution becomes quiescent until the next program review deadline is on the horizon.

Typically, there is little faculty or staff buy-in to the review process. They find the work uninteresting and time consuming and a distraction from more important work. To some, it may seem a coercive, top-down, and useless exercise that yields no immediate or long-term personal or professional benefit and takes resources away from other critical activities. It may even be viewed as dishonest, in the sense that carefully reasoned and sincere recommendations for change are ignored or whitewashed in the report sent to evaluators. These perceptions may even engender a hostile, passive aggressive response from the participants such that they fail to take responsibility for or cooperate with the review.

At the same time, most stakeholders do recognize that without institutional accreditation, their jobs may be in jeopardy and that allocation of external resources to and internal resources within the institution may be determined by the outcome. They understand that genuine improvement of the institution could make their lives better in general, and improvement in local conditions (classrooms, personnel at the departmental level) could benefit them directly. With a little prompting, stakeholders may also admit that program review is potentially a good opportunity for self-reflection and a rare opportunity for fertilization across functional boundaries (faculty/staff/administration/students).

One common approach to program review is to have each unit assemble a variety of documents: a statement of the college and units' missions; evidence/data from each unit showing that the mission is being supported/

achieved; a description of the strengths and weaknesses, and sometimes opportunities and threats (i.e., a SWOT or similar analysis) of each unit; and finally, recommendations based on this analysis. Unfortunately, the unit data are often collected with a silo mentality; that is, units do not share concerns with each other, because they see themselves as rivals for administrative attention and scarce resources and/or they are not provided with any low-stake opportunities for doing so. Recommendations coming from the analysis deal with individual components of the institution in isolation; no one is looking at the larger picture, the system, and how its components work (or don't) together. How the recommendations should be implemented is not thought through, and no one is held accountable for implementation. Sometimes, only external recommendations are taken seriously and other good ideas are forgotten. Finally, there is no follow-up to see that any implemented changes are working, until the next program review crisis.

Sometimes, the process may yield positive improvements such as getting new positions, reassigned time for the faculty, recruitment plans, and so on, but it all depends upon the administration. For example, a faculty member in another unit said that his department had done a tremendous amount of work over several years supported by the dean of the school. But when the dean was at odds with the president, the dean had to leave and along with him went the recommendations that he had made. The entire report went into the dust bin of history, causing frustration and pain to the affected faculty.

6.5.3 *How Can a TOC Analysis Improve a Program Review?*

The correspondence between a good program review process and a full TOC system analysis is probably intuitively obvious to the reader of this book. See Section 6.3 for details of the *five focusing steps*, discussed in the following:

Step 1: Identify the system constraint. (Apply TOC to find where the constraints are.)

Step 2: Exploit the system constraint. (Utilize the constraint to fullest extent. Help the constraint work better.)

Step 3: Subordinate everything else to the constraint. (Nonconstraint links must keep the constraint busy. Otherwise, stay out of the constraint's way.)

Step 4: Elevate the constraint. (Apply TOC to improve the productivity of the constraint. Expand the capacity of the constraint.)

Step 5: Do not let the inertia set in! (Find the next system constraint and repeat the previous four steps.)

Step 1: Identify the system constraint (the weakest link in a system, i.e., the Core Conflict).

The mission of the college is the strategic goal or objective of the system (Chapter 4), for example, to graduate students who are well prepared for further academic studies, careers, and life's personal challenges. The mission of each subunit might be considered the TOs (Chapter 4) which, when achieved, lead inexorably to accomplishment of the strategic goal. However, there are always obstacles standing in the way of achieving that goal—ask the various institutional stakeholders, from building and grounds staff to the president, what is not working and you will quickly get a long list of complaints. These are the UDEs of the system. We may need to add relevant statistics (facts of life) to clarify a given UDE. It goes without saying that an environment of mutual trust and safety needs to be created so that an honest discussion of the UDEs can occur. A suggestion as to how to achieve this is offered in Example 5.6.

From these UDEs, the Core Conflict Cloud can be extracted (see Section 3.6). This Core Conflict is the root from which all the other UDEs in the college arise. Connecting the UDEs logically to the Core Conflict gives us a very full picture of the current reality of the department/institution (the Current Reality Tree [CRT]—Section 2.4.1) and how its problems are *all related to each other*. Uncovering the connection among the parts is a strength of the TOC analysis.

Much attention should be focused on the Core Conflict and its resolution, since this conflict is the main constraint of the college system. This is where the college resources and efforts should be concentrated to do the most good. The solution is often startlingly simple, yet profound, and is revealed using the standard Cloud approach (Section 3.3). This approach also allows for logical and dispassionate consideration of the problem rather than, as is often the case, hostility traded among those considering it. Yet, few program reviews ever seek to or succeed in identifying this constraint, much less eliminating it.

Going beyond the Core Conflict, a graphical representation of What to Change is a holistic picture of the college system (see Figures 3.27 and 3.28) that can assist us in understanding what other critical problems need to be addressed. It shows where key interventions need to be made to eliminate negative branches and negative feedback Loops that are keeping the institution from reaching its goal (see Section 2.5). Creative interventions "injected" at the critical points are the self-study recommendations. These are TOCs Intermediate Objectives or various Tactical Objectives. The Current

Reality Tree (CRT) can show to all stakeholders how these interventions/ recommendations, if implemented, would significantly impact the college, and indicate where resources should be placed for maximum improvement of the institution (elevate the constraint, Section 6.3.2). The typical program review is not able to provide such a logical and broad overview of the system through consensus of the stakeholders.

Step 2: Exploit the system constraint.

By turning the UDEs into DEs (the logical opposites of UDEs), we can construct a map of what the institution would be like if all the issues were resolved. By adding injections at critical points, we can create our FRT summarizing what to change to (see Chapter 4). The DEs with their injections are conditions to strive for. Presenting this map publicly is motivating for stakeholders in so far as they can easily imagine a positive future for themselves and the institution. By contrast, a typical program review report may never be seen in its final form by those contributing to it.

Step 3: Subordinate everything else to the constraint.

This may be all that is needed for the self-study. However, it is insufficient for actually improving the college. All recommendations/interventions/ injections that are accepted need to be implemented with full support of the institution and in a nonrandom order. The PrT (Chapter 5 and Figures 5.9 through 5.12) allows the institution to determine the logical order in which the IOs or action plans should be pursued and allows the college to develop a timetable for doing so. Given that the implementation will typically depend on many people, accountability can be increased and task performance enhanced if the steps needed to reach each TO are explained in detail using an action plan developed as a TrT (see Section 5.6).

Step 4: Elevate the constraint.

Management of the entire program review process in an efficient and effective manner from an administrative point of view—from data collection to implementation of recommendations—can be handled using CCPM techniques (Section 5.4). Management of the human aspects of the process, that is, the interpersonal and interunit acute and chronic conflicts which will certainly arise, can be approached using the Cloud as a stand-alone tool (see Chapter 3). Addressing these issues elevates the constraint in terms of creating an environment and providing resources for increasing its productivity.

A TOC-inspired program review probably takes more time and sustained unemotional problem-focused cooperation among stakeholders than the typical program review demands or allows. It also requires at least some key players to be knowledgeable in TOC and its TP tools to help guide the process, and buy-in from top administration. But the TOC approach provides for a more complete and focused analysis of the systems of the college, from recruitment to graduation, and guides the development of detailed and logical solutions to the most pressing problems facing the institution. The logical maps created provide an easily accessible, public plan for improving the institution over the long term and a way to check on how successful any implementations have been.

Step 5: Do not let inertia set in!

The college is a dynamic system, and as one critical problem is resolved, another issue will become the new main constraint. Thus, the analysis will need to be revised and repeated based on current conditions (POOGI) and not written in stone until the next official program review is scheduled.

6.6 Strategic Planning in Higher Education Using TOC

As Benjamin Ginsberg, professor of political science and director of the Washington Center for the Study of American Government at Johns Hopkins University, has observed,

> Today, […] virtually every college and university in the nation has an elaborate strategic plan. Indeed, whenever a college hires a new president, his or her first priority is usually the crafting of a new strategic plan. As in Orwell's *1984*, all mention of the previous administration's plan, which probably had been introduced with great fanfare only a few years earlier, is instantly erased from all college publications and Web sites. (Ginsberg, 2011, pp. 1–15)

Ginsberg views strategic planning, typically practiced, as a waste of time. Other experts in the field are quick to point out that a strategic plan is more likely to fall short in terms of process—leadership, communication, and assessment—than in terms of content (*Strategic Planning in Higher Education: A Guide for Leaders*, n.d.). We argue that a TOC approach overcomes these shortfalls by empowering leaders and stakeholders, enhancing communication among the various components, and promoting ongoing assessment (POOGI). We would even like to suggest that a TOC-inspired strategic plan will outlast its authors and become a dynamic resource for positive organizational change. This has been our experience in the math department at MEC, where the TOC blueprint is still viable, 15 years after it was created.

What is a strategic plan?

According to a popular, albeit unauthoritative, source, "Strategic planning is an organization's process of defining its strategy, or direction, and making decisions on allocating its resources to pursue this strategy" (Strategic planning, n.d., p. 1). The strategic plan summarizes the outcome of this organizational process.

The Center for Organizational Development and Leadership is one of many organizations offering guidelines for preparing a strategic plan. In their view (*Strategic Planning in Higher Education: A Guide for Leaders*, n.d.), the plan should contain the following:

- A statement of mission, vision, and values of the institution
- Identification of stakeholders, internal and external
- An analysis of the internal and external *environment* of the institution
- Articulation of tangible institutional goals
- Action plans and general strategies/pathways for achieving the goals, with timelines
- The plan itself: a set of step-by-step procedures for implementing the action plans
- Outcomes and achievements—ongoing monitoring/assessment of the implementation and success/failures of the plan

A quick scan of some collegiate Strategic and related Action Plans ("A Strategic Plan for Barnard College," n.d.; "Charting a Course for the Future of York College: Institutional Action Planning," 2014; "Medgar Evers Institutional Strategic Plan," 2012) suggests that this model or something like it has been widely accepted in higher education.

6.6.1 Analyzing the Internal and External Environment

Traditional program review analysis typically breaks the college system down into its smaller units—programs/departments—and "analyzes" (i.e., collects data about) them. In Section 6.5, we suggested a TOC-based approach for improving such a review. The result of program review can feed into a strategic plan. Strategic planning, at its best, then analyzes the interrelationships/interdependencies among the constituent parts—the whole college system, shown in Figure 6.13.

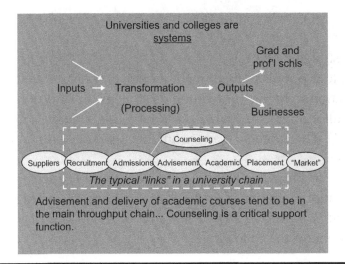

Figure 6.13   Universities and colleges are systems.

The first step in the analysis requires an understanding and acceptance by the college community of the *system diagram*, that is, the college's *business model*. This goes beyond even the most complex organizational chart; it attempts to describe the *flow* through the system—that is, in a college environment, students' passage from recruitment to graduation and employment or advanced studies (see Sections 1.1.2 and 6.1). As illustrated in Figure 6.14, it includes all the components and functions of the college, for example, financial aid, counseling, faculty scholarship, maintenance, the revenue it brings in and the expenses that it incurs. This model might be proposed by the leadership, but it should be modified and vetted by the key stakeholders.

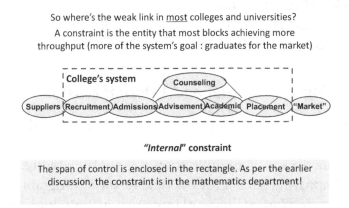

Figure 6.14   The weakest link in the system is in Mathematics (a department in Academics) affecting Placement as the next link connected to Throughput.

Once this flow diagram has been established, leadership should provide a safe environment in which stakeholders can identify the *S = strengths* and *W = weaknesses* in their areas. Note that a SWOT type of analysis, with the addition of opportunities and threats, would end here. However, a TOC analysis views strengths as links in the chain where there is no immediate attention required. But these strengths may also be affected by the weak links in the system as illustrated in Figure 6.15.

TOC views weaknesses as UDEs, looks for natural groupings or affinities among them, and distills key UDEs for further examination. The rules for identifying and stating UDEs are discussed in Section 1.4.

Example: In a workshop for counselors, advisors, and faculty in 2007, people listed weaknesses (UDEs) as shown in Figure 6.16. There are other general faculty and student UDEs listed in Section 1.2.4.

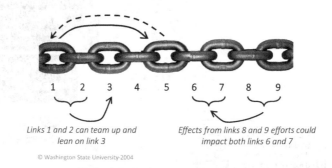

Figure 6.15   Interlinking of strengths and weaknesses of a system. Courtesy of Dr. James Holt, Washington State University.

Common problems

1. There is inconsistency of outcomes from freshman classes.
2. The non-academic challenges of students are not addressed.
3. The difference between an academic advisor and a counselor is not known.
4. More and more students have mental health challenges.
5. There are many turf wars.
6. The student service department experiences many disruptions.
7. Students don't see connections.
8. Students come to school hungry (no food, transportation, etc.)
9. College faculty are dismissive of students' personal issues.
10. Students who identify as LGBT are victimized.
11. Part-time faculty often do not attend to students' needs.
12. Some students fall between the cracks (a freshman seminar is not required of all students).

Figure 6.16   List of UDEs from workshop attendees.

With a TOC approach, the UDEs are not viewed simply as individual problems needing solutions. Rather, the UDEs are logically linked to each other using "if–then" (sufficiency) logic to create a CRT, a graphical representation of the whole system (discussed in Chapter 2). The CRT, as shown in Figure 6.17, reveals that some UDEs are more fundamental than others; they seem to govern the whole system. The Core Cloud was constructed from the UDEs.

The Core Cloud forms the key constraint of the system, which, if addressed, will eliminate the UDEs. Recall that all the UDEs were connected to the Core Cloud that gave rise to the CRT (see Figures 6.18 and 6.19).

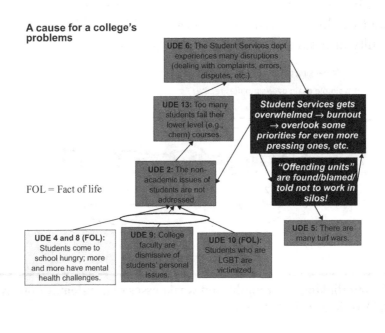

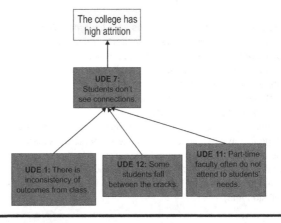

Figure 6.17 Core conflict based on faculty issues.

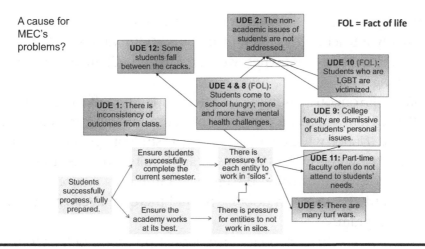

Figure 6.18   CRT of common problems: part 1.

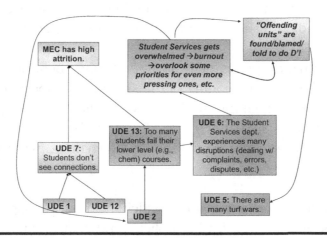

Figure 6.19   CRT of common problems: part 2.

The Bright Idea or injection to address the Core Conflict here is D′ = not to work in silos!

In developing the CRT, is it important to make explicit the assumptions, policies, and measurements that *drive peoples' behavior in the system*. These should be articulated for each UDE.

■ *Assumptions*. Assumptions are often hidden and are the underlying values/beliefs of the leadership and stakeholders that may not be true. These are often embedded in the *values, mission, and vision* parts of the typical strategic plan. Examples are: "Our student population is the same as it was 10 years ago," "Funding will decline in the future," "Our students are underprepared and unwilling to work hard," "Faculty do as little as possible," "Administrators interfere with faculty work," "We are primarily a teaching/research institution," "Our values and mission are the same as they were when we started," and "Change is always a negative thing."

■ *Policies.* Erroneous assumptions often underlie ineffective institutional policies. Here are some examples of questions that can help to reveal policies: "Under what circumstances can students get an incomplete grade?" "How many days per week are faculty expected to be on campus?" "How is information disseminated in the institution?" "Does the president have an 'open door'?" "Should there be a 'capstone' course in every program?"

■ *Measurements.* Inappropriate institutional policies can lead to the establishment of irrelevant metrics. Questions that reveal metrics: "What are faculty/staff rewarded for at the institution?" "How are students graded?" "How is funding related to enrollment?" "How are administrators evaluated?"

■ *Behaviors.* Inappropriate metrics can encourage behaviors that are detrimental to the functioning of the system. Examples of detrimental behaviors are: unqualified students are enrolled to beef up statistics, students cheat to get better grades, faculty publish at the expense of good teaching, and administrators require chairs to write too many reports.

Figure 6.20 illustrates how a single widely held but perhaps incorrect institutional assumption can lead to policies and measurements that in turn lead to behaviors.

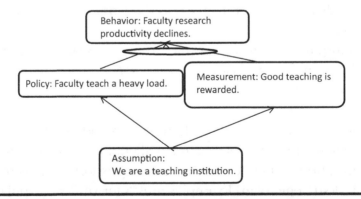

Figure 6.20   Example of the relationship among assumptions, policy, measurement, and behavior.

6.6.2 *Finding the System Constraint*

IDENTIFY the system constraint.

To complete the analysis, the most important UDE, or constraint, of the system has to be identified. In a SWOT analysis, this is the "*T*" or most significant threat to the system. Neglected *weaknesses* are also potential *threats*. As shown in Figure 6.14, the internal threats are in our area of control, and we can take care of them. In TOC, this is the first step in the Process of OnGoing Improvement: IDENTIFY the system constraint. This analysis can be approached intuitively by looking for obvious internal bottlenecks in the throughput of the system; for example, the doors to the building don't all open, so students are lined up and are late getting to class; there are not enough staff people available during registration to process students quickly; class sizes are so large that writing instructors have to cut down the number of assignments that they give; and there is one office that everyone seems to have to go to in order to move forward [or blame] if students don't graduate on time. Or, the blockage could be something external to the college; for example, the number of college-age students in the neighborhood has declined significantly, or the state legislature has cut the budget for the university. Another approach is to get the most experienced stakeholders to determine what function is *most* vital to graduating students; for example, math is required for graduation, but most students fail remedial math more than once, so their graduation is delayed, or students' significant personal issues keep them from succeeding in their studies. The latter issues were found to be significant constraints at our college (see Chapters 2 and 3).

The most rigorous approach, however, is to go through the three-Cloud process, described in Chapter 3, which will provide the *base* of the CRT, the root conflict from which all other UDEs arise. Briefly, the strategic planning leadership identifies three UDEs reflective of serious problems in different functional areas of the college, for example, counseling, registration, remedial instruction, or from the perspective of different stakeholders—for example, students, faculty, staff, and administrators. They create a Cloud for each of the key UDEs and then develop a Core Conflict Cloud using the three Clouds. If this is done correctly, the Core Conflict Cloud will form the base of the Current Reality Tree, and all the UDEs will be seen to emerge from D and/or D′. Stakeholders may quickly see places where an intervention or injection could "trim" a negative branch (see Chapters 2 and 4). **In a SWOT analysis, these injections are the**

opportunities. The Core Conflict can be resolved using TOC techniques described in Chapters 3 and 4 to remove the most significant impediment to moving students through the pipeline. In sum, the CRT analysis, a collaborative effort of the college community, shows us what we need to change (what to change) and where we need to focus our energies in order to improve the college.

A detailed CRT for students and faculty issues on attrition has already been described in Chapter 3.

6.6.3 Setting Goals and Objectives: EXPLOIT the System Constraint

Of course, it is not enough to simply analyze the current college situation. A direction for the college's future and a pathway to get to it must be determined. **The TOC step 2 of POOGI, is to EXPLOIT the constraint identified in the analysis, that is, help the constraint to work better and utilize it to the fullest extent.** To do this, we develop an FRT to map out what a positive future for the institution would look like if the Core Conflict were resolved and the injections were applied. To do this, all the UDEs in the CRT are transformed into DEs, logical opposites of the UDEs. The DEs are states or conditions at the college that we want to achieve, arranged to show their logical relationships. Injections are provided to ensure achievement of the DEs. The FRT shows the overall goals and objectives of a strategic plan—what to change to—and should be shared with the college community.

The FRT in Chapter 4 clearly indicates the critical activities that students, instructors, tutors, counselors/advisors, and administrators must take to reduce attrition and improve graduation rates. There has to be effective communication between the administration and all other stakeholders. In an ideal situation, the administrators play the role of facilitators to implement the change of the system.

6.6.4 Carrying Out the Plan: SUBORDINATE Everything Else to the Constraint and ELEVATE the Constraint

Identification of the goals and objectives (DEs and injections), however rationally achieved, does not tell us how to implement change. **In TOC, the next step in improving the system is to SUBORDINATE everything to resolving the Core Conflict and fulfilling the goals embodied in**

the FRT. This means that the nonconstraint links must keep the constraint busy and/or stay out of the constraint's way. *Action plans* demanded by accrediting bodies to accompany the grand strategic plan can provide only an outline of the proposed change process. However, TOC provides a tool, the PrT, discussed in Chapter 5, that uses necessity logic to determine the key steps needed to reach the intermediate/strategic/TOs identified in the FRT (discussed in Chapter 4). A well-constructed PrT can be mapped onto a timeline to provide a project plan.

We must also elevate the constraint; that is, expand the capacity and productivity of the constraint using TOC.

The PrT brings out the obstacles to attaining various objectives. Removing the obstacles is useful in increasing the capacity of the constraint. Thus, the PrT is useful for the committee charged with actually implementing changes. Detailed instructions with explanations as to why things should be done can be provided with the TrT discussed in Chapter 5. The TrTs describe the detailed, logically rigorous action plans.

6.6.5 Assessing and Monitoring the Plan: Don't Let Inertia Set in!

Most would agree that no strategic plan is complete without some proposal for monitoring the implementation and actual achievements of the college based on its plan. Once articulated, the job of assessment often falls to the Office of Strategic Planning, the Office of Assessment, or the moral equivalent. In the worst case, there is no such office or functional area, and/or the task awaits the next official strategic planning process to begin. As suggested in the introduction to this section, the arrival of a new college president can both trigger a new planning process and erase the old plan at the same time. By contrast, **a TOC-based strategic planning process is focused on detecting and removing the next system constraint (elevate the constraint)—and there is always another big obstacle to overcome—and becomes an ongoing, iterative method to improve the institution (POOGI) regardless of who is at the helm.**

To **summarize,** the five focusing steps of TOC are as follows:

Step 1: Apply TOC to find where the constraints are. **Identify** the system constraint.

Step 2: Utilize the constraint to fullest extent. (Help the constraint work better. **Exploit** the system constraint.)

Step 3: Nonconstraint links must keep the constraint busy. Otherwise, stay out of the constraint's way. (**Subordinate** everything else to the constraint.)

Step 4: Apply TOC to improve the productivity of the constraint. Expand the capacity of the constraint. (**Elevate** the constraint.)

Step 5: Find the next system constraint and repeat the previous four steps. (**Do not let the inertia set in!**)

In this section, we have tried to show how to develop and implement a strategic plan that outlasts its authors and—unlike a SWOT analysis which produces only short-lived improvements in silos—sets a higher education institution on the path to continuous improvement.

References

A strategic plan for Barnard College | Barnard College. (n.d.). Retrieved January 22, 2017, from https://barnard.edu/about/vision-values/strategic-plan.

Charting a course for the future of York College: Institutional Action Planning for 2010. (2014). https://www.york.cuny.edu/president/institutional-effectiveness/middle-states/supporting-documents/institutional-action-planning-for-2010-updated-august-2014.pdf.

Cox, J., & Goldratt, E. (1986). *The Goal: A Process of Ongoing Improvement.* Croton-on-Hudson, NY: North River Press.

Cox III, J.F., Boyd, L.H., Sullivan, T.T., Reid, R.A. & Cartier, D. (2012). *The Theory of Constraints International Certification Organization Dictionary*, 2nd ed. NY: McGraw Hill.

Departmental Guidelines. (2013). Unpublished report, Department of Mathematics, Medgar Evers College, New York.

Ginsberg, B. (2011). The strategic plan: Neither strategy nor plan, but a waste of time. *The Chronicle of Higher Education*, 1–15.

Medgar Evers College Institutional Strategic Plan 2012–2017: Advancing the Spirit of Transformation, Realizing Dreams. (2012). http://www.hezel.com/images/resource-library/MEC_Strategic_Plan_ISPC_Final_Draft_Post_Rev_9-14-2012.pdf.

Nagarkatte, U. (2007). *A TOC initiative at MEC.* Unpublished report, Department of Mathematics, Medgar Evers College, New York.

Nagarkatte, U. (2013). Motivational guide. Retrieved June 11, 2017, from www.TOCforCollege.com: http://www.tocforcollege.com/motivational-guide.html.

Ricketts, J.A. (2007). *Reaching the Goal: How Managers Improve a Services Business Using Goldratt's Theory of Constraints.* Indianapolis, IN: IBM Press.

Strategic planning. (n.d.). Retrieved January 22, 2017, from https://en.wikipedia
.org/wiki/Strategic_planning.

Strategic Planning in Higher Education: A Guide for Leaders. (n.d.). Retrieved
January 21, 2017, from http://oira.cortland.edu/webpage/planningandassessment
resources/basicassessmentresources/RutgersPlanning.pdf.

Wu, H. (2009). What is sophisticated about elementary mathematics? *American
Educator*, 4–14. Retrieved January 21, 2017, from https://www.aft.org/pdfs
/americaneducator/fall2009/wu.pdf.

Chapter 7

Epilogue: How Did We Do?

7.1 Overview: A TOC Initiative at MEC, 2001–2016

Medgar Evers College of the City University of New York (MEC) has pioneered the broad application of TOC/TP to a college *system*. The current text is based on our experience over 15 years with TOC/TP, mostly in the Department of Mathematics. Briefly, using a TOC/TP approach, we have, among other things, (a) identified the constraint in the math department system blocking the movement of students through the math major, (b) restructured and aligned the content and scheduling of basic skills and algebra courses, and (c) published three related textbooks. For those interested in using TOC to improve their own college system, we summarize here our objective, measurable progress to date toward achieving the goal of *reducing student attrition*. This material is adapted from *A TOC Initiative at MEC* (Nagarkatte, 2007). Some repetition from the previous sections is necessary for the sake of logical connectedness of activities from 2002 to 2016.

7.2 Grant Development and Management

Once key players in the Department of Mathematics had received formal training in TOC at the Avraham Goldratt Institute, using TOC processes, they were able to guide the department in identifying its core issues and strategies for resolving them. These issues, strategies, and the TOC processes themselves—from CCPM management of the grants and tutoring to curriculum development—were then incorporated into a series of seven related grant proposals* that yielded almost $4,000,000 to support the department's initiatives from 2001 to 2016. The first author served as the Principal Investigator on most of these and the second author, as the evaluator. Over the years, the proposals extended from the MEC Math Department to local middle schools and high schools, other MEC departments and programs (Biology, Computer Science, and Environmental Science; Freshman Year Program and Student Services), and other colleges (Queensborough Community College).

---

* Details of grant proposals may be obtained from the first author. Brief descriptions of the grant objectives are given in the following:

1. 2001–2004 MSEIP Institutional Grant for $300,000. *Improving Mathematics Instruction by Extending the Reform Calculus Approach:* this project was intended to increase the number of minority students entering calculus and postcalculus courses by reducing attrition from preparatory credit-bearing math courses and addressing different issues of students and faculty.
2. 2004–2007 MSEIP Institutional Grant for $300,000. *Learning Environment in Advancing Progress (LEAP) in Mathematics* had a goal of increasing the number of mathematics and science graduates and increasing pass rates in precalculus and enrollment in calculus, postcalculus, and science courses that need precalculus and calculus.
3. 2005–2007 WEEA Institutional Grant for $320,000. *Learning Environment in Advancing Development (LEAD) of Women Students*: activities were extended to include tutoring in credit-bearing and remedial mathematics courses and included TOC workshops for instructors, academic advisors, and counselors.
4. 2010–2013 MSEIP Institutional Grant for $600,000. *A Problem-Solving Framework in Mathematics:* the main aspects were adapting the *Singapore Model Method* to college; TOC workshops to make students, tutors, counselors, and instructors proactive in student success; and writing components.
5. 2010–2013 MSEIP Cooperative Grant for $900,000. *A Learning Environment Advancing Development (LEAD) in Mathematics*: the LEAD program included Queensborough Community College. The main activity was dissemination—adapting the Singapore Model Method to college; TOC workshops to make students, tutors, counselors, and instructors proactive in student success; writing components; and extending Queensborough Community College's Service Learning to MEC.
6. 2012–2015 MSEIP Institutional Grant for $652,218. *A March from Post-Secondary to Post-Baccalaureate:* along with all activities in the previous grants, this aimed to work with middle and high schools, improve passing rates in basic skills courses, invite math graduate school recruiters, take students to various math recruiting fairs, and prepare students for the GRE.
7. 2013–2016 MSEIP Institutional Grant for $750,000. *An All Embracing Endeavor to Increase the Underrepresented in STEM* was designed to increase the number of mathematics and science graduates by (a) increasing the passing rates in basic skills courses and college algebra and increasing enrollments in precalculus and calculus and (b) preparing junior and senior students in mathematics, biology, computer science, and environmental science for success in STEM careers or graduate education.

7.3 Departmental Structure and Functioning

Gaining the support of faculty for a TOC approach was a lengthy process. The chair explained the findings for 15 minutes in monthly meetings while discussing all academic and nonacademic issues of students and faculty. Through TOC consensus building, the department developed and implemented departmental guidelines (Berenbom & Nagarkatte, 2013) beginning in 2002 for faculty, tutors, and students (available from the first author). This laid out the responsibilities of each stakeholder and helped to standardize processes and procedures in the department. This was of special value to new full-time faculty and the many part time adjuncts who taught in the department. A TOC-based *Motivational Guide* (Nagarkatte, 2013a) was first developed in 2008 to inspire and guide students in the pursuit of their educational and personal goals, particularly in math. More than 5000 copies were distributed in the college over the years. The Cloud process was used to resolve inter- and intradepartmental conflicts and to create a positive environment in the math department for faculty and students, acknowledged by both the Math Department's 2014 External Program Review and the college's 2016 Middle States Report. Most important, TOC and TP tools were used to create a long-term project plan to improve the department and reach the goal of reducing attrition.

TOC processes were used to make major structural changes in the department. The college president invited the first author and the TOC Team to train him and his cabinet in TOC in March 2008 in order to develop a plan for smooth transition of students from their first year to credit-bearing courses. The TOC team made weekly presentations to the president and his cabinet discussing the issues of students and faculty of both the basic skills (math) and mathematics departments, departments that had been separated for many years. At the conclusion of the sessions, the president decided to merge the two faculties and programs.

7.4 Faculty and Staff Development

Faculty and staff training in TOC/TP and related pedagogy was an important component of the project plan. MSEIP grants supported 3–5-day workshops taught off campus by professional TOC facilitators almost every year. They initially targeted math faculty and tutors, then basic skills instructors and math faculty, followed by mentors in the counseling and advisement areas, and, finally, faculty from the sciences as well as other disciplines, and administrators (president, provost, deans). Over 300 stakeholders participated in just one grant period (2004–2007). In the 2013–2016 grant period, TOCfE provided Level 2 training in the TOC Learning Connection program leading to certification for 15 first-year student advisors and the dean of students.

7.5 Curriculum Development, Textbooks, and Instructional Materials

The grant team developed a unified syllabus from prealgebra to college algebra in 2012 and implemented it in Fall 2014. They used a PrT to develop objectives for each topic, listing all obstacles that students typically have and arranging them logically. The PrTs can be used by students as a checklist for preparing for an exam and are linked to KhanAcademy.org videos, now used in many units of the City University of New York and other colleges around the country.

The first author and Joshua Berenbom (grant person 2012–2015) used the same obstacles to write the college textbooks *Prealgebra* (Nagarkatte & Berenbom, 2014), *Elementary Algebra* (Nagarkatte & Berenbom, 2016a), and *Intermediate Algebra and Trigonometry* (Nagarkatte & Berenbom, 2016b). The texts adapted the Singapore Model Method to a college audience and were informed by "How students learn: mathematics in the classroom" (National Research Council, 2005). Along with the texts, volunteer faculty explored new pedagogical approaches. In Fall 2014, the books and pedagogy were used in experimental sections of basic skills (MTH 009 with 257 students and in MTH 010 with 263 students) compared with Control sections using the standard textbooks and pedagogy. Table 7.1 summarizes the results: passing rates (P) were higher for students using the new approach.

Of the advanced algebra and trigonometry book, one student* commented, ". . . For generations students have pondered when would they need mathematical formulas in real life. The text answers that question again and again (and again!) . . ." (T. Braithwaite, personal communication, December 8, 2016). A retired IBM physicist who now works with prisoners in an upstate jail and participates in Rising Hope, Inc. (https://risinghopeinc.wordpress .com/) commented on ". . . the monumental contribution to the mathematical

---

* Excerpt from a student's review of Nagarkatte and Berenbom's *Intermediate Algebra and Trigonometry* textbook. He was a student in the first author's section of the course.

Table 7.1 Comparison of Pass and Repeat Rates in Experimental versus Control Sections of Basic Skills Courses (Fall 2014)

		P		*R*		*Total*
Prealgebra	MTH 009					
	Experimental	123	47.86%	134	52.14%	257
	Control	44	31.65%	95	68.35%	139
Elem. Algebra	MTH 010					
	Experimental	100	38.02%	163	61.98%	263
	Control	34	27.64%	64	52.03%	123

foundations through those 3 books . . .," and plans to use them to teach a leadership course to empower prisoners (M. Cheruvu, personal communication, December 18, 2016).

With the help of Computer Science students, grant personnel developed two websites: http://www.tocforcollege.com and http://www.calculusplus.com, used at MEC college, around the nation and abroad. The tocforcollege website provides basic information about theory of constraints concepts and TPs and is the repository for MEC TOC and TOCfE documents, events, and achievements. It has been accessed by academics in the United States, Europe, South America, Asia, and New Zealand. About the website tocforcollege, a student says, "Very exciting work. Reading the process of TOC, I was able to envision the body of work behind it. The student accounts were inspiring to read and their paths to success, thereafter, are testimony to the results of TOC. It seeks to address a very common problem among college students and works toward helping them solve it. I just want to say that I am very impressed and I am looking forward to the release of the book" (Jamal Lambert, personal communication to Oley, February 27, 2017).

Since 2015, the Calculusplus website hosting Maple labs used in the department has also been used for training high school teachers at 17 schools participating in the Pipeline Project at MEC.

In addition to the Calculusplus website, exercises for hands-on practice were developed for Precalculus, Calculus I, and Calculus II online homework using WeBWorK (http://webwork.maa.org/). This is a national problem library to which hundreds of mathematicians around the country have contributed. No two students get the same problem. Several wikis for course review and test preparation have also been developed.

With grant support, faculty developed writing activities for several math courses (http://www.calculusplus.com); the second author incorporated TOC concepts into some Introductory Psychology classes (Oley, 2013) and developed a short course in TOC for remedial math students; and both authors developed the curriculum for a TOC-based first-year student seminar and the manuscript for this book.

In collaboration with our MSEIP partner, Queensborough Community College, MEC faculty were trained and initiated Service Learning in the MEC Math Department. Our students and faculty now assist math students in the MEC Prep School, the MathMasters program for middle school (MS 61) students and teachers, and at-risk students in the Brooklyn High School of the Arts. For the first time in 20 years, two of the targeted MS 61 students were admitted to the Brooklyn Tech magnet school.

7.6 Tutoring and Support Services

The first author and his research students, Reginald Dorcely and Denver Jn. Baptiste, applied TOC to issues in tutoring. They discovered a breakthrough solution: it was necessary for the student to be proactive and to use Critical Chain Project Management (CCPM) for his/her mathematics course. MSEIP funding then allowed the department to train peer math tutors to help students manage their college-level math courses using CCPM/TP techniques. Additionally, the department synchronized instruction, tutoring, and counseling with trained counselors and advisors to help students use TOC/TP to become proactive. The Middle States Accreditation Team (October, 2006) noted the vibrant environment in the Math Department where students, tutors, and faculty were actively working together. By the end of the second grant period, tutoring use had gone up by 500%.

7.7 Increased Enrollment, Retention, and Improved Performance in Mathematics

The bachelor of science (B.S.) degree program in math started in 2000 with seven students and as of Fall 2016 had an enrollment of 50. During that period, more than 70 math majors and hundreds of other science students have graduated, increasing from 152 in 2010 to 263 in 2016. Forty students elected a math minor within 2 years of its initiation.

Grants beginning in Fall 2010 focused on improving the overall learning environment in the Math Department and on increasing the number of students enrolled in gateway and especially *upper-level math courses*, as these courses were the only ones under the direct control of the department. Following implementation of grant activities, enrollments in the Precalculus and upper-level math courses increased as shown in Figure 7.1.

As enrollments increased, pass rates also increased or remained stable, with the result that, once they entered, more students moved through the math pipeline. This represented a significant addition to the pool of minority mathematicians.

The retention rates in science, technology, engineering, and math (STEM) for the 5 years 2010–2015 are shown in Table 7.2.

In mathematics, retention increased by 15% in 5 years as a result of grant activities. Note that Associates in Science (_A_) major students typically continue on to study for Bachelor of Science (_B_) degrees.

In contrast to the upper-level math courses, at the beginning of the project, the pass and retention rates in the basic skills courses were chronically low, with 88.4% of incoming first-year student needing remedial work (either MTH 009 and MTH 010 or just MTH 010). Figure 7.2 indicates that, following MSEIP-supported curriculum improvement and tutoring in these courses, the passing rates increased.

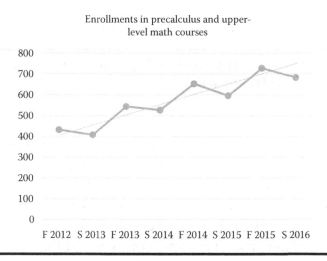

Figure 7.1   Enrollment in precalculus and upper-level math courses. Regression line, *y* **= 44.4t + 367 (rounded). The rate of increase is about 44 students per year.**

Table 7.2   Fall-to-Fall Retention Rate by Major

Dept	Deg major	F'10–F'11	F'11–F'12	F'12–F'13	F'13–F'14	F'14–F'15
BIO	_B _ 010_BIO	62.0	65.6	62.5	66.1	68.9
BIO	_A _ 011_SCI	55.4	55.0	58.8	62.9	61.4
PECS	_B _ 020_ENV	69.1	70.7	71.9	67.6	64.1
PECS	_A _ 050_CS	40.5	46.9	44.7	57.6	54.6
PECS	_B _ 051_CS	63.3	67.7	66.1	64.4	72.9
MATH	_B _ 080_MTH	61.8	64.5	71.1	80.9	76.8

Source: Office of Institutional Research, Medgar Evers College, CUNY, Brooklyn, NY.

Note: Ordered by dept, degree type (B—B.S., A—A.S. [Associate in Science]) and major code. Graduates are included as retained.

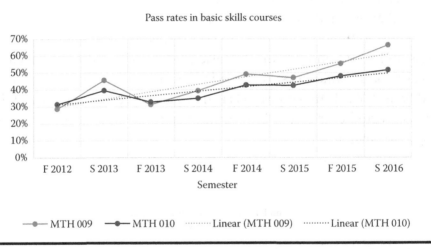

Figure 7.2   Pass rates in basic skills courses. Regression lines, with a slope of 21% for MTH 009 and 20% for MTH 010, point to a slow increase.

Grant activities increased our pass rates in intermediate and college algebra from 40% in 2004 to 65–70% in 2013–2014. This led to more students taking pre-calculus and calculus courses, from five sections in 2004 to 20 in 2014, where the pass rates ranged from 55% to 70%. Pass rates in basic skills courses had been about 30–35%; repeat and attrition rates were about 65–70%. Pass rates improved after merger of the basic skills and math departments in Fall 2012, from 25% to 42% in MTH 009 and from 25% to 37% in MTH 010. Table 7.3 shows enrollments and further improved pass rates for key math courses in 2015–2016.

Table 7.3   Course Enrollment and Passing Rates in 2015–2016

MTH 009 Prealgebra	MTH 010 Elementary Alg.	MTH 136/138 Interm./College Alg.	MTH 151 Precalculus	MTH 202 Calculus I	MTH 203 Calculus II
773	982	1500	419	251	188
61%	50%	70.1%	77.6%	70.1%	80.3%

Source: Office of Institutional Research, MEC.

7.8 Student Research

Research mentoring was strongly supported by MSEIP funding. In 2014 alone, 40 students and five mentors from three departments in the School of Science Health and Technology participated in summer faculty/student research. In 2015, 20 students and four faculty members participated in the National Joint Mathematical Meeting. Of recent note, Ligni Lugo won an award at the 2016 Annual Biomedical Research Conference for Minority Students conference in Florida for her presentation, and Janelle Walker participated in a Summer Program in Biostatistics and Computational Biology in the Department of Biostatistics at the Harvard T.H. Chan School of Public Health.

7.9 Graduate Success in Mathematics

One of the objectives of the grants was to increase graduate school readiness. By the end of 2015, more than 20 students—math and other majors, juniors, and seniors—were participating in graduate school prep activities. Our math graduates are strong in mathematics: Most have finished their masters and teach at community colleges, including the City University of New York, as full-time or adjunct faculty or in local schools. Some have become assistant principals. Those who are instructors at colleges have the highest pass rates and low attrition rates in their classes. Notable among our recent graduates, Andre Braddy (B.S. mathematics, August 2013), was selected by the Math for America Program and is now teaching in a neighborhood school while finishing his master of arts degree in Education at Teachers College, Columbia University. Cleveland Waddell (2012) is enrolled in a doctor of philosophy (Ph.D.) program at North Carolina State, and Kamal Barley (2010) earned his Ph.D. in Mathematics at Arizona State in 2016.

7.10 External Recognition

The following was discussed in Section 6.3.1 in Chapter 6. In 2005, after AGI facilitator Simpliciano's presentation about what the Department team had developed in formal TOC training, the president of the college, Edison O. Jackson, congratulated the math faculty for addressing the college's attrition problem and said: "I have never seen anything like this—conflict resolution, problem solving, decision making. Everyone at MEC needs to learn this starting with the counselors, basic skills instructors and middle management" (E.O. Jackson, personal communication, May 6, 2005).

The External Mathematics Program Review Team in April 2014 made the following observations:

> The Department Chair has aggressively and successfully sought significant external funding for activities central to the College mission, and leveraged those funds creatively to invest the faculty in those activities. The Department's tutoring program (which is crucial to an institution in which 87% of admitted students require at least one noncredit-bearing developmental mathematics course) appears to be funded almost exclusively by these grant funds. . . .
>
> Specifically, the MSEIP program has transformed the department into a technologically advanced operation which provides significant support for mathematics majors and general university students who are enrolled in developmental and service courses. (Finston and Lott, 2014, pp. 1 and 4)

It should be noted that the MSEIP activities were all based on the TOC project plan developed in January 2002 and improved over the years.

In May 2016, in recognition of the success of our unique project, Dr. Bernadette Hence, the MSEIP senior program officer, asked us to create a short video on *college success.** This was developed with the participation of the president, provost, faculty, alumni, and students.

Our findings have been presented at numerous TOC conferences (Nagarkatte, 2012; Nagarkatte, 2013b; Nagarkatte et al., 2006; Nagarkatte et al., 2007; Nagarkatte & Oley, 2014; Oley, 2006; Oley, 2013) and are available online or from the authors.

---

* The video "Medgar Evers College Math Dept Video" is available from the first author.

7.11 Challenges and Lessons Learned

Guided by the TOC-developed project plan, there were positive changes in the structure, ambiance and functioning of the math department, improvements in curriculum and pedagogy, and strengthened support services for math students. These have resulted in increased enrollments, increased passing rates, and increased retention in our higher-level math courses. The major challenge remaining is to apply our approach to benefit the students of basic skills mathematics and students in gateway and capstone courses in STEM.

The importance of obtaining buy-in to the TOC process from faculty, staff, and especially administration cannot be overemphasized. The buy-in process initiated by the appropriate unit head establishes a single goal for the unit. The math department first worked only within its area of control and domain of influence. Once the college president became committed to the TOC approach, it was possible to extend efforts to other departments and programs and to work quickly toward institutional change, for example, a merger of basic skills math into the math department. The next administration carried out the intended merger but failed to provide the required human and physical resources, with unfortunate consequences. The subsequent administration also gave the plan low priority. As noted by the External Review Team in 2014, staff positions, space, and other resources were needed to continue improvements but were not forthcoming:

> . . . The integration of the developmental mathematics program into the department has increased departmental responsibilities and removed two faculty lines. Faculty hires are required in order to complete the mission of the department.
>
> . . . a coordinator of developmental and pre-Calculus mathematics at the rank of Higher Education Officer (HEO) [is needed]. The size of these programs and the integration of developmental mathematics into the department make this position necessary. An adequately trained HEO can make informed recommendations to the Chair on space needs, course to course articulation, coordination of content, etc.
>
> . . . The university must allot funds to continue to support (via salaries, summer research programs, conferences, staff, equipment, venues, etc.) those services which are currently funded by MSEIP.
>
> . . . The tutoring program is a significant component of the academic program for students and should be provided with increased

space and funding. Current funding is from the MSEIP grant and the allotted space is inadequate. (Finston & Lott, 2014, page 5)

One of the important challenges is that external grant funding cannot be sustained unless departmental initiatives are institutionalized, but departmental initiatives do not get institutionalized because changing administrations have their own agendas and often ignore the progress made by departments.

As duly noted elsewhere, the discovery of a *breakthrough* solution and the development and unfolding of the project plan was a long and complicated process. Anything that could shorten this journey would be welcome, especially in academia, notorious for its slow, deliberative processes, and many changes in administrations with different agendas. We are pleased to note that research into TOC/TP is ongoing and that faster, more efficient methods are being tested and are changing the TOC landscape. The reader is referred to the work of Alan Barnard (Barnard, 2016; Barnard & Immelman, 2010) for his treatment of UDEs and the three-Cloud process and also for his suggestions as to how to use TOC to improve argumentative essay writing (Alan Barnard, personal communication, February 24, 2017).

References

Barnard, A. (2016). Why good people make bad decisions. TOCICO White Paper Series. http://www.tocico.org/resource/resmgr/white_paper/change_matrix_cloud_process_.pdf.

Barnard, A., & Immelman, R.E. (2010). Holistic TOC implementation case studies: Lessons learned from the public and private sector. In J.F. Cox, III, & J.G. Schleier, Jr. (Eds.), *Theories of Constraints Handbook* (pp. 455–498). New York: McGraw-Hill.

Berenbom, J. & Nagarkatte, U. (2013). *Departmental guidelines.* Unpublished report, Department of Mathematics, Medgar Evers College, Brooklyn, New York.

Finston, D., & Lott, D.A. (2014). *Medgar Evers Mathematics Department External Review Draft Report.* Unpublished report of the Department of Mathematics, Medgar Evers College, Brooklyn, New York.

Nagarkatte, U. (2007). *A TOC initiative at MEC.* Unpublished report of the Department of Mathematics, Medgar Evers College, New York.

Nagarkatte, U. (2012, October). *Holistic use of TOC in a university.* Paper presented at the TOCfE Virtual Conference. Retrieved from http://www.tocforcollege.com/downloads/Holistic%20Use%20of%20TOC%20in%20a%20University.pdf.

Nagarkatte, U. (2013a). Motivational guide. Retrieved January 22, 2017, from www
  .TOCforCollege.com: http://www.tocforcollege.com/motivational-guide.html.
Nagarkatte, U. (2013b, April). *Implementation of theory of constraints and thinking
  processes.* Paper presented at the 14th TOCfE International Conference. Baltimore,
  MD. Retrieved from http://www.tocforcollege.com/downloads/14th%20TOCfE%20
  International%20Conference.pdf.
Nagarkatte, U., & Berenbom, J. (2014). *Prealgebra.* Ronkonkoma, NY: Linus Learning.
Nagarkatte, U., & Berenbom, J. (2016a). *Elementary Algebra.* Ronkonkoma, NY: Linus
  Learning.
Nagarkatte, U., & Berenbom, J. (2016b). *Intermediate Algebra and Trigonometry.*
  Ronkonkoma, NY: Linus Learning.
Nagarkatte, U., & Oley, N. (2014, October). *The use of TOC to address student attrition
  at an urban college.* Paper presented at the TOCfE Virtual Conference.
Nagarkatte, U., Movasseghi, D., & Oley, N. (2007, November). *The theory of constraints
  (TOC) initiative at Medgar Evers College to reduce student attrition—A progress
  report.* Paper presented at the TOCICO Conference, Las Vegas, NV.
Nagarkatte, U., Movasseghi, D., Berenbom, J., & Oley, N. (2006, September).
  Implementing TOC—How a department makes an impact on an urban college.
  Paper presented at the 9th TOCfE International Conference, Leon, Mexico.
National Research Council. (2005). *How students learn: Mathematics in the
  classroom.*
Oley, N. (2006, September). *Improving faculty satisfaction.* Paper presented at the
  9th TOCfE International Conference, Leon, Mexico.
Oley, N. (2013, April). *How TOC can enhance students' writing and reasoning skills at
  an urban college.* Paper presented at the 14th TOCfE International Conference,
  Baltimore, MD. Retrieved from http://www.tocforcollege.com/downloads/TOCFE
  %202013.pdf.

Appendix: TOC for Education*

TOC for Education, Inc. (TOCfE), http://www.TOCforeducation.com, was founded in 1995 by Eli Goldratt who donated his knowledge of TOC for the use of educators. This organization has done a tremendous amount of work on all continents under the leadership of Kathy Suerken. It serves as an umbrella organization for all TOC activities in education and arranges international annual conferences around the world. It has influenced central boards of education in many countries and educational reforms mainly at the kindergarten, elementary, middle, and high school levels. It has also provided resources and training to community groups, churches, and prison reformers.

We subscribe to its mission statement and ethical code, as described in Chapter 1, for work at the college level. To simplify teaching the thinking tools, TOCfE has simplified the thinking process tools to *Cloud, Branch,* and *Ambitious Target Tree*, as illustrated in Figure A1.1. The branch includes *sufficient condition* processes used in the *Current Reality Tree* and *Negative Branch Reservations.*

An Evaporating Cloud (EC) or Cloud is a TOC thinking tool that analyzes the details of a conflict, meaningful action, and a decision, in a concise and nonprovocative way.

The Cloud helps to resolve a conflict (see Figure A1.2). A conflict is well defined when two possible opposing actions (wants) are present to achieve a common goal. Both actions are logically linked to the goal by two different needs. The two needs are general and do not oppose each other. If the different needs are met, then the conflict is resolved with a *win–win* solution.

---

* Kathy Suerken, President of TOCfE, has given permission to use/modify her copyrighted materials.

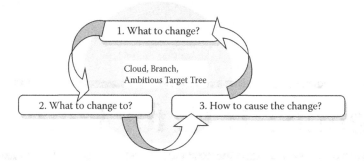

Figure A1.1   Three questions of TOC and three thinking tools.

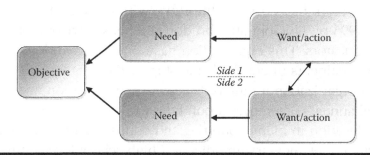

Figure A1.2   Cloud's structure.

The Cloud analyzes the details of the conflict by asking *five* guiding questions:

What do I *want*?
What does he or she *want*?
What is my *need*?
What is her/his *need*?
What *objective* do both sides have in common?

The cloud may be internal to an individual. For instance, a mother may need to resolve the conflict: "to cook dinner or to study."

The Cloud's structure is built of five boxes connected by logical arrows. Each box answers one of the five questions to help describe the conflict.

- The double sided arrow symbolizes the conflict—the wants or *actions* cannot both exist at the same time.
- The need is the real reason why each side insists on getting what he or she wants. In order to satisfy the need, it is necessary to achieve the want.
- The objective is a situation both sides wish to have, but in order for it to exist, each side must satisfy his/her needs.

The CLOUD

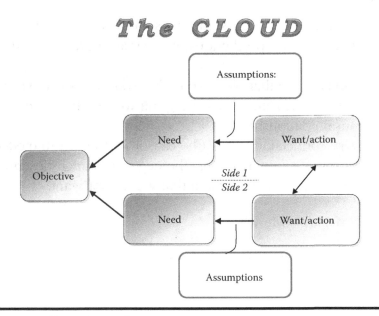

Figure A1.3   Revealing assumptions.

The arrow connecting the want/action and the need is based on many assumptions. If an assumption is invalid, then the want or action is not necessary for the need. If the want is not necessary for the need, it means that there is an alternative way to satisfy the need.

In order to reveal the assumptions (shown in Figure A1.3 as unshaded boxes waiting for text), we ask why getting the want or taking the action is necessary to fulfill the need. Then, we examine each assumption to determine if it is really valid and whether we can do something to make it invalid.

Finding win–win solutions

A win–win solution is a solution that enables both sides to satisfy their significant needs. The problem is that in order to satisfy its needs, each side usually insists on getting its conflicting wants. Thinking within a win–win framework requires us to shift the focus from getting what we want to obtaining what we need.

The Branch

The branch is a TOC tool used to logically analyze and explain a logical structure of cause–effect connections.

The branch is used to understand cause–effect links between actions and consequences, make predictions, and create new and better solutions.

In order to make sure that we have built a sound branch, we should read out loud the diagram in Figure A1.4 using the words: "If ... then ...," which express the causal relationship.

We read every connection: "If ... (the cause) ..., then ... (the effect). ..." By drawing cause–effect connections, the negative branch describes how an idea could lead to a negative outcome that we do not want.

To construct a negative branch

We use the negative branch to understand and analyze our concerns about implementing an idea.

1. First, define the idea.
2. Then, create a list of negative outcomes.
3. Finally, connect the idea to significant negative outcomes using cause–effect connections.

Then, we use the negative branch to find a way to implement the idea without suffering the negative implications (consequences).

4. Add explanations to the connections: If it rains, then the road is wet, *because* rain falls to the ground.

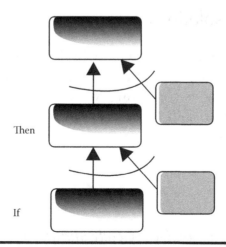

Figure A1.4 Branch.

5. Check to see if the explanations are necessarily valid: If rain does not fall to the ground (the ground is covered), then if it rains, the road is not necessarily wet.
6. Find a way to negate one of the explanations and thus break the connection.

Examples: Case histories are available as pdfs or PowerPoint slides on http://www.tocforeducation.com in addition to Chapter 2.

Ambitious Target Tree

The Ambitious Target Tree is a TOC tool used to analyze and sequence the steps needed to achieve a goal.

An ambitious target is a positive and desirable objective that, at first glance, seems unreachable.

The stages in constructing the tree are as follows:

1. Define the ambitious target.
    a. Before we start the discussion about how to achieve the target, we should always make sure that there is agreement among the team members that the target is desirable!
    b. Different team members may give a different meaning to the general terms and thus have a different mental image of the target. When that happens, many arguments are likely to occur about the ways to achieve the target.
    c. The third reason for carefully defining the ambitious target is to provide focus. If we do not define the ambitious target clearly, the objective may become vague.
    d. What is important is to verify that everybody understands the target and agrees that the target should be achieved.
2. Identify obstacles which block us from achieving the target.
    a. An *obstacle* is something that prevents or significantly inhibits the successful achievement of a target.
    b. After we define the ambitious target, we need to define the obstacles that prevent its achievement.
    c. In order to understand whether a specific action will move us toward the target, we should check to see if this action overcomes an obstacle that we believe prevents us from achieving the target.

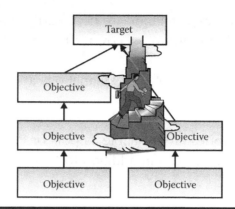

Figure A1.5   Ambitious Target Tree (ATT).

3. Verbalize intermediate objectives (IOs) according to the obstacles raised.
   a. *An IO is a situation reached after overcoming an obstacle.* IOs are landmarks or stepping stones between the present situation and the ambitious target.
   b. For each obstacle that we have identified, we need to verbalize IOs that will overcome it.
4. Arrange the IOs (in Figure A1.5 IO is labeled as 'objective') in a prerequisite order.
   a. A *prerequisite order* indicates which IOs must be achieved before others and which can be achieved in parallel.
   b. After verbalizing the IOs, we need to arrange them in a prerequisite order.

There are plenty of examples for children, parents, administrators, and community groups on the website: http://www.tocforeducation.com

Index

Page numbers followed by f and t indicate figures and tables, respectively.

M

Mathematics departments; *see also* Medgar
　　Evers College TOC initiative
　case study, 134–137
　constraint departments, 236
　curriculum and syllabus development, 164
　Departmental Guidelines, 168
　elevating constraints, 239–240
　faculty buy-in, 233
　Future Reality Trees (FRTs), 137–139,
　　138f, 139f
　implementation in mathematics tutoring,
　　177–181, 177t, 181t
　institutional problem solving example,
　　100–101
　Prerequisite Trees (PrTs), 164–169,
　　165–166t, 166–167t, 188f, 189f
　progression through an educational
　　institution, 227f
　service departments, 228–229
　sphere of influence, 24
　subordinating everything else to the
　　constraint, 237–238
Measurements
　Conflict Cloud Reality Trees (CCRTs), 106
　Current Reality Trees (CRTs), 255–256, 256f
　half-baked ideas, 59, 60, 60f, 61
　institutional initiatives, 218
　numerical measures of performance,
　　241–245
　paradigm shifts, 216
Medgar Evers College TOC initiative;
　　see also Mathematics departments
　challenges and lessons learned, 273–274
　curriculum development and
　　instructional materials, 266–268
　departmental structure and functioning,
　　265
　external recognition, 272
　faculty and staff development, 265–266
　graduate success in mathematics, 271
　grant development and management,
　　263–264
　mathematics enrollment, retention, and
　　performance, 268–270, 269f, 270f,
　　270t, 271f

　pass and repeat rate comparison, 267t
　student research, 271
　success of, 18–19
　tutoring and support services, 268
Minority Science Engineering Improvement
　　Program (MSEIP), 265, 268, 271, 272
Mission statement of TOC for Education,
　　Inc., 16, 277
Movasseghi, Darius, 18
Multitasking game, 172–175, 173t

N

NBRs, *see* Negative Branch Reservations
　　(NBRs)
Necessary conditions, 25–28, 26f
　Ambitious Target Trees (ATTs), 30f
　application of, 28–31
　Evaporating Cloud structure, 75f, 78–79
　needs statements, 73–74
　Prerequisite Trees (PrTs), 144–145
Needs
　Evaporating Clouds, 73–74, 77
　shifting focus from wants, 79–80
Negative branches, 51, 53
　chronic conflict resolution, 93
　persuasive essay writing, 119–120
　TOC for Education, Inc., 280–281
Negative Branch Reservations (NBRs), 51, 67
　developing the branch, 62–64, 62f
　half-baked ideas, 57–60, 59f, 60f, 61f
　justifications, 58–59, 63, 63f
　policy implementation issues, 59–61, 60f,
　　61f
　template, 68f
　trimming, 132–134
Negative feedback loops, 54–55, 72, 108
Numerical measures of performance, 241–245

O

Obstacles
　curriculum improvement example,
　　154–155t
　Department of Mathematics
　　implementation example, 165–166t
　identification, 281–282